HARPER

NEW YORK • LONDON • TORONTO • SYDNEY

The End of

Fashion

How Marketing Changed the Clothing Business Forever

TERI AGINS

A hardcover edition of this book was published in 1999 by William Morrow and Company, Inc.

First Quill edition published 2000.

Designed by Gretchen Achilles

The Library of Congress has catalogued the hardcover edition as follows:

Agins, Teri.
    The end of fashion : the mass marketing of the clothing business /
Teri Agins.
        p.   cm.
    Includes bibliographical references and index.
    ISBN 0-688-15160-4
    1. Clothing trade.   2. Clothing and dress—Marketing.   I. Title.
HD9940.A2A35   1999
687'.068'8—dc21   99-27075
                                                                   CIP

ISBN 0-06-095820-0 (pbk.)

08 09   18 17

to my parents,
Gene and Phyllis Agins

contents

a c k n o w l e d g m e n t s

JUST LIKE THE fashion designer who bows alone on the runway, the book author is rewarded with a byline in boldface, when backstage there are many individuals whose deeds are indispensable to such endeavors.

I cannot adequately expess my gratitude to the scores of designers, retailers, publicists, consultants, and analysts whom I have enlisted during the past ten years that I have covered the fashion beat at *The Wall Street Journal,* especially those who weighed in during the nearly three years I spent researching and writing this book. Their trust and willingness to "open the kimono" have been a godsend in my quest to get the story right. I hope that I have succeeded in depicting their situations in a truthful and even-handed way.

I wish to acknowledge my agent, Joel Fishman, of Bedford Book Works, who first approached me to write this book and was a terrific sounding board and hand holder along the way. Joel introduced me to Paul Bresnick, executive editor at William Morrow, and his associate editor, Ben Schafer, who demonstrated their unflagging support and keen interest in my project. Two skillful freelance editors, Charles Flowers and Ed Shanahan, helped me to whip the manuscript into shape.

The Wall Street Journal, my professional home for the past fifteen years, is a repository of America's best reporters and editors who continue to challenge and inspire me. Managing editor Paul Steiger generously granted me a twenty-month book leave and put me back on the fashion beat when I returned.

I am fortunate to have many close relationships at the *Journal,* including Johnnie Roberts (now at *Newsweek*), Alexandra Peers, and Wade Lambert, who came through in the crunch with critical suggestions, while veteran book writers George Anders, Jeffrey Trachtenberg, and Roger Lowenstein shared their experiences. Reporter Wendy Bounds kept the *Journal*'s fashion coverage lively during my absence. Bruce Levy, the *Journal*'s most valuable researcher, unearthed valuable nuggets, and computer whiz Phil Chan rescued my lost files on several occasions. Among my *Journal* colleagues who deserve my thanks are copy editor Betty Hallock, and editors Cynthia Crossen, Ellen Graham, David Sanford, Carolyn Phillips, Ron Alsop, Mike Miller, Laura Landro, and Dan Hertzberg.

Jane Berentson, a lifelong fashionista and big-picture editor, volunteered to help me map out the book and kept me on track. Veteran fashion writer Cathy Horyn is the world's most unselfish reporter, whose extraordinary talents are matched only by her friendship of a decade.

I've sharpened my fashion instincts by tapping the experts: Caroline Rennolds Milbank, Vicki Ross, and at the Costume Institute at the Metropolitan Museum Richard Martin, Deirdre Donohue, and Stephane Houy-Towner. I miss my mentor, the late Alan Millstein—the Quotron—who knew the ways of Seventh Avenue better than anybody else. Joan Kron, who first carved out the fashion beat at the *Journal* in 1983, came through and hooked me up with Andrea Miller, a skilled transcriber, and editor Ed Shanahan. In Paris, Pamela Golbin, of the Musée de la Mode et du Textile, was also an invaluable resource.

Several leading fashion journalists shared their astute insights: Bernadine Morris, Constance White, Robin Givhan, Mary Lou Luther, Ruth La Ferla, Christy Ferer, Elizabeth Snead, Anna Wintour, the late Elizabeth Tilberis, and *WWD*'s Patrick McCarthy, who permitted me to use the archives at Fairchild Publications.

Every nonfiction work benefits from having a broad range of key sources, and I am indebted to them all, including those who asked not to be named. My profile subjects kindly granted me extensive interviews and their staffers obligingly responded to my many inquiries: Ralph Lauren, Tommy Hilfiger, Emanuel Ungaro, Giorgio Armani, Zoran, Dan Skoda at Marshall Field's, Isaac Mizrahi, John Idol, and Robert Gray.

I gleaned pertinent insights from many others, listed here in no particular order. In New York: Bud Konheim, Joel Horowitz, Philip Miller, Victor Lipko, June Horne, Audrey Smaltz, Gary Galleberg, Hamilton South, Mallory Andrews, Jim Fingeroth, Dennis Walker, Jerry Chazen, Rick Rector, Bill Blass, Henry Hacker, Josie Esquivel, Faye Landes, Michael Toth, Christy Ferer, Carl Steidmann, Domenico De Sole, Maryanne Wheaton, Arnold Simon, Stephen Ruzow, Arnold Aronson, Allen Questrom, Terry Lundgren, Catherine Fisher, Michael Sondag, Craig Reynolds, Silas Chou, Lawrence Stroll, Kim Johnson Gross, Jeff Stone, Martha Nelson, Lynn Wyatt, Grace Mirabella, Michael Clinton, Tom Julian, Ted Marlow, Michael Gross, and Hal Rubenstein.

In Paris: Carlo Valerio, Ferrucio Ferragamo, Laura Ungaro, Rene Ungaro, Nino Cerruti, Ralph Toledano, Karl Lagerfeld, Didier Grumbach, Robert Bensoussan-Torres, Bernard Arnault, Tom Kamm, Amy Barrett, Pier Filipo Pieri, Jacques Babando, André Leon Talley, Denise Dubois, Robert Forrest, and Jacques Mouclier.

In Milan: Pino Brusone, Kevin Doyle, Maria Sturani, Rosita and Tai Missoni, Aldo Pinto, Pierfilippo Pieri, and Luigi Maramoti.

In Chicago: Sharon Stangenes, Genevieve Buck, Dorothy Fuller, Sugar Rautbord, Teresa Wiltz, Judy Byrd, Homer Sharp, Phyllis Collins, Connie Jackson, Gloria Bacon, Gary Witkin, and Dayton Hudson Corp.'s Michael Francis and Gerry Storch in Minneapolis.

In Los Angeles: Lisa Bannon, Wanda McDaniel, Michael Sharkey, and Bob Mackie.

Friends, indeed, are those who shared my pain and raised my spirits on the phone and through E-mails, and my tribe is the best: Wendy Urquhart (who came up with the idea for the book cover), Gay Young, Diane White, John Dwyer, Veronica Webb, Benjamin Borwick, Christine Bates, Peter Greenough, Chuck Stevens, Kevin Merida, as well as my sister Genie Agins, her husband, Chris Nunes, and Aunt Dorothy Wilson. Back home in Kansas City where I grew up, Bette Dooley, my stylish next-door neighbor, taught me to love high fashion.

Finally, I count as my biggest blessing, my parents, Gene and Phyllis Agins, whose love, guidance, and sacrifices have allowed me to pursue my dreams.

TERI AGINS

WHAT HAPPENED TO FASHION?

*S*upermodel Naomi Campbell has a killer body, a sassy strut, and a $10,000-a-day attitude. Famous for being fashionably late for work, she has left more than a few designers in the lurch right before a big show, wondering when—or if—she would appear. But the supermodel wasn't quite so cavalier when it came to Isaac Mizrahi, her buddy and the darling of America's designers. Nobody lit up a runway the way Isaac did during the 1990s. His witty, high-energy fashion shows were always the highlight of the New York collections.

On the evening of April 10, 1997, Mizrahi's fashion spectacle took place near Madison Square Garden, at the Manhattan Center on West 34th Street. At a quarter to six, with more than an hour to spare, the diva of the catwalks made her entrance, in sunglasses, $500 Manolo Blahnik stilettos, and a stunning spotted coat. On cue, bounding down the stage steps, emerged the man in black, Isaac Mizrahi, brandishing a Camel Light like a conductor's baton.

"There she is! *Na-o-mi!*" he exclaimed, swooping in to buss her on both cheeks. "Fab-u-lous." Mizrahi ooohed and ahhed, checking out her genuine leopard wrap. Evidently, the antifur era was over and out. Campbell was sporting the most politically incorrect of furs; leopards had been an endangered species since before she was born.

Naomi did a little pirouette, then swung open her vintage coat. The bronze satin lining was embroidered with the name of its famous original owner: Ann-Margret. "I got it in Los Angeles from this dealer," she explained in her girlish-British lilt. Suddenly, André Leon Talley, *Vogue*'s main man-about-Paris, stormed in to boom: "Girl, that coat is *major!*" The trio huddled for a dishy chat, then Mizrahi scooted her off backstage to get made up with the rest of the "girls," models like Kristen McMenamy and Shalom Harlow. As Campbell slipped away, her Hermès tote let out a "brrring," from her cellular phone. A cigarette ash fell to the floor as Mizrahi spun around, his arms flying as he jabbered some directions to his backstage crew. "I just *love* this," he muttered to no one in particular.

This drive-by vignette from fashion's fast lane harked back to *Unzipped*, the lively 1995 documentary that followed Mizrahi through the exhilarating fits and starts during the months when he prepared his 1994 fall collection. *Unzipped*, which won the audience award at the Sundance Film Festival, captured all the hyperbole, razzle-dazzle, and parody of high fashion, juiced up by the ebullient Mizrahi, a showman so delicious you couldn't make him up.

Straight out of Brooklyn's well-to-do Jewish enclave, Mizrahi got fixed on fashion early in life. His elegant mother decked herself out in Norman Norell and Yves Saint Laurent, while his father, a children's-wear manufacturer, bought Isaac his first sewing machine when he was still in grade school.

By the time Mizrahi was fifteen, he was stitching up a storm, designing a collection called "IS New York" which he sold to friends and a few neighborhood boutiques. He was also an imp and a cutup who in the 1970s starred onstage at the High School of Performing Arts and as an extra in the movie *Fame*. After studying fashion at New York's Parsons

School of Design, he moved on to Seventh Avenue, where he became an assistant to designers Perry Ellis, Jeffrey Banks, and Calvin Klein.

Ambitious and fast-tracking, Mizrahi was ready to do his own thing by the time he reached twenty-five. He invested the $50,000 trust fund his late father had left him to launch his eponymous fashion house in a brick-walled loft in downtown SoHo. His March 1988 debut runway show was one of those rare and unforgettable moments that left fashion editors agog. They knew they had just witnessed the start of something big.

That spring, Bloomingdale's rushed to put Mizrahi's debut collection in its windows on Fifty-ninth Street and Lexington Avenue, where Mizrahi showed up in person to greet shoppers. The most enthusiastic fashionistas swallowed the hype and splurged on their first Mizrahis. Kal Ruttenstein, Bloomie's fashion director, remembered: "We sold Isaac to the customer who was aware of what he was doing."

What Mizrahi was doing was cool and high-concept. He had a sophisticated take on American sportswear, inspired by fashion's modern masters, Claire McCardell and Geoffrey Beene, with a nod to Mary Tyler Moore, Mizrahi's favorite TV muse. But he also pulled a few tricks from up his own sleeve.

Throughout the 1990s, Mizrahi stood out as America's most prolific idea man, turning out one innovation after another, in a splash of Technicolor delight: paper-bag-waist pants, a tartan kilt strapless dress, fur-trimmed parkas, and boxy jackets. He spiked his fashion-show programs with puns to describe fabrics and colors: "Burlapse," "Fantasy Eyelet," "Lorne Green," and "James Brown." The fashion editors lapped it up, with page after page of pictures and kudos. But among retail buyers, there was decidedly less of a consensus. Barneys New York and Ultimo in Chicago were among the handful of stores whose fashion-forward clientele craved the labels with the most buzz. Accordingly, such retailers could move a few racks of Mizrahi's $800 jackets and $350 pants most every season. But Mizrahi barely caused a blip at chains like Neiman Marcus and Saks Fifth Avenue, where his spirited fashions got buried in the broad mix of up-and-coming designer brands.

Gilding the Mizrahi mystique was his colorful, megawatt persona. With a bandanna headband taming his frizzy black hair, he was an adorable cartoon. Isaac was fashion's funniest Quotron, who chirped frothy declarations with the push of a button, just like Diana Vreeland, the legendary *Vogue* editor of the 1970s whose snappy sound bites ("Pink is the navy blue of India") have entered fashion's lexicon. "Le Miz"—as *WWD* dubbed fashion's wonder boy—once exclaimed about a chubby fake fur jacket: "It looks *divine* in beast." He held forth to *WWD* about his 1992 spring collection: "It will be all about irresistible clothes. The *only* kind that will sell."

But what merchandise actually sold was of little concern to the members of the Council of Fashion Designers of America and other fashion industry groups, who showered Isaac with a number of "best designer" awards during his first years. All Mizrahi needed now was solid capital backing to take his business to the next stage. "All my life, I dreamed of a design house like that of Calvin Klein, Armani or Yves Saint Laurent," Mizrahi once wrote in a pitch letter to potential financiers. His dream seemed like a foregone conclusion by 1992 when the venerable house of Chanel in Paris stepped in to help, signing on to become Mizrahi's financial partner. Chanel certainly had the expertise, having successfully staged its own renaissance in the 1980s, with management's deft handling of Chanel's perfumes and accessories, bolstered by the ingenious Karl Lagerfeld, who had become Chanel's couturier in 1982. Chanel was poised to parlay Mizrahi's marquee image into profits with the 1994 introduction of "Isaac," a bread-and-butter department store collection of $150 dresses and $300 jackets.

Meanwhile, Le Miz continued to reign as Mr. Fabulous on the high-fashion runways, as he mined his bottomless pit of creativity. And after his wacky performance in *Unzipped*, a star was born. Among his TV and movie credits, playing a fashion designer, naturally, was his bit part in the Michael J. Fox comedy *For Love or Money*. He was also a jovial guest on the TV game show *Celebrity Jeopardy!*, where he was the winner.

But while Isaac, the stylish personality, was in high demand, his clothes weren't. By 1996, Mizrahi's runway collections weren't wowing the fashionistas anymore, as Gucci and Prada were now the favorite flavors of the moment. Meanwhile, the Isaac collection on which Mizrahi banked his future just didn't click with shoppers, who were far too savvy to fork over $150 for a cotton shift designer dress when chains like Bebe and The Limited were turning out similar styles for as little as $49.99. As reality bit harder, Mizrahi had no choice but to close his Isaac division at the end of 1997, leaving his struggling fashion house hanging by a thread.

That's fashion. And that's the curious way success plays out in the fashion world. A designer can be deemed hot by buzz alone—as Mizrahi was from the start—even though the sales of his collections were barely tepid. But people outside the fashion loop would never be the wiser, because fashion coverage in newspapers and magazines was all about style, not substance.

The fact that Mizrahi's sportswear was thoroughly modern should have worked to his advantage, but his business habits were pretty old-fashioned. He saw himself as a latter-day couturier who designed for supermodels and the coolest fashionistas—but not ordinary women. Mizrahi couldn't connect with the critical masses because he didn't relate to them. For example, when retail buyers once begged him to repeat one of his few best-sellers—paper-bag-waist pants—Mizrahi couldn't bring himself to do a rerun. "I just got *bored* with them," he later recollected.

Flashing back to the final scene in *Unzipped*, Mizrahi showed what really mattered to him. There was Mizrahi, in post-fashion-show anxiety at a Manhattan newsstand, hovering over a copy of *WWD*, which applauded his latest collection, proclaiming "the man has a hit on his hands." The camera zoomed in on a giddy Mizrahi, who was bouncing down the street. But what was missing from this happy ending was the only review that counted in the real world: sales in stores.

Mizrahi, aloft in a cloud of chiffon, had yet to get serious about the bottom line. He was an artiste who refused to become another Seventh Avenue garmento. "Look, it is all I can do to make fabulous collections and fabulous clothes," he explained in July 1997. "That is *all* I can do. You know I can't imagine after all these years, *I can't imagine* how it will translate at retail."

On October 1, 1998, the curtain finally came down on Mizrahi's fashion show. Ten years of terrific reviews added up to little; the House of Mizrahi chalked up no more than an estimated $15 million at its peak in 1996—and zero in the profit column. The money men at Chanel, realizing that Mizrahi's moment had passed, slammed the door on America's most beloved Little Fashion House That Could. Mizrahi unzipped played like an obituary across the bottom of the front page of *The New York Times*. Out of fashion and headed toward a career in Hollywood, Mizrahi was sanguine—leaving the door open for his possible comeback. "I will always have a great love of fashion. I'll always be a fashion designer," he told *WWD*.

There's no better example than Mizrahi to show what has been happening lately in the real world of fashion. It's not only the end of the millennium, but the end of fashion as we once knew it.

Mizrahi is a direct descendant of the trickle-down school of fashion, the aspirational system in which high-fashion designers, their affluent clients buoyed by scads of publicity in *WWD* and *Vogue*, dictated the way everyone dressed. The old order was starting to unravel when Mizrahi first went into business in the 1987. But failing to read the shifts in the marketplace, Mizrahi became the quintessential fashion victim; he arrived on the scene just when fashion was changing. By the early 1990s, a confluence of phenomena arising from retailing, marketing, and feminism began transforming the ways of fashion forever.

For all of its glamour and frivolity, fashion happens to be a relevant and powerful force in our lives. At every level of society, people care greatly about the way they look, which affects both their self-esteem and the way other people interact with them. And it has been true since the beginning of time that people from all walks of life make the effort to dress in style.

Yet fashion, by definition, is ephemeral and elusive, a target that keeps moving. A clothing style becomes fashionable when enough people accept it at any given time. And conversely, fashions go out of style when people quit wearing them. Traditionally, the fashion system has revolved around the imperative of planned obsolescence—the most familiar examples being the rise and fall in skirt lengths, and for men the widening and narrowing of trousers and neckties. Every few years, when the silhouettes change, women and men have been compelled to go shopping and to rebuild their wardrobes to stay in style.

In America's consumer society, which burgeoned after World War II, apparel makers, designers, retailers, and their symbiotic agents, the fashion press, were the omnipotent forces pushing fashion's revolving door. They have been responsible for creating new fashion trends and inducing people to shop until they dropped, to scoop up the novelties the industry promoted. This order was a mighty mandate that prevailed throughout the 1980s, a system which established a consensus that kept millions of consumers moving in lockstep. Perhaps that's what William Shakespeare foresaw when he wrote: "Fashion wears out more apparel than the man."

But in recent years, a number of circumstances caused a revolutionary shift that upset the old order and wrested control away from the forces in the fashion industry. In 1987, designers missed the boat when they failed to sell women on short skirts. They misfired again, a few seasons later, with the somber "monastic" look and other fads, resulting in millions of dollars of losses to the industry. By the mid-1990s the forces of fashion had lost their ability to dictate trends. Increasingly, the roles have reversed. The power now belongs to us, the consumers, who decide what we want to wear, when we buy it, and how much we pay for it. And nowadays, consumers are a lot savvier and more skeptical when it comes to fashion.

Four megatrends sent fashion rolling in a new direction.

• *Women let go of fashion.* By the 1980s, millions of baby-boomer career women were moving up in the workplace and the impact of their professional mobility was monumental. As bank vice presidents, members of corporate boards, and partners at law firms, professional women became secure enough to ignore the foolish runway frippery that bore no connection to their lives. Women began to behave more like men in adopting their own uniform: skirts and blazers and pantsuits that gave them an authoritative, polished, power look.

Fashion's frothy propaganda no longer rallied the troops. The press beat the drums for a decade, but the name Isaac Mizrahi still drew a blank with millions of American women who hadn't bothered to notice.

A defining moment in high fashion occurred in 1992 with the closing of Martha, the venerable dress salon on Park Avenue. Starting in the 1930s, Martha Phillips, a feisty entrepreneur with impeccable taste, began her reign as one of America's leading standard-bearers for snob appeal and Paris originals. And for nearly six decades, elegant women beat a path to the pink-walled emporium on shopping trips that took hours as Phillips and her attentive staffers put their clients together in head-to-

toe perfection. Such was the drill during an era when rich women derived much of their self-worth from wearing the best couture labels.

Martha's demise was the latest casualty in a rash of salon deaths, coming just months after the closing of such salons as Loretta Blum in Dallas, Amen Wardy in Beverly Hills, and Sara Fredericks in Boston. Martha Phillips and her exquisite counterparts couldn't hack it anymore because the pace-setting socialites who once spent a fortune on their wardrobes no longer devoted so much time and money to getting dressed up. Park Avenue style maven and decorator Chessy Rayner, who used to be a front-row regular at the Paris fashion shows, was among those who had made the conversion from clothes horse to fashion renegade. In 1992, she recalled: "Today my style is totally pared-down and non-glitz."

As such salons folded, many of their suppliers, namely the couture houses in Paris, faced a precarious future. For most of the twentieth century, Paris designers had set the standard, introducing the full-skirted "New Look" after World War II, the "sack" silhouette of the fifties, the "space age" sleek of the sixties, and the "pouf" party dress in the eighties. Such were the trends that Seventh Avenue manufacturers slavishly copied and adapted for the mass market. But by the 1990s, most Paris designers couldn't set the world's fashion agenda anymore. Styles were no longer trickling down from the couture to the masses. Instead, trends were bubbling up from the streets, from urban teenagers and the forces in pop music and counterculture with a new vital ingenuity that was infectious. The powers in Paris were taken aback when their captivated clients awoke from the spell of couture and defected in droves. And thus, the fortress of French fashion came tumbling down.

• *People stopped dressing up.* By the end of the 1980s, most Americans were wedded to jeans, loose knit tops, and Nike shoes, which became the acceptable standard of everyday dress even in offices. Leading the charge for informality were men, in their rejection of the business suit, which since the start of the industrial age had been the symbol of masculine authority and the uniform of the corporate workplace.

Starting in the 1980s, the bespectacled computer nerds at the helms of America's buoyant high-tech industries broke the pattern of stuffed-shirt formality in business. Microsoft Corp. founder Bill Gates emerged as the world's wealthiest man—and the personification of the Internet-set look, dressed for success in chinos and sports shirts.

In America's more traditional corporations, the men's fashion revolt first erupted in Pittsburgh, of all places. In the fall of 1991, Pittsburgh-based Alcoa, the giant aluminum concern, became the first major corporation to sanction casual office attire. The move came about after Alcoa had allowed employees who contributed to the United Way to dress casually during a two-week fund drive. The perk proved so popular that Alcoa decided to give its employees the option of never having to dress up again. Even Alcoa's top honchos stopped suiting up. One typical weekday morning in March 1992, Ronald Hoffman, an Alcoa executive vice president, was working in his suite on the thirty-seventh floor wearing a yellow V-neck sweater, an open-neck shirt, and slacks. "There used to be a time when a white shirt went with your intelligence," Hoffman told *The Wall Street Journal*. "But now there's no reason to do this anymore."

Before long, the rest of corporate America had shifted into khakis and knit shirts at least one day of the week, which became known as "casual Friday." Computer giant IBM went so far as to go casual every day, starting in 1995. Levi Strauss & Co., the world's biggest apparel maker, caught the wave in the early 1990s with its loose-fitting Dockers casual pants, which quickly became a popular wardrobe staple for men. It took less than five years for Dockers to explode into a $1 billion-a-year business.

Without enough suit buyers to go around, many of America's fine haberdasheries and boutiques suffered the fate of Martha. Charivari, a flashy New York chain known for its dressy and expensive European designer imports for men and women during the 1980s, planned to ride out the dress-down trend. In 1991, Charivari plastered on billboards: "Ripped Jeans, Pocket Tees, Back to Basics. Wake us when it's over. Charivari." Instead, seven years later, it was Charivari that was over—and out of business.

Indeed, it seemed as though not only dress-up clothes, but good taste, had fallen by the wayside as millions of Americans sank into sloppiness, wedded to their fanny packs, T-shirts, jeans, and clunky athletic shoes. "Have We Become a Nation of Slobs?" blared the cover headline of *Newsweek*, February 20, 1995. The accompanying article provided a mountain of evidence that people were no longer dressing to impress, including a Boston funeral director who said that some families were now asking for their loved ones to be buried without a coat and tie.

• *People's values changed with regard to fashion.* Most people used to put "fashion" on a pedestal. There was a sharp delineation between ordinary clothes from Casual Corner and Sears and true "fashion" from Paris couturiers and boutiques like Charivari and Martha. But such a divide existed before so many options for fashion became widely available at every price level. Stores like Ann Taylor, The Limited, Gap, Banana Republic, and J. Crew turned out good-looking clothes that deflated the notion that fashion belonged exclusively to the elite. In effect, designer labels started to seem like a rip-off. Increasingly, it became a badge of honor to be a bargain hunter, even among the well-to-do. Discounter Target Stores struck the right chord with this tagline in its ads: "It's fashionable to pay less."

Many people like Deirdre Shaffer, a thirty-one-year-old part-time psychotherapist from a New Jersey suburb, learned this lesson quite by accident. In 1994, Shaffer and her husband attended a cocktail party at their local country club to which she wore a black dress from Ann Taylor and $12.99 black suede sandals that she had just purchased from Kmart. Earlier that day, Shaffer didn't have enough time to comb the upscale malls where she usually bought her clothes. So, while she was shopping in Kmart for paper towels and toothpaste, she wandered over to the shoe racks, where she found the sandals. That evening, Shaffer was feeling quite satisfied with her budget find. "I got more compliments on the shoes than my dress," she recalled, noting that her friends were "impressed when I told them they came from Kmart."

Indeed, seeing was believing for Shaffer and millions of folks who wised up. It was akin to a Wizard-of-Oz discovery: Behind the labels of many famous name brands was some pretty ordinary merchandise. Increasingly, the savviest shoppers started paying closer attention to details like fabric, workmanship, and value—and thus became less impressed with designer labels. *Consumer Reports*, which is best known for its evaluations of kitchen appliances and cars, helped millions of shoppers see the light when the magazine began testing different brands of clothes for durability, fiber content, and wear. The truism "You get what you pay for" was proven false. In a 1994 test of chenille sweaters, *Consumer Reports* concluded that a $340 rayon chenille sweater from the upscale Barneys New York "was only a bit higher in quality" than a $25 acrylic chenille sweater from Kmart. In another trial in 1997, the magazine gave its highest ranking for men's polo knit shirts to Honors, a store brand that sold for only $7 at Target, but whose quality scored well above those versions by Polo Ralph Lauren at $49, Tommy Hilfiger at $44, Nautica at $42, and Gap at $24.

Marketing analysts describe consumers' new embrace of the most functional and affordable clothes as the "commoditization" of fashion. Beginning in the 1980s, more apparel makers shifted most of their manufacturing from the U.S. to low-cost factories in the Far East, where they were able to provide more quality at an attractive price: good-looking polo shirts and other apparel that were perfectly acceptable to most people—with no sustainable difference between one brand or another. As more people had no reason or burning desire to dress up anymore, they had no qualms about buying their clothes wherever they could get the best deal—just as Deirdre Shaffer did at Kmart.

The commoditization of clothes coincided with the most popular clothing trends of the 1990s: the "classics," "simple chic," and "minimalism." This comes as no surprise. Such mainstream styles are far easier for designers to execute on a commercial scale, in that they are cheaper and safer to produce, with less margin for error in the far-flung factories in China, Hong Kong, Korea, and Mexico, where much of today's apparel is made.

Furthermore, there's a whole generation of people under forty who don't know how to discern quality in clothes. Generation X-ers born in the 1970s didn't grow up wearing dresses and pantyhose in high school, nor did they own much in the way of "Sunday clothes." These young people are largely ignorant of the hallmarks of fine tailoring and fit. Jeans, T-shirts, stretch fabrics, and clothes sized in small, medium, large, and extra-large are what this blow-dry, wash-and-wear generation have worn virtually all of their lives. While their mothers and grandmothers donned slips and girdles—and pulled out the ironing board before they got dressed—these young people had already formed the habit of wearing comfortable, carefree clothes.

• *Top designers stopped gambling on fashion.* Isaac Mizrahi mistakenly believed that there were enough fashion mavens still willing to put their trust in his taste level. But the best-selling designers nowadays know better. Liz Claiborne, Polo Ralph Lauren, and Tommy Hilfiger are among the fashion houses that grew into billion-dollar empires of apparel, handbags, cosmetics, and home furnishings. Such fashion houses just also happen to be publicly traded companies, which must maintain steady, predictable growth for their shareholders. The upshot: The big guns can't afford to gamble on fashion whims. Fashion as we have known it requires a certain degree of risk-taking and creativity that is impossible to explain to Wall Street. Even though the leading designers tart up their runways with outlandish, crowd-pleasing costumes, they are grounded in reality. The bulk of the actual merchandise that hits the sales floor is always palatable enough for millions of consumers around the world, thus generating the bottom line that Wall Street expects.

WITH SO MUCH consumer rejection of fanciful fashions, will the world turn into a sea of khakis and T-shirts? Will Paris couture and the likes of Mizrahi and Charivari ever rise again? And moreover, will fashion ever matter as it used to?

"The fact is that women are interested in clothes, but the average consumer isn't interested in the 'fashion world,' " observes Martha Nelson, the editor of *In Style* magazine. Women want attractive clothes that function in the real world, "not something that is impossible to walk and drive in. You know, clothes that fit into your life."

So, that's why we've come to the end of fashion. Today, a designer's creativity expresses itself more than ever in the marketing rather than in the actual clothes. Such marketing is complicated, full of nuance and innovation—requiring far more planning than what it takes to create a fabulous ballgown, as well as millions of dollars in advertising. In a sense, fashion has returned to its roots: selling image. Image is the form and marketing is the function.

Nowadays, a fashion house has to establish an image that resonates with enough people—an image so arresting that consumers will be compelled to buy whatever that designer has to offer. The top designers use their images to turn themselves into mighty brands that stand for an attitude and a lifestyle that cuts across many cultures. Today's "branding" of fashion has taken on a critical role in an era when there's not much in the way of new styling going on—just about every store in the mall is peddling the same styles of clothes. That's why designer logos have become so popular; logos are the easiest way for each designer to impart a distinguishing characteristic on what amounts to some pretty ordinary apparel.

Having burnished his image through millions of dollars of advertising, Calvin Klein towers as a potent brand name and leverages his CK logo across a breadth of categories—$6.50 cotton briefs, $1,000 blazers, and $40 bath towels—even though there are plenty of cheaper options widely available.

Image, of course, works in conjunction with the intrinsics—the style, quality, and price of each actual item—and image comes from everywhere: the ambiance of the location where the clothes are sold, the advertising, the celebrities who wear the clothes, and so forth. Image is how the Gap sells a $12.50 pocket T-shirt, how Ralph Lauren pushes a $40 gallon of wall paint, and how Giorgio Armani moves $1,500 blazers.

These designers assault the American public with their ubiquitous advertising, most typically seen in the fashion press. But the roles have reversed there as well. Fashion publications like *WWD*, *Vogue*, *Harper's Bazaar*, *GQ*, and the rest have lost their power in their editorial pages to make or break fashion trends—the same power designers have lost to the consumer. Nowadays, the mightiest fashion brands, by virtue of their heavy-duty advertising, take their message directly to the public—unfiltered by the subjectivity of the editors: Ralph Lauren's ten-page advertising inserts in the front of *Vogue* and *Vanity Fair* are more arresting than any fashion spread featuring his clothes in the editorial pages of the magazine.

It was always confounding, this business of selling fashion. And now the industry has become fragmented into so many niches in which scores of companies churn out more and more merchandise at every price range, season after season. The fashion-industry powers at the head of the class prevail because they swear by retailing's golden rule: The consumer is king.

The following chapters capture some of the industry's best-known players in recent years, as they've succeeded—and sputtered—in their quest to make fashion for profit, as well as for glory. Fashion, which began in the hallowed ateliers of Parisian couture, now emanates from designers and retailers from around the world, reaching the masses at every level. In today's high-strung, competitive marketplace, those who will survive the end of fashion will reinvent themselves enough times and with enough flexibility and resources to anticipate, not manipulate, the twenty-first-century customer. There's just no other way.

PARIS: THE BEGINNING AND
THE END OF FASHION

We will know twenty years from now what fashion is in Paris. Right now, there is general confusion.

KARL LAGERFELD, April 24, 1998

he stock market crash of October 19, 1987, left the world in stunned suspension, as millions of people pondered how their lives would inevitably change after nearly a decade of fast fortunes, high living, and conspicuous consumption. Just days after the big bombshell, New York's financial district erupted again—but this time for a glorious celebration inside the World Financial Center, the gleaming new office towers that were the home of American Express, Merrill Lynch, and Dow Jones and Co., the publisher of *The Wall Street Journal.* On the evening of October 28, New York's social glitterati headed downtown to pay homage to Christian Lacroix, French fashion's *it* man of the moment.

Except for the unlucky timing, the venue was perfect. Overlooking the Hudson River in lower Manhattan, with a distant view of the Statue of Liberty, the World Financial Center's glass-covered public courtyard provided a glamorous backdrop for a fashion-show stage and dozens of candlelit tables arranged around the sixteen live palm trees that rose forty-five feet from its marble floors. Partygoers would long remember the Lacroix gala, which concluded with a fireworks show as exuberant, excessive, and eerily off-key. It was an event where over-the-top fashion mirrored Wall Street, on the verge of collapse.

To the fashion establishment, the arrival of Lacroix had been like the second coming. With his dark, slicked-back hair and cherubic face, he was an extraordinary talent with a heavy-handed flair for the baroque. He had come to save haute couture, the pinnacle of French fashion, whose legendary practitioners included Yves Saint Laurent, Hubert de Givenchy, and Emanuel Ungaro. Lacroix had burst on the scene initially as the couturier of the house of Patou in the early 1980s, when haute couture was suddenly back in style for the first time in years. Luxurious suits and party frocks that cost as much as suburban homes became the badge of wealthy Arab ladies, nouveau riche trophy wives, and international socialites, who delighted in supporting high fashion's noblest tradition. "The fact is that fashion needs Lacroix—needs somebody new to bring along the next generation of couture customers," Holly Brubach raved in *The New Yorker*.

Serving as chairwoman of the Lacroix benefit, Blaine Trump, the beautiful, blond sister-in-law of real estate mogul Donald Trump, decked herself in a purple brocade Lacroix confection, in keeping with the fairytale frippery Lacroix sent down the runway that night: enormous *fichu* portrait collars, bustles, farthingales, pouf overskirts and underskirts—in a riot of vibrant colors, festooned with embroidery and jeweled trimmings. Balancing strange headdresses atop their tightly coiffed updos, the models moved gingerly down the catwalk. Also laboring under the weight of Lacroix luxe—and suffering gladly through the night—

were a number of guests, such as millionairess Gloria von Thurn und Taxis, who was done up in a black bustle number. Sitting next to Donald Trump, she whispered: "You know, you can't go to the bathroom in these dresses."

Lacroix took his runway bow to a shower of bravos and red carnations. No one was prouder than Lacroix's French benefactor, Bernard Arnault, a thirty-seven-year-old mogul on the rise. With the help of investment bank Lazard Frères in 1984, Arnault had acquired the bankrupt Agache Willot, whose most valuable asset was the Christian Dior fashion house. A couple of years later, he bankrolled the House of Lacroix, with an initial $8 million commitment. Over the next years, Arnault would become the luxury world's most active predator, creating, through a series of hostile takeovers and buyouts, LVMH Moët Hennessy Louis Vuitton, the world's largest luxury-goods empire. By 1998, the $8-billion-a-year LVMH had amassed a formidable lineup, including Hennessy Cognac, Moët and Dom Pérignon champagne, airport Duty Free Shops, as well as other fashion houses: Louis Vuitton, Céline, Givenchy, Loewe, and Kenzo. But Lacroix was Arnault's favored son, the only enterprise he had started from scratch. From the start, Arnault held high hopes, especially after Lacroix garnered so much breathless publicity for his signature pouf gown. He was destined to become the next Yves Saint Laurent.

But despite his triumphant debut, Lacroix would turn out to be the soufflé that refused to rise. No one had expected that there would be a run on $40,000 Lacroix ballgowns. But even Lacroix's earliest enthusiasts got cold feet—and cooled on the couturier. Georgette Mosbacher, the red-headed wife of U.S. Commerce Secretary Robert Mosbacher, admitted that she felt forced to buy a Lacroix dress, but never wore it, and ended up donating it to a museum. Likewise, the retail collections Lacroix created were fanciful eye-candy—but flops on the sales floor. The definitive proof that there was no more helium left in the pouf came when Lacroix brought out his first signature perfume, C'est La Vie, in 1994. Despite its Calvin Klein–size $40 million marketing sendoff, C'est La Vie retailed so poorly that Lacroix pulled the fragrance from the market.

During its first five years of business, the house of Lacroix waded in red ink—more than $37 million in losses. Profits were still elusive in 1997 when Lacroix, at forty-six, celebrated ten years in business, having run through almost as many managing directors.

Unapologetic, the earnest couturier vowed never to surrender to commercial pressures. He wrote in his fashion show program in July 1997: "I believe I have not given in to systems whatever they might be. . . . A Lacroix style has been born and even if it doesn't appeal to everyone, so much the better. The barefooted, jewelry-less woman, skimpily dressed in worn-out togs, creates a ghost-like vision that only satisfies the most pessimistic, of which I am not one. . . ."

Bernard Arnault wasn't so much pessimistic as he was frustrated by the couturier who couldn't be king of French fashion. By the end of the 1990s, Arnault would be forced to face the naked truth: that Lacroix was the end of fashion.

Bernadine Morris, the former *New York Times* chief fashion reporter, admitted years after the fact that she, too, had gotten carried away by what was a Lacroix moment. "When I wrote [my reviews], I believed it at the time. When you see an extraordinary collection, it does set you up. What we didn't know was what the fallout was going to be from the stock market crash. And now, looking at Lacroix ten years later, the demise of couture was irrevocable at that stage, the kind of elaborate clothes which looked so exciting in a show just weren't conducive to modern life."

THE TANKING OF Lacroix summed up all that had been going wrong with Paris fashion in the last decade. As the ranchers like to say in Texas: Big hat, no cattle. Throughout the 1980s, the Paris fashion establishment had many glossy components—haute couturiers, famous ready-to-wear designers, and loads of perfumes, handbags, and trinkets flashing their logos.

But underneath French fashion's broad brim was a sinking industry, outmoded and out of touch, suffering from hubris and denial. The upbeat reports that couture had bounced back during the 1980s were greatly exaggerated because the couture houses were still losing millions on such collections. With few exceptions, French designer clothes in general were too contrived, too uptight, or just too weird looking. "It's the same ten old men doing a boring rehash of what they've already done, like the hobble skirts that are too tight and too expensive," remarked Vicki Ross, an independent buyer for retailers in Asia.

The state of French fashion was shaky in the 1990s, but Paris still stood on ceremony as the fashion capital of the world. To be sure, the City of Light prevailed as the world's most visible stage, where the international press and hordes of fashion groupies converged every season to cover the designer shows. But French fashion just wasn't selling the way it used to—having been upstaged by fashion labels from Italy and the United States. Nevertheless, the French, smug in their superiority, maintained that Paris would always be the guardian of high fashion, if not high commerce. But the reality was that by the mid-1990s, the French designers, who invented couture and set the standards for high style for more than one hundred years, were now hopelessly passé.

LIKE VINTAGE CHAMPAGNE, haute couture appointed the French as connoisseurs of the good life. It came as no surprise that the homeland of Versailles and Madame de Pompadour would serve as the birthplace of couture and high fashion. "Nowhere else in the world was elegance taken so seriously or supported by such a reservoir of talent, skilled craftsmen and cooperative clients," wrote Marilyn Bender in her 1966 study of pop fashion culture, *The Beautiful People*.

The couture industry began in the nineteenth century as a vehicle to stimulate growth in the French economy. In 1858, monarch Napoleon III summoned Charles Frederick Worth, an innovative English dressmaker practicing in Paris, to whip up a magnificent wardrobe for his wife, Empress Eugénie, who would become the world's first fashion model. Worth, who invented the bustle dress, came to design all of Eugénie's official court clothes and his label—the first in fashion history—bore the royal crest. Thus, Worth became known as the first Parisian couturier and the preferred dressmaker of the crowned heads of Austria, Italy, and Russia, which fueled the demand across Europe for fashion, jewelry, and other finery made in France.

French fashion stood for snob appeal and the height of elegance for ladies whose lives revolved around their wardrobes, the ones whom Parisian gentlemen playfully ordered: *"Sois belle et tais-toi,"* or "Shut up and be beautiful." By the 1920s, fashion would become France's second largest export, employing thousands of workers and establishing the benchmarks for quality and style around the world.

"The fashion system here is a reproduction of the aristocratic tradition in which the couture represents the establishment," observed Pascal Morand, an economist who heads the Institut Français de la Mode, a fashion industry graduate school in Paris. "Couture sells a luxury image that makes people feel that they are belonging to an elite. In the French vision, the creativity comes strictly from the product. But with the Italians and Americans, creativity concerns all parts of the business."

———

teri agins

DURING MOST OF the twentieth century, couture was a vital cog in the French economy, funneling big business to countless fabric mills and craftsmen trading in feathers, buttons, embroideries, and so forth. The French government lent a hand, providing subsidies and organizing the industry under the Chambre Syndicale de la Couture Parisienne, the powerful trade group that promoted high fashion.

As long as French couture was selling briskly, there was little incentive to industrialize the French clothing trade for the mass market. This was the stark contrast between France and the United States, where commercial apparel began to take on steam at the turn of the twentieth century alongside the nation's burgeoning department stores such as R. H. Macy in New York, Marshall Field's in Chicago, and John Wanamaker in Philadelphia. France had no such retailing boom, and thus the trade of handmade clothes and tailoring continued to thrive unfettered.

Even if department stores had cropped up across France back then, it was unlikely that the couturiers would have been inspired to sell to them. "They were all snobs," asserts Gerry Dryansky, a Paris-based journalist who reported on the couture houses for *Women's Wear Daily* in the 1960s. "Coco vowed she'd never do ready-to-wear because she didn't want to dress everybody. [The couturiers'] ambitions weren't so high. They were rich and lived well, but they never intended to build colossal businesses. Their snobbism was greater than their greed."

DESPITE THEIR AVERSION to outfitting ordinary women, the couturiers nevertheless did just that—in a roundabout way—as they opened their elite salons to American retailers and manufacturers, who went to Paris twice a year to get a few good ideas. These commercial clients gained admission into the French showrooms where fashion shows were held by paying a fee called a "caution," or by ordering one or two couture dresses, often priced a notch higher than what private customers paid.

Everyone who attended the shows back then knew the rules. Fashion-show guests were allowed to take discreet notes, with stubby gold pencils that were handed out with the printed programs. The members of the press agreed not to circulate photos or sketches from the shows until after the official "release" date one month later.

To further safeguard exclusivity, the couturiers staggered deliveries: The private clients received their orders first, about a month ahead of stores like Ohrbach's and Marshall Field's. In those days, all of Seventh Avenue breathlessly awaited for the couture samples to hit American shores. *Women's Wear Daily* reported on August 24, 1965: "The first batch of Paris couture models for New York is slated to arrive at John F. Kennedy Airport Wednesday at about 8 P.M. on Air France flight 051."

This crude form of protectionism, no better than a gentleman's agreement, was always prone to leaks. During one fashion show in the 1950s, Christian Dior darted out from backstage to confiscate one woman's notebook full of sketches. But most copyists didn't get caught. "Right after the shows at Chanel or Christian Dior, I'd run to the nearest sidewalk café and start sketching the collection from memory," said Shannon Rodgers, a designer who worked for a number of New York dress houses back then. His drawings came to life as affordable ensembles sold in the "French Room" at L. S. Ayres in Indianapolis.

Dior, who was one of the first couturiers to offer a mass-produced retail collection, fought a losing battle with the knockoff artists. As early as 1957, Dior wasn't moving fast enough; copies of Dior's hobble skirts were hanging on Macy's racks well before his couture customers got their originals. Retailers awaiting shipments from Dior's retail collection shifted into spin control, pleading for women to be patient, advertising that it was "better to wait for perfection."

The couturiers didn't need to convince French women about the virtues of fine craftsmanship, for their countrywomen had an affinity for custom-made clothes. Until the late 1950s, in fact, most middle-class Frenchwomen were still having their clothes made by local dressmakers, many of whom used bootlegged couture patterns. Most every French home or apartment contained a *lingerie*, a tiny room off the *boudoir* designed for the care of clothes, where seamstresses worked when they made house calls.

Thus, groomed in the habits of countless fittings and creative clothes-making, middle-class Frenchwomen dreamed of trading up, and eventually wearing the top-of-the-line couture. And before the cost of skilled labor rose sharply in the 1970s, which forced the couturiers to keep raising their prices, many Frenchwomen could afford to splurge occasionally on a simple couture outfit.

GREASING THE PATH for Parisian designers—and fashion in general—were the members of the fashion press, who were the best unpaid publicists a designer could ever want. Before the late 1970s, when designer brands became household names with million-dollar advertising budgets, fashion houses relied on powerful editors—Carmel Snow of *Harper's Bazaar*, Diana Vreeland of *Vogue*, and Eugenia Sheppard of *The New York Herald Tribune*—enthusiastic fashion buffs who relished their omnipotent role as kingmakers and arbiters of taste to the masses. The women of the fashion press were a clubby lot, who got used to being wined and dined and discreetly wardrobed—either at discount or for free—by fashion houses who were keen to curry their favor.

Raising her hand high, Carmel Snow did her part to ensure that the French couture houses, which had been shuttered during World War II, would rise again. She said: "I was no more willing to concede the permanent fall of Paris than was General de Gaulle. . . . Since fashion is the second largest industry in France, I felt my personal contribution to the Allied cause could be to help the revival of that industry." It was Snow, in fact, who coined the term "New Look" in her breathless description of Dior's pivotal 1947 collection of long, ankle-grazing skirts that rendered every woman's prewar wardrobe of short dresses obsolete.

Fashion journalism would always be known for its relentless boosterism, as fashion writers typically slanted their reviews to flatter their designer buddies with shameless flackery ("his best collection in years") and rarely a discouraging word.

"The women who covered fashion generally didn't do a good job," said James Brady, publisher of *WWD* in the 1960s and of *Harper's Bazaar* in the 1970s. According to Brady, "The major papers would send reporters to Paris twice a year to get competent fashion show reviews—and they got to lunch with the designers. But I'm not aware they ever did a serious business story. *Vogue* never did serious stories inside the fashion business. The average reader didn't know a helluva lot what was going on. Back then, women were fascinated by fashion trends and not by anything else."

Flexing its editorial muscle with stylish irreverence was the omnipotent *Women's Wear Daily*, the garment industry paper that turned into a lively social chronicle in the 1960s under the reign of John B. Fairchild, the Princeton-educated heir to Fairchild publications, the trade-newspaper empire founded by his grandfather in 1890. John Fairchild was twenty-seven in 1955 when he became *WWD*'s bureau chief in Paris, where he began transforming his sleepy, rag-trade rag into a gossipy must-read that raked over the personalities of high fashion: the couturiers and their socialite clients.

Becoming the editor and publisher of *WWD* in the 1960s, Mr. Fairchild, as he was always so respectfully addressed, drummed up delicious little dramas, pitting one designer against another—while blithely shunning those like Geoffrey Beene and Pauline Trigère, who didn't strike his fancy. The intrepid Fairchild weighed in annually with his famous IN and OUT list and his roast of the year's "fashion victims," those ladies who dared to wear the worst of fashion.

In his 1989 biography, *Chic Savages,* Fairchild writes: "The real issue is that in the fashion business, it's almost against the law to tell the truth, and anyone who steps behind the silk curtain to show how raw the business is can expect a rough time. Designers go to grotesque lengths to exaggerate their concepts to the press. And the press is just as guilty when it swallows the bait and spews forth huge headlines. The self-importance of our profession is appalling."

DESPITE THE GLAMOROUS world portrayed and promoted by the press, by the 1960s, the first hairline cracks in the couture world began to appear. Rising labor costs were steadily erasing profits, and in 1961, the French government stopped providing subsidies to couturiers who did not agree to use at least 90 percent French textiles in their collections.

But economics aside, Paris fashion was being upstaged by London, where the miniskirt was born. The impact of the mini was tremendous. Beyond its saucy, knee-baring silhouette, the mini represented a change in women's values as it rendered the matronly, hat-and-glove standard out of style. "What was amusing about the fifties was that women didn't care about looking young," recalled Karl Lagerfeld. "An eighteen-year-old wanted to look like a woman with jewelry and a mink coat because this was the fashion. The fashion of sexiness and youth didn't come until the sixties with the miniskirt and Brigitte Bardot."

Fashion's youthquake of the 1960s revolved around the joy of shopping, the onset of what was known as the "boutique mystique," as Marilyn

Bender noted in 1966: "From then on, most of the high and mighty fashion leaders wanted it known that their clothes came from the small shops with the low prices. . . . Shopping in boutiques was like altering the birthdate on a passport. It certified that a woman was a swinger."

The boutique phenomenon quickly spread to France in the 1960s, where such couturiers as Emanuel Ungaro and Yves Saint Laurent introduced ready-to-wear collections for their own shops. But this diversification turned into the quintessential catch-22: As more wealthy women got hooked on the more affordable frocks at boutiques, they began to lose interest in collecting expensive couture clothes.

AS THE FRENCH couturiers created boutique collections, they discovered that the easiest way to offset their mounting losses on couture was to sign up licensees, which provided a reliable money machine and a lifeline for their businesses. The father of fashion licensing was Christian Dior, who in 1948 signed up with Prestige, a New York hosiery company, which produced his Christian Dior nylon stockings. Dior rejected an initial offer of a flat $10,000 licensing fee and held out for a revenue stream—a sliding royalty based on a percentage of sales—which became the industry standard for such contracts in the future.

In fashion licensing, a designer collects a royalty payment—between about 3 percent and 8 percent of wholesale volume—from an outside manufacturer who produces and markets the merchandise. Licensing enabled designers to put their trademarks on handbags, jewelry, shoes, and bedsheets—as well as clothes—quickly and relatively painlessly. Millions of American women who would never see the inside of an exclusive Paris atelier nevertheless shared the allure of filling their closets with affordable designer merchandise that was blessed with a couture pedigree.

Long after Dior's death in 1957, the house of Dior continued to milk its vaunted trademark, with more than two hundred licensees by the late 1980s, when the royalties ran deep. "From 1983 to 1989 we had licenses that were getting 20 to 25 percent increases every year and we didn't understand why," said Marie Fornier, who worked at Dior at the time. "The system was so great; Asia was just opening and there wasn't a lot of competition outside the traditional designer brands. So it was, why not more? We even licensed Dior slippers with Aris Isotoner."

But "more" resulted in schlock instead of chic. Marc Bohan, Dior's couturier for nearly thirty years, became more and more disgusted as the Dior label ceased to reflect all that was elegant and chic. Once in the late 1980s when Bohan and Arnault were canvasing the floors of Bloomingdale's in New York, Bohan was aghast upon seeing "all that horrible luggage with the Dior name on it!"

While Arnault could take pride in Dior's popular fragrances such as Diorissimo and its chic Baby Dior infant's wear, the Dior trademark nevertheless suffered from "inconsistency," admitted Colombe Nicholas, who ran Dior's U.S. division in the 1980s and signed up many of its licensees at the behest of Paris headquarters. Quality control became exceedingly difficult to maintain because the licensees were more interested in making money than genuflecting to the House of Dior.

For example, the licensees refused to make merchandise that complemented the fashions designed by Marc Bohan. According to Nicholas, Bohan's "ready-to-wear [collections for Dior] never sold well in the U.S. because the clothes were all wrong—too expensive, too formal, too French-looking, and not lifestyle-driven. Marc would set styles; he would say, for example, that green was the color of the season and half of the licensees would say 'you can't give away a green coat in America.' So, they tended to ignore him, rightly or wrongly."

But the licensees were driven to safeguard their profits by any means necessary. They were already on the hook to pay Dior guaranteed minimum royalty payments, regardless of sales or profit levels. So it was in their best interest to jack up sales—to cut corners on quality, to make a handbag in a vinyl-trimmed canvas, for example, so that the handbags could retail for a lower price, making them easier to unload to department stores. Most high-fashion designers barred their licensees from shipping their merchandise to discounters like Loehmann's. But if nobody was watching—and the French fashion houses were lax when it came to monitoring—the licensees would surreptitiously ship merchandise to any stores they pleased.

In fashion licensing, Nicholas said, "It is very difficult to balance image and to make money. The challenge is standing up to the licensees, telling them that whatever limitations in price, there should be a certain quality level. But when you are sitting across from a licensee with whom you do $100 million of business, it is a difficult position to be in. They tell you, 'You don't know what you are talking about.'"

The licensing boom saturated the world with designer merchandise that hardly lived up to its prestigious labels—polyester scarves and handbags stamped with brassy logos. Hurting the French mystique even further was the flood of illegal counterfeit T-shirts and handbags hawked on the streets of big cities like New York. By the late 1980s, American shoppers in particular had had their fill and were no longer fascinated by most French designer labels.

WITHOUT A DOUBT, Pierre Cardin took fashion licensing to dizzying new lows. By the late 1980s, Cardin had signed up a staggering eight hundred licensees worldwide, in apparel, cosmetics, chocolate, home furnishings, and appliances. Cardin raked in the millions, selling his name so many times over that his cursive signature itself was a valued commodity. There was always a manufacturer somewhere in the world ready to slap "Pierre Cardin" on hair dryers, alarm clocks, bidets, and frying pans. "My name is more important than myself," Cardin once said.

Pierre Cardin became the couturier the French loved to hate—an artist who got swallowed by marketing madness. Cardin's gold-plated credentials dated back to 1947, when he was a top Dior assistant and renowned as the author of Dior's best-selling "Bar" suit—a fitted white jacket over a full black skirt. Cardin was also a trailblazer in menswear, the Giorgio Armani of his time. In 1961, when smartly dressed gentlemen favored the boxy suits from Savile Row, Cardin broke the mold with his dandy Edwardian-cut suits, with high armholes and nipped waistlines, that were soon worn by everybody from the Beatles to Rex Harrison.

Cardin, the son of Italian working-class immigrants, was always disdainful of couture's aristocratic pretensions. He could hardly wait to begin selling to the masses after he opened his own couture house in 1949, at the age of twenty-seven. Eight years later, he cornered the Japanese market, staging his first fashion show in Tokyo. And on the heels of President Nixon, Cardin conquered China in the early 1970s, where the screaming Chinese mobs awaiting Cardin's arrival mistook him for the president of France. "Cardin is a very excellent promoter and he was a salesman before anything else," said Henri Berghauer, who managed Cardin's business back in the 1950s. "Pierre realized early that he wanted to be more of a label than a designer. He wanted to be Renault."

Cardin's road to riches was paved with licensing contracts from a reported ninety-four countries—deals that the intrepid couturier made so fast and furiously that he had trouble keeping up with all the products he licensed. His haphazard ways landed him in court, when he was forced to pay $600,000 to settle a dispute over Pierre Cardin cigarette lighters, which he had mistakenly licensed to two different parties.

In 1981, Cardin paid $20 million to buy Maxim's, the legendary Paris restaurant, on which he lost millions as he turned it into a licensing machine. Nevertheless, Cardin was still filthy rich, one of the wealthiest individuals in France, with an estimated net worth of more than $300 million in 1987. Cardin-label products reached an estimated wholesale volume of about $1 billion in 1991, according to his biographer Richard Morais, who concluded: "His fortune was built on the back of rapidly changing media, which in the period of his lifetime had shrunk the world into one easily accessible market."

The eccentric tycoon was still on the move well into the 1990s, running his far-flung empire from Paris. In January 1997, he was taping a TV interview at Espace Cardin, the theater and exhibition space he owned across the street from the American embassy in Paris. Pale, thin, and angular in a drab gray business suit, Cardin feigned utter indifference to the plight of the French fashion houses in the 1990s. "I don't understand what they're doing. It makes no sense." He shrugged. "Anyway, I already did all of that."

As the septuagenarian spoke, his head tilted cockily to the side, he wasn't exaggerating. Indeed, the designers in Paris were now scrambling to pursue the same path he had pioneered twenty years earlier. "Pierre was considered too rough for this market at the time, but nevertheless, in the end, everybody wants to sell," said Berghauer. "You look at what has happened to these big fashion labels. They aren't selling caviar; they are selling T-shirts, jeans and underwear."

WHILE CARDIN, FRENCH fashion's most colorful enigma, was in a class by himself, it was left to the reigning king of couture, Yves Saint Laurent, to wave the flag for French fashion. After Dior's sudden death in 1957, it was the twenty-one-year-old Saint Laurent, Dior's able apprentice, who carried on designing the Dior collections without missing a beat. The fragile and introverted Saint Laurent founded his own fashion house in 1962, together with his shrewd and tough-as-nails business partner, Pierre Bergé.

For more than twenty years, Saint Laurent was revered as French fashion's most progressive designer for modern women, in the spirit of Chanel. Saint Laurent prospered as a couturier and a retailer through his chain of Rive Gauche boutiques, where he marketed such liberated looks as "safari" pantsuits, *le smoking* tuxedos, and pea coats.

But the house of Saint Laurent, too, couldn't resist the siren call of licensing, stacking on more than two hundred licensees, including YSL cigarettes. Bergé pontificated on the excesses of fashion licensing as practiced by the likes of Cardin, telling *The Wall Street Journal* in 1984: "A name is like a cigarette, the more you smoke it, the less that is left." Naturally, he avoided discussing the slew of mediocre Saint Laurent–labeled umbrellas, scarves, and handbags—not to mention cigarettes—that were dragging the trademark down.

Saint Laurent managed to hold on to his prestige longer than Cardin and Dior because of his stunning success in marketing perfumes. Years before Calvin Klein took over the perfume counter, Saint Laurent had already scored a blockbuster with his 1978 fragrance Opium. A spicy Oriental scent that was as exotic as its controversial name, Opium made its New York debut with a splash: Saint Laurent hosted a lavish bash on the *Peking*, a Chinese junk moored in the East River. Opium continued to be a bestseller for more than a decade, joining the ranks of dozens of other popular French designer perfumes.

French perfumes, whose essences were composed of the exotic flowers from France's southern Grasse region, used to be prized by women around the world. Thousands of American G.I.s returned from World War II with bottles of Chanel No. 5 for their mothers and sweethearts.

For years, perfumes had been a nifty, image-enhancing sideline for couturiers, producing such legendary classics as Arpège from the house of Lanvin, Joy by Jean Patou, and L'Air du Temps—in its famed René Lalique–designed bottle—by Nina Ricci. But in most cases, the perfume sideline threw couturiers off the track from their fashion main line and eventually became a distraction, albeit a profitable one.

"The perfume business is the worst thing that ever happened to French fashion," observed Patrick McCarthy, the editorial director of *WWD*. "Once perfume came on the scene, the French didn't have to worry about selling clothes. Any major fashion house, if you had a reasonably successful perfume, you could do what you wanted. The designer could tell the stores, 'I'm not changing the way I'm cutting the dresses; I am doing whatever I want.' The money would still be coming in from that little perfume license.

"That's why somebody like Giorgio Armani could come in and change the way men and women all over the world dress and take over all the space in stores," said McCarthy. Meanwhile, "the French were still selling some perfume—but nobody was buying their clothes."

Nevertheless, Saint Laurent and Bergé would go on to make enormous sums in their fashion house, which was valued at $500 million when it went public on the Paris Bourse in 1989. In the next years, Saint Laurent himself would visibly deteriorate, the legacy of more than three decades of nervous breakdowns and bouts with depression. In the early 1990s, he teetered and trembled down the runway, underscoring speculation that his future was precarious.

In 1993, cosmetics giant Elf Sanofi bought the house of Saint Laurent for $650 million, leaving Bergé and Saint Laurent in charge of the couture operations and with employment contracts for several more years. But Elf Sanofi made it clear that its long-term future was in its still-buoyant YSL fragrances and cosmetics. Elf Sanofi's chief executive, Jean François Debreq, told *Vanity Fair:* "If he dies, I think I make even more money because then I stop the [couture] collections." He said at the time that the couture was losing $5.4 million a year.

LICENSING WAS INDEED an opiate that had greatly enriched the French houses while handicapping them for the long run. By handing over their trademarks to licensees, the French designers escaped the rigors and nuances of mass production, international retailing, and marketing. So when the licensing bubble finally burst, the couture houses were hard pressed to find a new way to whip up a heady froth to revive their brands.

While the French were on their licensing binge in the 1980s, the Italian fashion industry was steadily making inroads, having gained its footing in Milan, in close proximity to the country's leading textile mills in the Lake Como region and factories that promote homegrown talents such as Giorgio Armani, Gianfranco Ferré, Krizia, and Genny. The Italian manufacturers, who had a history of competition and cooperation with the apparel, footwear, and textile sectors, "developed a marketing plan to increase Italian exports with the objective to make a large footprint in Italian fashion in the U.S.," asserted Armando Branchini, a Milanese management consultant.

"In one sense, the Italians have won the battle of fashion," wrote *WWD*'s John Fairchild in 1989, noting that French designers Emanuel Ungaro, Christian Dior, Christian Lacroix, Sonia Rykiel, Claude Montana, and Jean Paul Gaultier all manufactured much of their apparel in Italy. "The Italian monopoly is even more complete because in addition to clothes, the Italians are responsible for designing and producing some of the most beautiful fabrics in the world."

The French didn't worry much about the rise of the Italians during the 1980s because couture had gotten a shot in the arm with a new generation of fans from the Middle East and America. The couture revival coincided with the OPEC oil cartel in the 1970s, when wealthy Arab ladies began taking their petrodollars to Paris for shopping sprees. Middle Eastern women loved opulent couture gowns and they bought liberally, especially for weddings, for which they also bought couture dresses for their young daughters. In 1984, Arab women represented only about 15 percent of the clients, but they bought more than half of the reported $24 million of garments sold by the twenty-three official Paris couturiers that year. The Middle East gravy train continued until couture sales dropped dramatically with the outbreak of the Persian Gulf War in January 1991. Ironically, most of the couture ensembles destined for the Arab world hit a dead end, never to be photographed and never to be worn in public. As was the custom in Muslim countries, women wore their couture finery behind closed doors, only in the company of other women.

By the early 1980s, the Arab ladies were joined by the Americans, the Reagan-era charity-ball set—women like Ivana Trump, Ann Getty, and Lynn Wyatt—who headed to Paris via Concorde for the couture shows. Such clotheshorses were known to blow $100,000 or more on a couture wardrobe on a single Paris trip.

DURING THE EIGHTIES the rising couture tide lifted all French fashion, as Parisian designers like Claude Montana, Jean Paul Gaultier, Sonia Rykiel, and Thierry Mugler flourished alongside the couturiers.

The designer boom was running at full gallop and sparking a new type of rivalry: the war on the catwalks. It was Pierre Cardin who had paved the way back in the 1960s when he first began filling his runways with outlandish costumes, as he cleverly sensed that a sensational runway picture was worth far more than a thousand words.

The international fashion circuit included women's and men's designers who staged fashion shows twice a year in Paris, Milan, New York, and London. By the early 1990s, there were a staggering 1,500 major showings on the calendar. Television cameras joined the parade, capturing runway footage for such fashion news programs as CNN's *Style with Elsa Klensch*. High fashion turned into high entertainment. And always, the loudest noise was coming from Paris, where avant-garde Japanese creators like Issey Miyake, Yohji Yamamoto, Kenzo, and Rei Kawakubo joined the local lineup.

The shows took on a life of their own as everyone tried to outdo each other with seminude costumes, strange hair and makeup, and gimmicky staging—starring those $10,000-a-day playmakers known as supermodels. Jean Paul Gaultier, Paris fashion's kilt-wearing enfant terrible, was idolized by avant-garde fashion groupies, only to be one-upped from time to time by Thierry Mugler, whose 1994 fall fashion show, televised live, was a sci-fi spectacle of Jetsons-like creations, featuring celebrity model Patty Hearst and soul singer James Brown in a musical finale. The reported cost: $3 million.

Mugler could afford to splurge on such lavish shows, which were partially underwritten by Clarins, his publicity-hungry perfume licensee, who was glad to oblige as long as the shows created a big buzz. And the fashion magazines just couldn't seem to get enough of the wild and crazy images from the Paris catwalks.

Distracted by all that fashion-show hoopla, French designers missed out on the shift that began in the late 1980s when sales of high fashion stagnated and American retailers began searching for new ways to sell designer clothes. Retailers came up with a new marketing vehicle known as "bridge"—collections that carried a designer label but were priced at least 30 percent less than the top designer lines. Bridge jackets, for example, retailed at $350 to $650, compared to designer jackets at $700 and up. The bridge brands enabled American department stores to generate big volume in designer brands, without selling the most expensive goods. In 1996, bridge brands such as Donna Karan's DKNY, Anne Klein II, and Ellen Tracy accounted for about $4.7 billion, or 12 percent, of all women's wear sold at retail and represented the top price range at most department stores. By comparison, top-tier designer lines accounted for about $1 billion in retail sales and were available only at select locations at Saks Fifth Avenue, Nordstrom, Neiman Marcus, and Barneys New York, as well as the designers' own boutiques.

Given that French suppliers were accustomed to selling to independent boutiques rather than big American chains, most houses didn't grasp the bridge concept. Instead of shifting more of their production to the Far East, where most bridge brands were made, the majority of French designers continued to use high-cost factories in France or Italy. Thus, French designer brands weighed in at the loftiest prices, which virtually locked the French out of U.S. department stores and, consequently, the world's primary clothing market.

There was another fundamental problem: the look of the clothes. Retailers agreed that too many French designers had made some bad fashion calls. Even when Mugler, Montana, and Gaultier eventually marketed so-called *"diffusion"* or bridge-style brands, the styles were usually too avant-garde for most women—and were cut too tight for American bodies.

"Mugler and Montana were sexy and hot in the 1980s, but now women want something that is more contemporary and less aggressive," said Armand Hadida, the owner of Eclaireur, a seventeen-year-old chain of four high-fashion Paris boutiques. As for Jean Paul Gaultier's whimsical designs, Hadida considered them ridiculous. "Gaultier is doing only theatrical collections for the *défilé* [fashion shows], which are good for a moment, but try to sell this. Nobody wants to buy it. . . . It is a joke."

More affluent American women were gravitating toward bridge brands—and increasingly ignoring the noise coming from the high-fashion shows, which played on warp speed. The Paris shows continued to be media happenings, chock-full of buyers, press, and miscellaneous stylish groupies. This was the clubby world of the fashionistas, the women who dress alike in all-black, in a sea of studied nonchalance. The fashionistas reinforced each other's importance by being there, in the thick of the action, during a glorious, expense-account whirl, to cover the shows twice a year under the pretext of fashion news.

The American newspapers covering the shows—*The New York Times*, *The Washington Post*, the *Los Angeles Times*, and *The Dallas Morning News*—were caught in a tougher bind. They were passing judgment on clothes that would never be seen again—and that their readers thought were ridiculous. So the fashion writers strained to characterize fashion as a high art form—and they looked hard for any common themes on the runway that they could pinpoint as the coming trends that would soon trickle down to department stores. But once readers saw the pictures and read the copy, they knew high fashion was more and more a series of publicity stunts.

In 1995 *USA Today* stopped covering the shows in Europe and New York altogether, at the suggestion of Elizabeth Snead, *USA Today*'s fashion editor at the time, who volunteered to quit going. "I just couldn't justify going anymore. It didn't make sense to call the shows fashion 'news' when they weren't anymore." Snead transferred from New York to Los Angeles, where she started covering fashion on movie stars and celebrities, who had become the new fashion role models of the 1990s.

Retail buyers continued to ply the international circuit, but they were grounded by what their stores could actually sell—and not what fashion editors considered cutting-edge. "We're really not influenced by what we read," remarked Joan Kaner, fashion director of Neiman Marcus. The

Dallas-based retailer bought as much as 70 percent of its collections in the showrooms *before* watching a single fashion show, with most of their choices being the styles that the designers thought were too bland to be shown on the runway.

BY 1995, FRANCE was facing a bleak economic climate that affected fashion and other local industries. Consumer spending was down, unemployment stood at 12 percent, and the overvalued franc was hurting France's ability to increase exports of consumer products, from automobiles to clothes. Moreover, the French image was taking a bruising in the U.S. as many treasured symbols of French refinement came under siege. Sophisticated New Yorkers no longer treated themselves to classic French cuisine; Italian food—lighter, healthier, and more creative—was now the preferred choice of many. Champagne was still divine, but more connoisseurs also respected fine wines from California, Italy, and Spain. And on Mother's Day, men were more likely to buy their wives Beautiful by Estée Lauder than Joy by Jean Patou. The French mystique simply wasn't holding up.

In a telling sign that struck closer to home, French President Jacques Chirac appeared on the cover of *Paris Match* in an oxford-cloth, button-down-collar dress shirt with a Ralph Lauren polo-pony logo on his first day on the job in May 1995. (Lauren's officials back in New York sent Chirac a thank-you note and a box of shirts.)

The French mystique could no longer coast on inertia alone. French fashion needed to be repositioned, updated, and most of all marketed to a new generation of sophisticated consumers. "When you look back to the 1950s and 1960s, Paris designers had an ability to create a fashion look that everyone wanted to have," observed Carl Steidtmann, a New York retail industry economist. "The French felt they didn't need to market to consumers because their brands were very strong. But now that the focus has shifted away from designing, and if you have enough money and are good at marketing, you can create a strong brand."

Throughout Paris in department stores such as Galeries Lafayette, a number of the world's most powerful fashion marketers like Gap, Calvin Klein, and Ralph Lauren began winning over Parisian shoppers. In 1995, Calvin Klein had brazenly splashed his sexy underwear ads on billboards all over town and planted his retail flagship on the swank Avenue Montaigne—the best shopping street in Paris—directly across from Christian Dior. Klein's success didn't come from creating *true* fashion, maintained Didier Grumbach, the managing director of Thierry Mugler, who declared in 1997: "It is better to be known for a beautiful embroidered dress than for underwear."

By the mid-1990s, fashion's klieg light shone brightly on Milan with the onslaught of Italy's big three: Giorgio Armani, Prada, and Gucci. Ever chauvinistic, the powers in France ignored the Italians—at least for the record. The prevailing French group-think went like this: stay the course in promoting traditional French savoir faire, which will outlast them all. The Chambre Syndicale trade group took Paris runway shows on the road to such places as Belarus, Beijing, Shanghai, and Budapest, where the locals remained enthralled with classic French labels and now had the freedom to buy them.

Just as Arnault's LVMH went about acquiring the house of Givenchy in the 1990s, other fashion industry investors in France were also keen to revive couture's most fabled names from the 1940s and 1950s— namely Balmain and Balenciaga—instead of starting from scratch with an unknown designer. "Fashion in France is considered a national patrimony," said Morand, the economist. "You don't even pose the question whether one of the traditional houses is obsolete or not. That is why you have some financial people who will be ready to buy brands that don't mean anything anymore, because they are linked with history and status, whether or not they have a concept which is still valid."

But valid or not, reviving a long-forgotten couture brand was no different than launching a new name; both scenarios required millions in marketing and advertising to position the brands in the public consciousness. But heavy-duty advertising simply wasn't the French way, least of all in the fashion sector, where designers had long put their faith in the free plugs they got in the fashion press. Counting on getting a steady blast of publicity from one of Seventh Avenue's most beloved designers, the House of Balmain hired Oscar de la Renta to be its couturier in 1995. While Balmain did draw more business from de la Renta's American socialite clients as a result, the Balmain trademark and its Ivoire perfume remained in obscurity.

FOR ALL THEIR bluster about their eminence the beleaguered French houses were becoming more prickly and paranoid about their future. Perhaps that's why certain designers suddenly became obsessive about stopping knockoffs, which were the oldest gambit in fashion. Knockoffs had always provided the grist for countless fashion dramas as designers staked their reputations and won awards from their peers— by being original, by being first with the next Big Idea, whether they made money on it or not. The irony of it all was that designers around the world had stopped staring at Paris to get their best ideas. The most successful houses were pragmatists, grabbing trends from the present, from the past, and from the trendy kids on the street, making it impossible for any designer to claim ownership of a particular style. In any event, the end of fashion in the 1990s made pedantic arguments over creativity and originality irrelevant.

Nevertheless, the powers at the Chambre Syndicale decided to get tough on knockoffs, zeroing in on the hundreds of freelance photographers and video cameramen whom French designers had accused of leaking fashion-show photos to their foreign competitors. In 1995, the Chambre Syndicale dreamed up a regulation in which photographers attending the Paris shows were told that they could publish photos only for "journalistic information," and not on the Internet. Then the Chambre Syndicale instituted a throwback from the 1930s: an official photo "release date," three months after the shows were held. An impossible dream in today's media age? "*Mais non*," vowed Jacques Mouclier, director of the Chambre Syndicale. Mouclier claimed that "a French prosecutor" was all set to press charges against *First View*, a website that published fashion-show photos during the collections. "We are seeking to make an example," he asserted in 1997. But *First View* said that other than receiving a few threatening letters from Mouclier, nothing happened.

In 1994, a knockoff war erupted over a sleeveless tuxedo gown between Yves Saint Laurent and Ralph Lauren. Saint Laurent charged in a French court that Lauren's $1,000 tuxedo gown was a spitting image of his $15,000 couture version. (Ironically, though it wasn't widely known, Saint Laurent himself was a convicted plagiarist, who had been fined in 1985 after a French court found him guilty of copying a toreador jacket credited to couturier Jacques Esterel.) Sleeveless tuxedo gowns had been on the market for years, but that didn't stop a French judge from concluding that Lauren was guilty as charged and slapping him with a $411,000 fine. To further shame the American, the judge ordered Lauren to advertise the court decision in ten publications.

The judge, Madelaine Cotelle, wasn't a lawyer but a fashion expert of sorts, by virtue of her ownership of two boutiques in suburban Paris. During the proceedings, live models paraded through the courtroom dressed in both versions of the tuxedo gown. Judge Cotelle's remarks during the trial left little surprise as to Lauren's ultimate fate. "I know something about fashion," Judge Cotelle said. "Clearly there are differences in the two dresses. Saint Laurent's dress is made of a different fabric and has pockets, unlike Lauren's. And his buttons aren't gold, while Mr. Saint Laurent's are. The Saint Laurent dress also has wider lapels and I must say is more beautiful, but of course, that will not influence my decision."

Eagerly awaiting an expected victory in court, Saint Laurent's Bergé gloated. He told *WWD* that Lauren was "ripping off" the Saint Laurent tuxedo dress "line for line, cut for cut." Judge Cotelle ruled that his premature outburst defamed Lauren and fined Bergé $93,000. Indignant, Bergé later crowed that Saint Laurent's victory was a "great shot in the arm for our fellow designers. It's a clear warning that so-called designers, especially from America, cannot get away with lifting original ideas of true creators of fashion." (The case was eventually settled with both parties paying lower fines, and Ralph Lauren wasn't forced to run ads to publicize the decision.)

IT HAD BECOME increasingly harder to make a case that French fashion had kept up with modern women, including those from France, who were searching for practical fashion solutions, not just prestige, from a label. In 1994, Faces International, a Paris-based market research firm, surveyed three hundred European women about their attitudes toward fashion. The French respondents sounded just like American women, as they unanimously agreed that their "dream world of fashion" was "designer labels at affordable prices," and not couture. Answering the question "Who or what do you emulate when you try to be fashionable?" only 2 percent said "the models in magazines," while 70 percent said: "No one. I just want to maximize me."

ANY DISCUSSION ABOUT the stamina of French fashion always came back to Chanel, the house that underwent a spectacular makeover during the 1980s with the help of designer Karl Lagerfeld, who began creating Chanel's collections in 1982. By the end of the decade, Chanel was more than just viable—it was red hot, more popular than it had been under Coco Chanel, who died in 1971. By the mid-1990s, the Chanel empire, which included forty-one boutiques, had racked up an estimated $1 billion a year in clothes, cosmetics, and accessories—without enlisting a single licensee.

While Lagerfeld would get a lot of the credit, the fact was that Chanel owed its renaissance to a confluence of circumstances. Before Lagerfeld, Chanel was a prestigious, if faded brand that hadn't been compromised by the far-flung licensees that bastardized Dior's image. Chanel also benefited from its stash of enduring marketing symbols created by Coco Chanel: the tweed suit, the camellia, the interlocking CC logo, the quilted chain handbag, and the famous, black-tipped slingback pump.

Above all there was Chanel No. 5, the most popular designer fragrance of all time. Alain Wertheimer, who took over the Chanel empire in 1974, began aggressively marketing the famous fragrance in clever TV commercials, such as the one featuring a morphed image of Marilyn Monroe holding a gigantic bottle of Chanel No. 5.

Meanwhile, Lagerfeld got busy tarting up Chanel's dowdy tweed suits to make them status symbols for executive women. With his white powdered ponytail, sunglasses, and black Yohji Yamamoto suits, the German-born designer was the most experienced hired gun in high fashion. Since the 1970s, Lagerfeld had designed collections for Chloé in Paris and for Fendi in Rome, as well as his own namesake collections.

Chanel also got plenty of tailwind from Lagerfeld's close friendship with one of the most influential people in fashion, *Vogue* editor Anna Wintour, who frequently wore Chanel suits and practically lived in oversize Chanel sunglasses. "Karl is a terrific designer; he has everything going for him," said Bernadine Morris, the veteran fashion journalist. "He knows how to sell, how to seduce the press—he does it in five languages."

Lagerfeld admitted that he came to Chanel at the right time, in the early 1980s when he was able to concentrate on revamping Chanel's image with substance rather than pure hype. "All this media stuff didn't exist when I started at Chanel," he observed. "I made over the image with things that would sell. I didn't have to be outrageous."

While Lagerfeld resided most of the time in Paris, inside a splendid eighteenth-century estate on the Left Bank, he considered himself a foreigner and an outsider to the French fashion establishment, which he loathed because the French kept clinging to the past, while the rest of fashion had moved on.

Consumers around the world, Lagerfeld maintained, are "no longer impressed with the prestige of Paris. The Italians are very clever marketers and the Americans are making modern and interesting clothes, capturing the right mood of today. . . . You don't think of French perfume; you think of Calvin Klein, which the Europeans are also buying."

OBSERVING CHANEL WITH a mixture of envy and admiration was Bernard Arnault, the hard-charging chairman of the LVMH fashion empire. Arnault had spent about thirteen years building LVMH, exercising his penchant for strong-arm tactics. Everyone who had observed the unflappable Arnault wrangle one company from the grip of another wondered if he could also marshal his executives to master the subtleties of the high-strung world of high fashion. Arnault was considered a maverick whose steamroller style was anathema to France. "Behind his angelic appearance there lurked an authoritarian proprietor," wrote Arnault biographers Nadege Forestier and Nazanine Ravai in *The Taste of Luxury* in 1992. "He liked to increase tension in his various companies. His managerial credo became American-style management. He was not worried about charisma. What mattered to him was efficiency."

Born in 1949 to a wealthy family in northern France, Arnault majored in math at École Polytechnique, the prestigious French university that bred corporate titans and government ministers. Arnault spent three years in the United States to develop his family's real estate business in Florida before returning to France in 1983, when he began to build LVMH, starting with Christian Dior in 1984.

People close to Arnault believed that his original strategy was to recast Dior as a mirror image of Chanel. Colombe Nicholas, who oversaw Dior's U.S. operations in the 1980s, recalled: "There was always some envy when he looked at Chanel, which stayed pure without licensees and secondary lines, and Arnault is saying to himself, 'Dior is just as good a name and I'm going to make it pure again.' "

Tall, gangling, and pale, with heavy, dark eyebrows, Arnault was low-profile, aloof, and mysterious. He sat on the front row at fashion shows, stone-faced and silent, his bodyguards planted nearby. An accomplished pianist whose second wife, Hélène, was a concert pianist, Arnault never professed to be a fashion expert. He did profess that his obsession to collect so many of the world's top luxury brands dovetailed with his love of money. Arnault once said: "My relationship to luxury goods is really very rational. It is the only area in which it is possible to make luxury profit margins."

While he struggled with his pet project, Lacroix, Arnault put his faith in Dior, which had a thriving perfume and cosmetics business that would generate revenue and visibility for the brand as he went about canceling most of Dior's licensees in an effort to reposition Dior to be as upscale as Chanel.

Starting around 1994, designer handbags suddenly became the rage in fashion and Dior was lucky enough to ride the wave with its Lady Dior handbag, a quilted box in buttery lambskin, distinguished by the gold-plated letters D-I-O-R dangling from its double handles. At $1,200, the Lady Dior bag was a pricier version of Chanel's $960 quilted bag. But what a difference Princess Diana made! French First Lady Bernadette Chirac gave the Princess of Wales a Dior bag in 1995 and she began carrying it everywhere, within full view of the paparazzi. Before long, retailers had a hard time keeping Lady Dior handbags in stock and more than 100,000 Lady Diors flew off the shelves in 1997.

Employing his adopted American sensibilities, Arnault took advantage of the power of publicity. He recruited a few of the darlings of the fashion press to design for LVMH's brands. From London came John Galliano, who went to Dior, and Alexander McQueen for Givenchy. Arnault chose three Americans for LVMH's other leather-goods divisions: Marc Jacobs for Louis Vuitton, Michael Kors for Céline, and Narciso Rodriguez for Loewe. None of the new charges had couture experience, nor had they run financially successful fashion businesses on their own. Whatever their talents were as designers, they all held the promise of generating lots of press. Indeed, in the case of Rodriguez, he had made his name on a single dress. As an assistant at Cerruti 1881, Rodriguez created the much-photographed slip wedding gown worn by Carolyn Bessette when she married John F. Kennedy Jr. in 1996. Labeling McQueen and Galliano as "two of the greatest creators of our time," Arnault told *Paris Match* that he chose them "for the simple reason talent has no nationality."

The fashion world watched in awe while Arnault went about his grand restructuring. *WWD*'s McCarthy observed in December 1997: "It is a massive investment and it's fascinating to watch. For every ten times you try, there is one time you succeed. Who knows if Galliano will make Dior sing again? This is the biggest gamble anyone has taken in fashion in a long time."

Galliano—a Salvador Dalí caricature with a skinny mustache and alternating wavy and dreadlocked hairstyles—had a fitful start, first spending a year at Givenchy only to be shifted to Dior by Arnault. Known for his dramatic bias-cut evening gowns, Galliano staged many theatrical fashion shows, including a 1998 couture show with a Pocohontas theme, complete with a moving train. Rumors flew that the artisans in Dior's workrooms despised Galliano, and retailers conceded privately that his clothes weren't selling.

As for McQueen, the chubby son of a taxi driver, his claim to fame as a London designer were his low-riding, cleavage-revealing "bumster pants." The impudent McQueen liked to shock the French establishment, such as the time he told *Le Monde* that handmade couture embroidery looks "like vomit." His retort to his many critics was a dismissive "Fuck you." After the press criticized his first quirky-looking collections, McQueen lashed out: "People aren't going to get wonderful things overnight. I don't expect everyone to do what I do right away. . . . I do what I do and people can take it or leave it." Arnault was obviously taking it; he signed McQueen to a three-year contract in October 1997.

While the fashion press stopped short of writing off the designing Brits, other observers were pointedly dismissive. Lagerfeld sized up McQueen as "crude and vulgar," while David Wolfe, a New York retail consultant, pounced: "For Bernard Arnault to hire McQueen to do Givenchy is such an exercise in bad thinking; it goes against every idea of common sense and marketing imaginable. If any publicity is good publicity, then this works. But I will be surprised if it does."

If Arnault had learned anything from Lacroix, he knew that fashion shows would take Galliano and McQueen only so far. Colombe Nicholas wondered: "What is the press value of couture? If you have a strong accessory business your brand will work. Galliano is getting a lot of press but is the twenty-year-old buying that product? I don't think so. I don't understand where it will lead to."

Arnault had little to worry about with Louis Vuitton, the $1-billion-a-year leather-goods company that no young turk designer could destroy. Yet he believed that a Vuitton fashion collection would put some sizzle back into Vuitton, the same way that Tom Ford had done for Gucci in the 1990s. That's why Arnault chose Marc Jacobs, the New York designer who put the downtown grunge look on the runways when he worked for Perry Ellis in 1989.

Jacobs, a cute, chain-smoking favorite of fashion editors, began locking horns with Vuitton's strait-laced executives right from the start. It was an uneasy fit: Jacobs was a high-concept designer working for Vuitton, which catered to conservative, bourgeois tastes. In his first months at Vuitton in 1997, Jacobs had experimented with a boiled, matted cashmere that he adored because it was "guaranteed to pill with age; beautiful but a little fucked up." Jacobs delivered a few samples of his cashmere scarves, which Arnault passed out to his friends. They didn't get it. But Arnault told Zoe Heller of *The New Yorker* that Jacobs would nevertheless bring a "trendy, fashionable edge to Vuitton," which would broaden its traditional base. "It is an easy idea," Arnault said.

AROUND THE CORNER in 1998 was a new, jarring reality that nobody in Paris was ready for: the collapse of Asia. The most buoyant market for luxury French designer brands was suddenly hit with a monetary economic crisis that effectively froze consumer spending on fashion brands across the board. The Japanese superconsumers, who once collected Chanel handbags as if they were trinkets, put the brakes on their spending. Scores of designer shops in Singapore, Hong Kong, and Thailand closed. Economists predicted that the Asian crisis would last for a while, at least through 2000, before any recovery would begin. And everyone knew that once the crisis subsided, the Asians would return to the marketplace with a sobering new mindset—just as the Americans had done when they shifted from ostentation to practicality in the aftermath of the 1987 stock market crash. In the midst of the crisis, Japanese shoppers were getting into the habit of buying simple, affordable sportswear from Gap, which opened ten stores across Japan in 1998.

The so-called Asian flu stung the luxury-goods sector badly in 1998, when LVMH's earnings plunged 29 percent, dragged down by $37 million in operating losses from its Duty Free Shops division, which was hit hard by the weaker yen and reduced Japanese overseas travel.

In the meantime, Bernard Arnault, the protector of French high fashion and luxury-goods raider who some dubbed "the wolf in cashmere," took a stunning detour in 1999. Instead of simply hiring a few more British and American designers to pursue LVMH's French agenda, Arnault began aggressively shopping for American and Italian fashion brands to call his own.

During a March 1999 interview at Dior's Fifth Avenue showroom, he explained his new, multinational strategy. "It isn't a question of country, but a question of power of the brand and its capacity to be developed on a worldwide scale. Fashion is very different in today's world. It is very important to link up with each other."

In 1999, LVMH spent $1.5 billion to secure a 34 percent stake in Gucci Group, the Florence-based leather-goods and fashion house that was among the hottest, most profitable fashion brands in business. Arnault coyly explained that his interest in Gucci was a friendly attempt to forge a partnership. But his sneaky way of buying up all those Gucci shares without launching a formal bid for all of Gucci was viewed as a "creeping takeover"—an approach that incensed Gucci's CEO, Domenico De Sole, who began waging a down and dirty fight to escape LVMH.

As if Gucci didn't keep him busy enough in 1999, Arnault extended his overtures in March to another Italian designer, Giorgio Armani, to effect some type of "partnership" with LVMH, presumably to link up with Armani's connections with some of the best Italian factories. Praising Giorgio Armani to the hilt, Arnault called him a "fantastic designer and a businessman whom I admire very much. He is an incredible talent and extremely successful worldwide. I don't see any other brand that can compare with Armani with so many different lines with a separation between them. Armani is a unique example."

Arnault was also teeming with pride with regard to his best hire so far, Michael Kors, who had accomplished in a little more than a year something that Galliano, McQueen, not to mention Lacroix, had failed to accomplish. Under Kors, Céline was starting to attract significant retail business from American stores. Arnault was so pleased with Kors, in fact, that in March 1999, LVMH bought a 50 percent interest in the modest fashion business Kors continued to operate in New York.

Unlike the artistically obsessed Lacroix, "Michael Kors is very interested in commercial success," Arnault observed. "He goes to the Céline shop to talk to the customers. The reason to be a designer is to sell. Fashion is not pure art. It is creativity with the goal of having as many customers as possible wearing the product."

LVMH rounded up more American companies in March 1999, buying a 70 percent interest in a trendy New York spa called Bliss, and curiously, a 25 percent stake in Gant, a solid but undistinguished maker of men's sports shirts sold in department stores.

The new-look LVMH, stacked with more Americans and perhaps a couple of Italians around the corner, heralded the end of French fashion as the world knew it.

FASHIONING A MAKEOVER FOR

EMANUEL UNGARO

The great question which I have not been able to answer despite my
thirty years of research into the feminine soul is
"What does a woman want?"

SIGMUND FREUD (posted beneath a picture of Freud in the studio of Emanuel Ungaro)

On the balmy morning of July 8, 1996, about an hour before his couture show at the Paris Intercontinental Hotel, Emanuel Ungaro was at peace, and oblivious to the backstage commotion of models and makeup and hair people rushing around like Keystone Kops.

For thirty-one years, Ungaro had performed this drill to perfection. Dressed in a black turtleneck tucked into black pants, he slipped past the racks of the exquisite creations he had worked on for nearly four months. Short and sturdy, Ungaro wore facial stubble, his thick, graying hair in a brushed-back shag setting off his heavy-lidded blue eyes. He was a sexy, good-looking sixty-two. A charming gallant, given to hand-kissing and to passionate analogies, he made fashion his mistress. "My colleagues always tease me when I plunge my nose into fabric," he once said. "I caress it, smell it, listen to it. A piece of clothing should speak in so many ways."

Keeping his distance backstage, Ungaro found a quiet spot where he sat down and closed his eyes to meditate, as he always did before the storm on the runway. He had more on his mind than usual. Just days earlier, he had announced that he had sold his fashion house to Salvatore Ferragamo SpA, the Florence-based footwear and fashion empire owned by the Ferragamo family.

The takeover of the House of Ungaro was far from hostile. It was actually more like a marriage of two businesses that, by all appearances, dovetailed quite neatly. Ferragamo's marketing and international retailing expertise enhanced Ungaro's extraordinary skill at making fine garments.

The House of Ferragamo respected Ungaro's heritage and promised to preserve his couture and possibly to strengthen it, even though couture would inevitably generate losses. Ferragamo saw high fashion as an invaluable legacy that would enhance the cachet of the Ungaro trademark (as well as that of the Ferragamos)—and would keep Emanuel Ungaro toiling away happily for years to come.

So Ungaro was ready to take a big—and belated—step into the brave new world of high-fashion marketing. Ferragamo was prepared to roll out a new generation of Ungaro boutiques, to overhaul Ungaro's licensees, and to position the couture house in a more modern way. Ungaro looked forward to a prosperous new future. "I want this house to grow, to reach its fullest potential," he said.

Yet while he talked a big marketing game, Ungaro remained an old-school couturier who had a lot to learn. Handbags were now the hottest designer trinket on the market. But to Ungaro, a handbag wasn't a stand-alone that got stamped out by the thousands; he created a handbag to *accessorize* a particular outfit. Selling the fashion house he built from the ground up was "very difficult, both from an objective and sentimental perspective," he told *WWD* in July 1996. "It was a decision that took a long time. I *did not* and *do not* want to change the house."

But changes were inevitable. As Ungaro pondered the many possibilities in those moments before his fashion show, he was also thinking about his new partners, the Ferragamo family, who would be in the audience ready to view their first Ungaro collection.

EMANUEL UNGARO WAS a proud member of that rarefied circle of haute couturiers who started in the sixties: Andre Courrèges, Yves Saint Laurent, and Paco Rabanne, among others. Ungaro had burst onto the scene in 1965 with kicky minidresses—and not ballgowns. He was the renegade whom *WWD* had nicknamed "the terrorist" and the "new cat for couture."

During the mid-1980s, Ungaro reigned as one of couture's finest artisans, whose trademark burned the hottest when such international socialites as Lynn Wyatt in Houston snapped up his body-hugging, draped silk dresses which came in a kaleidoscope of layered prints and patterns. "Emanuel had such a definite style, a focus. Those jackets were unforgettable. You *knew* what you were looking at," remembered Grace Mirabella, the editor of *Vogue* from 1971 to 1989 and Ungaro's most enthusiastic sponsor in the fashion press.

Ungaro had indeed made it, but he never reached the critical mass that would have made him a household name. By 1995, Ungaro had only nineteen shops, with just three in America, and his once-popular Diva perfume had fizzled and was practically forgotten. Nearly all of the House of Ungaro's $280 million revenue in 1995 had come from royalties from twenty-five licensees, many of which were in Japan. Ungaro's first love would always be couture, of which he sold only about three hundred outfits a year, at a loss of $3 million.

With his 1996 marriage to Ferragamo SpA, Ungaro, a proud perfectionist, became one of the last couturiers to sell out, joining Dior and Givenchy—both owned by LVMH, Bernard Arnault's luxury goods conglomerate, and Yves Saint Laurent, which became a division of Elf Sanofi, the big pharmaceutical concern. "These are huge financial powers with lots of means," Ungaro said. "I cannot really compete by myself in this situation."

After watching the venerable business of his contemporary, Hubert de Givenchy, lose its identity after being swallowed up by LVMH, Ungaro was determined not to allow his trademark to lose the classy, romantic French image that had always been the signature of the house.

EMANUEL UNGARO'S JULY 1996 couture show took place in one of the most magnificent venues in Paris, the Salon Imperial at the Hotel Intercontinental. A baroque ballroom with a frescoed ceiling, the Salon was designed in 1878 by Charles Garnier, the architect of the Paris Opera house—a heritage underscored that day by Ungaro's choice of music, which included the recorded arias of Maria Callas, one of his favorite artists.

The Salon resembled a regal theater, its mottled mirrored walls reflecting the endless runway bisecting the room. A glossy crowd of fashion's high court of socialites, private clients, fashion editors, and other international guests streamed in, creating a multilingual din of French, English, Italian, and Japanese. They took their assigned places in tight rows of gilt chairs lining either side of the runway, with each seat bearing a name card written in calligraphy, and secured with a fuchsia ribbon—Ungaro's signature color. As the room grew stifling from the bright overhead stage lights and the clash of perfumes, shiny-faced women fanned themselves furiously with their fashion show programs.

Milling around the doorway, the fashion paparazzi snapped the usual couture suspects, the tucked and titled social X rays now in their sixties, such as Park Avenue socialite Nan Kempner and the swan-necked Viscountess Jacqueline de Ribes, who ran her own couture house for a while in the 1980s.

French actress Anouk Aimée was greeted by a bolt of flashing strobes when she entered. Aimée had had a long love affair with Ungaro in the 1980s, and she provided the inspiration for his Diva perfume, which she helped him promote at its introduction. Although they were no longer a couple, they remained such friends that she always made it to his shows. Wearing huge sunglasses atop her chiseled cheekbones, the sixty-two-year-old actress was just as fetching as she had been more than thirty years earlier, starring in *A Man and a Woman.*

Three members of the Ferragamo family had flown in from Florence for the show, but they were nowhere to be seen. Pier Filipo Pieri, Ungaro's plucky public relations man, had stashed them in the hotel's coffee shop—a little scheme he hatched to heighten the drama when the Ferragamos entered the packed Salon just moments before the lights went down.

Right on cue, the photographers swooned at the sight of the Ferragamos. First came Wanda Ferragamo, the sixty-eight-year-old matriarch, a short woman with wavy reddish hair, in a crisp summer dress. Her modest demeanor belied her stature as the executrix who had spent the last thirty-five years steering her family's firm to international prominence following the death of her husband, Salvatore.

She was followed by her son Massimo, who ran Ferragamo in the U.S., his wife, Chiara, and her eldest son and heir apparent, Ferrucio, age fifty, who managed to look distinguished on crutches, his right leg in a cast after a soccer injury.

It had been Ferrucio's idea to buy Ungaro. Investment advisors had brought the parties together, and then Ferrucio and Ungaro negotiated in secret for about nine months. During that time, Ungaro and Ferrucio communicated using the code name "Rosa"—roses were the flower Ungaro often used in his advertising.

It was easy to see why they clicked, for Ungaro and the Ferragamos had a lot in common. Ungaro's parents were Italian; he was married to an Italian and his CEO, Carlo Valerio, was Italian. Ferrucio and Ungaro spoke to each other in Italian, and they were like-minded in their serious and conservative approach to business—both were committed to quality and the snob appeal of high fashion. Salvatore Ferragamo SpA bought a controlling interest in Emanuel Ungaro S.A., which had an estimated value of about $40 million, leaving Ungaro with a minority stake and an employment contract that left him in place as couturier through 2002.

As the searing soprano of Maria Callas permeated the Salon Imperial, the fashion show was under way. The Ferragamos watched attentively, marveling at the fifty-four couture confections under the trademark that now belonged to them. Out came the models in Ungaro's gold-embroidered decorative jackets, worn with flowing silk pants. The evening gowns were opulent, festooned with handmade lace and intricate beading. The grand finale was a magnificent pearl-encrusted wedding gown.

The applause swelled and a few people rose to their feet as Ungaro, beaming and blushing a bit, came down the runway to take his bow. All eyes in the room watched as he paused midway to extend his hand to the Ferragamos, who looked happy, yet reserved. They joined Ungaro backstage for champagne after the show to greet well-wishers Aimée and other clients.

A couple of hours later, the Ferragamos met with Ungaro for their first joint board meeting in the conference room back at Ungaro's atelier at 2 Avenue Montaigne. There wouldn't be a whole lot to discuss. The Ferragamos weren't ready to make any moves yet; they had just hired Bain management consultants in Boston to do an extensive study of the couture house. So Ungaro had to sit tight for a while. All he could do now was go along for the ride. And keep meditating.

EMANUEL UNGARO WAS born in 1933, in Aix-en-Provence, in the south of France, where his Italian parents, Cosimo and Concetta, had emigrated during the 1920s to escape Mussolini's Fascist regime. In Aix, Cosimo Ungaro, a tailor, opened a storefront haberdashery, where the eldest of their six children, Eugenio, began his grooming to take over his father's shop when he was fifteen. His second son, Emanuel, first sat down before a Singer machine when he was five and quickly took to the craft of making men's suits. The Aix shop was a serious yet jovial workplace where *La Bohème* filled the air, as rendered by Cosimo Ungaro, who "had a perfect voice for Rossini, a lyric tenor light, seductive and airy that he coached us in at work in our tailor's shop," Ungaro later recalled.

Emanuel inherited his father's passion for opera, but by the time he was a teenager, he already had set his ambitions far from Aix, in Paris, where he dreamed of designing couture for the world's most elegant women. Emanuel was twenty-three in 1957 when he arrived in Paris, settling in the Montparnasse district, the community known for its artists, intellectuals, and musicians. The next year Ungaro got his big break. He was hired as an assistant to the legendary couturier Cristobal Balenciaga, at the recommendation of one of his assistants, Andre Courrèges. For the next six years, Ungaro toiled under the wings of the great master, who was the archetype of the suffering artist. Ungaro once wrote: "What I can try to describe is the emotional effect of my encounters with him, the genuine and powerful feeling of having been brought into contact with knowledge, rigor, strength and greatness."

Even in the lofty leagues of Paris high fashion, Balenciaga towered above them all. Coco Chanel once asserted, "Balenciaga alone is a couturier in the truest sense of the word. Only *he* is capable of cutting material, assembling a creation, and sewing it by hand. The others are simply fashion designers." Balenciaga had first made his name in his native Spain, where at age forty he opened his first couture shop in Barcelona in 1935. Two years later he had established another atelier in Paris on the exclusive Avenue Georges V, which for more than thirty years attracted the world's most elegant and discerning clients, women like Gloria Guinness and Babe Paley.

Balenciaga ran a modest but thriving business between his Paris and Spanish workrooms, where he toiled relentlessly in silence, for he tolerated no talking at the office. Balenciaga marched to his own exigent drummer as he invented styles like his famous chemise, or sack dress, that flattered the rounded, matronly figures of the ladies who sought him out. Where Balenciaga led, buyers followed, like Beverly Rice, who ran the French room at L. S. Ayres department store in Indianapolis during the 1960s. Back then, Ayres hosted a chic luncheon, "Paris Calling," where local ladies listened as Rice, via transatlantic hookup, breathlessly related the latest news from the runways. "When Balenciaga changed the width of a seam, *that* was news," she recalled.

The Balenciaga mystique was further heightened by his inaccessibility and indifference to the rest of high fashion. The reclusive master took no bows on the runway, nor did he give interviews. He refused to introduce retail collections and rejected all licensees, except for perfumes. Resigned that the future of fashion was in retailing—and not couture—Balenciaga abruptly shuttered his couture workrooms in 1968 and died four years later.

Indoctrinated in the ways of Balenciaga, Ungaro rose to become his chief assistant. Courrèges left Balenciaga to open his own house in 1961 and Ungaro left a couple of years later, but then spent a few months helping out Courrèges, to whom he was indebted for having recommended him to Balenciaga.

Finally, in 1965, Ungaro was ready to go on his own. He scraped together a few thousand dollars and opened his business with his partner and girlfriend, Sonia Knapp, a fabric artist. Knapp hocked her blue Porsche to raise enough money for three months' rent for a tiny Right Bank studio on Avenue Macmahon. Ungaro's atelier-on-a-shoestring included three seamstresses and Knapp, who helped design fabrics and served as the house model. Meanwhile, Ungaro wore many hats as couturier, bookkeeper, delivery man, and janitor, sweeping up all the pins and fabric scraps after hours.

By then, Courrèges had made a splash as the hottest couturier in Paris, by virtue of his 1964 futuristic "space" collection of white minidresses worn with short white boots. After Courrèges's instant fame, the fashion world anxiously awaited the debut of another promising Balenciaga protégé. Days before Ungaro's July 1965 show, *WWD* reported: "One name on everyone's mind is Emanuel Ungaro. Paris needs a new force. The press needs a new attraction and Emanuel Ungaro is here." He didn't disappoint.

Ungaro's collection of twenty shift minidresses and coats in double-faced wool in pastel colors would have made Balenciaga proud. It was now Ungaro's turn to be the toast of Paris, as influential clients such as

Marie Hélène de Rothschild and Jacqueline Kennedy rushed in for fittings at his studio. And *Vogue* began its love affair with Ungaro, prominently featuring his creations in its fashion spreads.

Alongside his popular couture, Ungaro signed his first licensee, Gruppo GFT, to make a boutique collection called Parallèle in 1967. Based in Turin, Italy, GFT began in 1865 as a manufacturer of uniforms for the Italian army. Military uniforms were among the first apparel mass produced after the sewing machine was invented in the 1850s, ushering in the era of commercial clothes making. A century later, Ungaro would take his couture expertise inside GFT's factories to spearhead the company's diversification into women's wear. "GFT said, 'Here is a factory and 200 people. Do it,' " Ungaro recalled. "I spent three days a week in Turin teaching them how to make the clothes. I was a pioneer; I paved the way for the others," which included Giorgio Armani and Valentino, who later also became GFT licensees.

By the seventies, GFT was also turning out Ungaro menswear, under the direction of Ungaro's younger brother, René. But the couturier wouldn't wear his own label, preferring instead the fine hand-tailoring of his other brother, Eugenio, who made all of Emanuel's suits at their father's shop in Aix.

DESPITE HIS PIONEERING moves into industrial clothes making, Ungaro adhered to the doctrine of Balenciaga. "He makes what he wants—the best," explained Catherine de Limur, the director of Ungaro's couture salon from almost the beginning. "He designs like a writer writes a book. He's not commercial; he's a couturier." Consequently, Ungaro didn't factor in the feedback he got from his clients. "Research just shows what women liked in the past," he explained. "I project myself into the future. I don't even remember my last collection."

INSIDE UNGARO'S SECOND-FLOOR design by studio on Avenue Montaigne, daylight streamed in from a wall of windows where creativity took place in the Balenciaga tradition. Even the short lab coat Ungaro worked in had a ceremonious cut, featuring an unusual kimono armhole. Hanging from a cord around Ungaro's neck was a flat, beige pouch containing a stash of straight pins and a tiny pair of scissors.

Balenciaga taught Ungaro to design by working first with the fabric and then sketching afterward—which was just the opposite of the way almost every other designer created. Ungaro began by cutting toile, or muslin, after he had his "dream," or concept, figured out. Using a live model, Ungaro used hundreds of pins to baste every seam, pleat, and tuck. His smooth, blocky hands were nimble and quick, as he took the utmost care when he got to the armholes. "I sew the sleeves myself; I have a *passion* for the sleeves," Ungaro murmured.

As the weeks went by, a long rack of toiles—so full of pins that each piece stood stiffly at attention—sat in the studio's hallway, ready to come to life in whatever fabric Ungaro chose. Pamela Golbin, the curator at the Musée de la Mode et du Textile, the fashion museum at the Louvre, said of Ungaro: "Everything evolves from the fabric, so your relationship with the fabric will change the outcome. If you choose chiffon or wool—two fabrics that have nothing to do with each other—the result of each will be different. Balenciaga and Ungaro let the fabric dictate what will happen, as opposed to using a technician to figure out how to produce a garment from a sketch."

Not surprisingly, Ungaro cut and pinned in twelve-hour stretches, in solitary confinement, while chamber music by Beethoven and Wagner played in the background. The act of designing was exhilarating at times, but always, he sighed, "full of suffering."

Over the years, his private clients also suffered—before and after they received the invoices for their couture garments. The pinnacle of fashion perfection required patience—a client had to troop over to Ungaro's atelier at least three times for fittings. On the floor below Ungaro's studio were his two primary workrooms where the *petit mains*, the "little hands," in white lab coats actually fabricated the garments. There were sixteen sewers specializing in the *flou*—dresses and gowns—and fourteen other seamstresses in the *tailleur*—jackets and suits. They used irons and sewing machines—but only to stitch the primary seams on each garment. Everything else—the buttonholes, the zippers, the pleats, and the tucks—were sewn and finished entirely by hand.

Et voilà! Perfection was indeed divine: an exquisite garment that looked as beautiful turned on the inside as it did on the outside. Couture garments were often embellished with hand embroidery or beading, work that was farmed out to a dwindling breed of artisans around Paris. A simple daytime dress took a few weeks to make; an embroidered gown took months. The high cost of such exacting handwork was what drove up the price of couture, which in the 1990s ranged from about $15,000 to $150,000 for the fanciest beaded and embroidered gowns.

Couture had been the calling card of his atelier, and Ungaro doubted that his couture workrooms could survive without him. He was confounded by the limitations of his assistants, who could sketch well enough but couldn't sew. "I try to teach to young people [that] to be able to do what I am doing means that you have to work twelve hours a day every day of the week. They don't do it anymore. They don't have patience for a fitting. There is a young man here who has fantastic taste but he can't control the construction of the drape. Maybe, if he has a good *premier* [first assistant], he could tell him how to do it. It is very complicated."

And even more complicated than producing couture was making couture viable again after the go-go eighties, when Ungaro seemed poised to take off internationally.

"The Heat Is On. Fashion Goes Feminine and Ungaro Leads the Way," blared a coverline on an April 1988 *Newsweek* in which Somalian model Iman was pictured in Ungaro's polka-dotted pouf cha-cha dress. "After twenty-three years of perfecting a combustible formula of silk fabrics and a seductive fit, his draped dresses are the hit of the year," wrote *Newsweek*'s Jennet Conant.

The eighties had been good to Ungaro. One of his most devoted clients, Lynn Wyatt, said: "Emanuel puts a woman on a pedestal and that's why I feel so feminine and romantic in any Ungaro gown." Wyatt, the perky, petite wife of Houston oil mogul Oscar Wyatt, made a stunning entrance at Count Volpi's ball in Venice in 1988, dressed in Ungaro's yellow-and-black tartan ballgown.

Such famous fashion plates adored Ungaro, but the workaholic, reclusive couturier didn't hobnob with them. Before he was married, Ungaro continued to live as a haute-bohemian in a rented studio apartment, and he drove around Paris in a beat-up Austin Mini Morris. He had season tickets to the opera and to the symphony, and his big indulgence was a country house in his hometown of Aix-en-Provence, which he decorated with Italian baroque furniture and flea market antiques he liked to collect.

Not surprisingly, Ungaro was on "the miserly side," remarked *WWD*, noting that in 1986 he drew a yearly salary of about $500,000 but ran around the office turning off lights. "I have complete freedom in this house," he said. "I'm not working under the pressure of finance. I use my freedom in the haute couture."

While couture always conferred prestige on the Ungaro trademark and some one thousand pages annually of editorial spreads in fashion magazines, Ungaro was still largely unknown—undoubtedly because he never spent more than $1 million to advertise his fashion lines at a time when other houses were spending tens of millions on advertising by way of their perfume licensees. Ungaro would have to wait until the 1990s for his name to become a bona fide hit in America—and his commercial coup didn't come from couture or Parallèle. Instead, Ungaro scored with his lowest-tier label, Emanuel, a women's bridge collection of $475 silk blazers and $250 pants—a collection that he didn't design.

Introduced in 1991, Emanuel vaulted Ungaro ahead of all the other French fashion brands, to become *the* top-selling French apparel brand in American department stores, selling more than $150 million at whole-sale in the late 1990s.

Emanuel was a tale of "The Licensee Knows Best." Watching its sales of $2,000 Parallèle ensembles decline steadily, licensee GFT dreamed up a new cash cow for American department stores called "Emanuel by Emanuel Ungaro." Emanuel went from being a literal in-terpretation of Ungaro's bright prints and romantic styling in its first sea-sons to becoming a polished, tailored collection of suits, jackets, and vests in neutral shades. "We have a living French couturier, which is our heritage, but we had to make something that would sell in the States," said Maura De Visscher, the founding president of the Emanuel division. "Ungaro trusted us and gave us the license to make the right decisions."

Ungaro was immensely proud of Emanuel, even though he hadn't done any of the heavy lifting. Still, this was a man who got off on psychic rewards, not fat royalty checks. It must have galled him that most American women didn't know who the Emanuel behind Emanuel was. Actress Kyra Sedgwick, hired in 1997 by GFT to appear in Emanuel's advertising, was initially among the clueless. "I knew the name but I wasn't that familiar with the designer," she said. Before she became the poster girl for Emanuel, the wide-eyed blond actress said her wardrobe consisted "mostly of vintage clothes from secondhand shops."

WITH THE STABILITY and prestige that Emanuel delivered, Ungaro celebrated his twenty years in business by designing a family life for himself. In 1990, the fifty-six-year-old couturier married the well-connected Laura Fafani, a thirty-year-old divorcée from Rome whose father was the director general of Italy's three state-owned TV stations. The couple said they hit it off at their first meeting, during a business lunch, when Laura was a publicist for GFT. *Vanity Fair* pictured the happy newlyweds on their wedding day, and writer Ben Brantley noted that "hearts were shattered in Paris" when the news of Ungaro's marriage broke. "Here, after all, was the end of the long bachelorhood of fashion's most flaming heterosexual, a man who claimed to make clothes and love with monomaniacal devotion to the unfathomable in women. 'I design dresses for women I would like to take in my arms,' he said. . . . Laura represented 'one of the few times in my life that I seduced the woman [rather] than her seducing me.' " The Ungaros had a daughter whom they named Cosima, after Emanuel's father.

Slender, pretty, and highly animated, Laura Ungaro became director of communications for her husband's house, where she became the modern muse Ungaro now needed. Laura imparted her own sense of style to Ungaro's socialite look. When she tossed on Ungaro's exquisite embroidered jackets over a T-shirt and a pair of tight pants, she made them look sassy and very youthful. She had her own discreet way of dropping fashion hints to her mate. "I like to play a little game with him," she said, recalling the mornings when she got dressed in something that wasn't designed by Ungaro. "I may ask him to zip me up." Ungaro, of course, wouldn't utter a word, but Laura would discover later that he had been asking his assistants about her clothes.

Laura worked alongside Carlo Valerio, the seasoned, forty-six-year-old Milanese executive whom Ungaro hired as his first managing director in 1993. Bringing in Valerio was Ungaro's first step toward modernizing his business. The professorial Valerio, who favored blue oxford-cloth shirts and sweater vests, had a degree in nuclear engineering and was previously an executive at Ratti, the giant Italian fabrics producer. He set about developing a restructuring plan for Ungaro, which culminated with the sale to the Ferragamos.

Ungaro was among Ferragamo's first outside acquisitions in a diversification plan designed to provide future positions for nineteen members of the youngest Ferragamo generation who were coming of age and were expected to join the family empire. As with Ungaro, the story of shoemaker Salvatore Ferragamo was one of ambition and big dreams. Born in 1898, Salvatore was the eleventh of fourteen children who grew up in poverty in the Neapolitan village of Bonito. He was just nine years old when he crafted his first footwear: white shoes in canvas and cardboard, made specially for his little sister's first communion. At sixteen, Salvatore was already a skilled shoemaker on his way to Boston, the capital of America's footwear industry, to learn about mass production.

But Salvatore Ferragamo was frustrated when he saw the tradeoffs required to execute factory-made footwear. The mass-produced American shoes were "heavy, clumsy and brutal, with a toe like a potato and a heel of lead," a far cry from what he was capable of turning out by hand.

So he headed to the West Coast, where he opened a handmade-shoe shop in Santa Barbara, California, in the shadows of the motion picture industry. Salvatore became famous for his innovative and comfortable footwear used in movies. His private clients included screen legends

Douglas Fairbanks, Mary Pickford, Greta Garbo, and John Barrymore, who relied on the Italian cobbler to resolve his problem of flat feet. Salvatore perfected his signature fit by taking anatomy courses at the University of Southern California, where he learned everything he could about the foot.

When Salvatore Ferragamo returned to Italy in 1927, he had retail orders from Saks Fifth Avenue and Marshall Field's—and a burning desire to grow. He began to expand with the help of dozens of shoe contractors around his Florence headquarters. He later married Wanda Miletti, the daughter of his hometown mayor. During his fifty-seven-year career, Salvatore Ferragamo created some twenty thousand styles of handmade shoes, including his patented cork wedge heel, an innovation he concocted during the leather shortages of World War II. Later, in the 1950s, he invented the first pair of stiletto heels for Marilyn Monroe, in alligator skin.

In 1960, Salvatore died after a long illness at age sixty-two and left his homemaker widow in control of his business. With the help of her children, Wanda continued her husband's dreams of building Ferragamo into a full-line fashion house that dressed men and women from "toe to head" by adding scarves, men's silk ties, sweaters, and other sports wear. While these collections rounded out the Ferragamo empire, they were fairly staid, never matching Ferragamo's innovations in footwear.

That's why many fashion insiders jumped to the same conclusion when they learned of a Ferragamo-Ungaro partnership: How could Ferragamo, which had no track record in high fashion, orchestrate a makeover at Ungaro when Ferragamo's own collections were so conservative? In apparel, Ferragamo's bestsellers included men's silk ties and a wool cardigan sweater with gold-logo buttons, a perennial in its line for more than a decade.

Set against Prada and Gucci, which marketed trendy fashions alongside their core leather goods, Ferragamo never became a force in apparel. It wasn't as if Ferragamo hadn't tried. Steven Slowick, an American designer and former Calvin Klein assistant, was barely in his twenties when the Ferragamos hired him in 1989 to create its women's collections. Slowick, who reported to Giovanna Ferragamo, Ferrucio's older sister, had tweaked Ferragamo's conservative look in his fashion shows, but neither the merchandise in the boutiques nor the advertising seemed to reflect his new mood. His first fall collection in 1990 had a sixties/Andy Warhol mood, with mirrored-fabric minidresses and lots of leather. He recalled: "For *them*, it was too forward, but for the press, it wasn't crazy. After that fashion show, Giovanna told me how the family members felt: 'This is too extreme for us. We have to, kind of, tone it *down*.' "

Slowick, who left Ferragamo in 1996 to open his own fashion house in Paris, has fond but mixed feelings about his years at Ferragamo, where change occurred at a snail's pace. "They are great people, very serious and all that, but they are not fashion people," he reflected in July 1997 from his modest studio on the Left Bank of Paris. "Their view of fashion is very conservative. Very, very conservative. And my personal view is that you have to be a little out there. You can make a product that's really classic that you can sell to a twenty-year-old and an eighty-year-old. That's hard to do, but Hermès does it. But you have to make an image. I told [Ferragamo], 'You have to do something about that image because it's the pits. People think you're an old-lady house.' I think of my grandmother when I think of Ferragamo.

"I worked the best I could within the structure of the family and the company. It was more like, 'Well, we don't want to lose our old customers; we don't want to confuse them, but we want to get more modern.' Which I can understand. But at some point you have to go a bit one way or a bit more the other way. I would say to myself, 'Be patient—you know this is the way this family works.' But other times my American business side would come out and say, 'Oh, why can't you just change things quicker?' "

Likewise, at Ungaro the Ferragamos were locked into their cautious Goldilocks strategy: Not too fast, not too slow, just right. But in fashion, where momentum counted for much, they needed to strike while the irons were hot. Instead of making a great leap forward, the Ferragamos liked to enlist outside consultants to study their situation. The Bain review, which came out a year later, didn't contain any monumental revelations. The only bit of new marketing came in the October 1997 fashion show, when a model in a floral dress bounced down the runway caressing a huge bottle of Fleur de Diva, a new Ungaro perfume launched in a joint venture between Ferragamo and Bulgari, the Italian jeweler. But for a fragrance sendoff, Fleur de Diva's was altogether pitiful; the perfume wasn't even advertised in America, Ungaro's prime market.

While Ungaro's name was still on the door and Valerio was the managing director, the de facto CEO was Ferrucio Ferragamo, the formal and often terse micromanager who acted as if he knew more about high fashion than he probably did. During the summer of 1997, Ferrucio took several early morning flights from Florence, arriving at Ungaro's atelier at about 9:30, ready for a full day of board meetings with Ungaro and Valerio. Ungaro always detested these drawn-out meetings, which took him away from his work in the studio, yet he sat through them, mindful that he had to be involved in planning the future of his house. Aware of his short attention span, Ferrucio avoided the minutiae of profit margins and market share when he was in the room. "We know he gets a little bored, so we try to make the meetings as interesting as possible," Ferrucio said.

But during the meetings, the person who was squirming was Carlo Valerio, whom Ferrucio had effectively pushed out of the loop. After Ferragamo bought Ungaro, Ferrucio had dispatched one of his accountants to work in Paris, bypassing Valerio altogether.

Meanwhile, in New York, Peter Arnell, the fashion advertising wunderkind who had produced the first ads for Emanuel, had read about Ferragamo's big plans for Ungaro and thought it might be time to check in. But when he called Valerio in Paris in the summer of 1997, Valerio admitted that he didn't know what was up: "The decision process has suddenly become very slow."

Valerio had been eager to start rolling out Ungaro boutiques, while gradually phasing out certain licensees. But Ferrucio's plan was to sever most of the licensees immediately, especially the ones in Japan. The Ferragamos, who owned all but three of their fifty signature boutiques, didn't believe in licensing in most cases; all Ferragamo merchandise was made in Italy through a network of selected contractors, and tightly controlled through a central distribution center in Florence. Valerio worried that if Ungaro canceled so many licensees, the company would lose not only a royalty stream, but visibility at retail. Valerio preferred to phase out the licensees slowly, while simultaneously promoting Ungaro on other fronts.

But it was clear that Ferrucio would prevail and that Valerio would soon be out of a job, substituted by a managing director of Ferragamo's choosing. Valerio resigned quietly, having accomplished his goal of finding a financial partner for Ungaro. While Ungaro didn't balk at Valerio's leaving, privately his associates said he was upset, yet resigned that he was no longer running his company.

Ferragamo wasted no time cleaning house. The first licensee to go was a line of Ungaro bathroom tiles made in Italy, which had yielded "zero for the bottom line or our image," Ferrucio explained. As expected, the House of Ferragamo immediately took over production of Ungaro's shoes and leather goods, canceling Ungaro's licensee in Europe.

The next group to tackle were the twenty-five Japanese licensees representing about $100 million, or 44 percent, of Ungaro's 1995 revenue. Ferragamo had sound reasons for wanting to discontinue most of the Japanese licensees. The Asian business had come at a heavy cost to Ungaro's image. Over the years, Ungaro had allowed Takashimaya, the Tokyo retail giant and its main Japanese licensee, to adapt the look of Ungaro's clothes to appeal to a broad range of Japanese shoppers. But Takashimaya, wearing two hats as licensee and retailer, always had a conflict of interest. There was little incentive for Takashimaya to sell Ungaro merchandise to Japanese retailers that competed with its own stores. Consequently, in Japan, most people saw Ungaro as a Takashimaya house brand—a fact that was underscored because the fashions by Ungaro carried a "made in Japan" label. As a consequence, when Japanese tourists visited Paris or London, for example, they weren't inclined to shop for Ungaro fashions they thought they could find at home.

Ferrucio's strategy centered around moving all of Ungaro's production either to France or to Italy, with the exception of Solo Donna by Ungaro, a women's brand sold only in Japan through Takashimaya.

Initially, Ferrucio had considered Japan the biggest problem area, but in 1997, Emanuel, Ungaro's U.S. juggernaut, took an unexpected body blow. American department stores were overstocked with bridge designer merchandise from Dana Buchman, DKNY, Ellen Tracy, and Emanuel that wasn't selling as briskly as it had in the past. But Emanuel's executives hadn't anticipated the retail slowdown when they charged ahead, aggressively shipping merchandise into department stores during the worst of seasons. As loads of Emanuel clothes languished on the markdown racks, Emanuel failed to meet department stores' profit benchmarks, obliging the company to pay steep rebates, known as "markdown money." The division had planned for sales of about $150 million, but less than half of that sold. The upshot: Ungaro would receive lower royalties for 1997—and again in 1998, when sales had slumped by a third, to an estimated $100 million.

Right before the Emanuel crisis came to light in early 1998, Ferrucio hired a replacement for Valerio. After a drawn-out search, he made an underwhelming choice: the reserved and soft-spoken Thierry Andretta, a forty-one-year-old former managing director at Belfe Group, an Italian outerwear maker whose biggest licensor was Giorgio Armani. Andretta was hardly the hard-nosed presence whom everyone expected Ferrucio to choose. Andretta said he was taken aback initially when the head-hunter from Egon Zendher International described the Ungaro position as a "difficult opportunity."

Looking more like an advertising creative director than a high-fashion mogul, the balding, sun-tanned Andretta favored Armani sport jackets paired with casual pants from Banana Republic. Andretta had five interviews with Ungaro in Paris, where they talked about the history of the house and his mentor, Balenciaga. "I like the history of Ungaro," Andretta said. "We had a lot of discussions about marketing. I see there is a lot of potential here, especially in menswear."

Andretta knew what Ungaro was up against: his own favorite designer. "Armani is the best industrial designer in the world," Andretta said. "There is a line, a signature look that he is always evolving. Ungaro has a history of creativity. It is hard to make a comparison because these are two different worlds of the fashion business. It is more simple for Armani; he changes a few details, whereas Mr. Ungaro, he makes a lot of new things each season."

In April 1998, Andretta moved into Valerio's old office at the atelier and got busy carrying out Ferrucio's orders, signing up new licensees— all Italian companies—for eyewear and jeanswear. It had now been nearly two years since the Ferragamo takeover, and nothing major had happened to jump-start the Ungaro trademark. Other than a few paparazzi shots of *Vogue*'s Anna Wintour and actresses Elizabeth Hurley and Sharon Stone wearing Ungaro out on the town, there was no buzz. Instead of opening new stores in 1998, Ungaro was closing shops in Bangkok, Singapore, and Jakarta, where the Asian economic crisis had hit hardest. By contrast, Calvin Klein, Dior, Gucci, and Prada were rolling out new boutiques and running advertising everywhere you looked.

Meanwhile, the boss's wife had done her best to shake things up. Laura Ungaro hit the gas pedal, hiring five different parties to work on Ungaro's marketing campaigns, prompting Andretta to reel her in. Ever outspoken and anxious, Laura fretted, pointing to Ferrucio, who was holding things up. She spoke up one afternoon in the hallway of Ungaro's Paris atelier: "Ferrucio is more rational and cold, he is slower than me . . . maybe it is good, I give him the push to go forward, but he has to think about it. . . ."

Ferrucio, she insisted, was still on a learning curve. "There is the difference between the way you go with leather goods and haute couture and prêt-à-porter. You can't go slow and take your time in fashion. Since he has entered our world, only in a short time, Prada and Gucci are moving. He is starting to learn. It took a long time and now we begin to move forward."

Laura had a dream: "Money, money, money. I have a plan, we just need money to go fast and it will explode!" she exclaimed, rubbing her fingers together. "I feel that this is the right moment for Emanuel Ungaro. It is now. The company needs to invest in the priorities, the boutiques, the advertising campaign, because Ungaro—as far as the fashion crowd is concerned—is understood. He is following the needs of the market."

While Laura prattled on, her husband was upstairs, sequestered in his studio as usual, fixated on pinning another toile. Recovering from a cold, Ungaro looked weary and became testy when the question was put to him again: What was taking the Ferragamos so long?

"The Ferragamos are very clever, reflective people. They don't do things like that," he said, snapping his fingers for effect. "They have to be sure everything is good. They take their time, to think and to check. I am still the chairman and the family is part of the company. We make all our decisions together. We are completely compatible and complementary. I have a serenity about the future for the house. I'm not paralyzed with haute couture, I'm not mummified. Many houses aren't selling clothing. We are still selling clothing, two million pieces a year. I want this to be a young house. . . . The house is full of projects and energy and young people working all around me."

Ungaro was now concentrating on improving handbags and shoes, the weakest part of his business. "That is difficult—to find an identity with accessories is very difficult. We must find an emblem that is elegant and identifiable. We are working on a handbag now. I don't know when it will be ready; that is a dream. The moment you have it, that is fantastic."

BUT UNGARO NEEDED more than a dream and Laura needed more than just money. In addition to all those millions that Ferragamo had yet to spend on the House of Ungaro, the company desperately needed a deft, well-executed game plan—and some luck. Ferragamo's go-slow approach was designed to avoid making costly mistakes. But going too slow had also resulted in missed opportunities. Then there were those inevitable, unforeseen banana peels: the Emanuel setback and the Asian crisis.

What seemed inexplicable, however, was that the fashion house wasn't keeping its name in lights. Ungaro's solitary, one-page advertisement in the September 1998 *Vogue*—the most high-profile issue of the year—said it all. Ungaro was anonymous and becoming even more so.

Intense and reflective as he was, Ungaro must have second-guessed himself often. Had he erred in selling out to the Ferragamos? Clearly, the partnership was a good fit when it came to footwear and leather goods, but now it was clear that the Ferragamos were out of their league when it came to orchestrating a turnaround.

Ferrucio Ferragamo kept on taking his time while Ungaro was barely coasting on his famed couture heritage to keep his brand afloat. But the Italian owner made no apologies for sticking to his plodding approach. "We can't force the situation," Ferrucio declared during an April 1999 interview. He lamented that Ungaro had lost visibility and sales, after cutting off eighteen licensees. But he vowed that the next steps to remodel Ungaro's remaining boutiques, to expand further into menswear, and to introduce a unisex Ungaro fragrance in 2000 would bear fruit in due time. In three to five years, Ferrucio predicted, the Ungaro label would be back on track.

Following his penchant of enlisting outside professionals before making any costly move, Ferrucio called upon New York investment bankers at Goldman, Sachs & Co. to assist in negotiating a better deal with Ungaro's longtime licensee, GFT.

In the meantime, fashion insiders around the world were convinced that the House of Ungaro was stuck in a rut and steadily slipping off the radar. Ferrucio appeared to be unfazed: "Are we doing this for pride or are we doing the right thing to revive the brand? We don't want to waste money.

"It could be that [Emanuel] might be more anxious to have more visibility, but I told him that I will invest more money at the right time."

So for the short term, the House of Ungaro would lumber along without doing much to establish a more arresting and prominent image for the couturier who more than thirty years ago had basked in the reflection of the great Balenciaga. Until Ferrucio Ferragamo figured things out, Ungaro would likely remain a stagnant, fading brand, like so many others in France.

As for Thierry Andretta, the job that was originally pitched to him as a "difficult opportunity" wasn't worth the wait. He resigned from Ungaro in order to follow the big money and fast company at LVMH. Andretta jumped ship to run a business that by the looks of things was well on its way to becoming a player in the new millennium. In March 1999, Andretta became managing director at Céline, whose designer Michael Kors was now the darling of LVMH chairman Bernard Arnault.

chapter 3

BOUND FOR OLD GLORY:

RALPH LAUREN AND TOMMY HILFIGER

I don't respect Tommy Hilfiger as a designer. Everything he did
he got from me. He has nothing new to say.

RALPH LAUREN, April 1997

In July 1998, Ralph Lauren took ownership of the American flag for a cool $13 million.

Not since eighteenth-century seamstress Betsy Ross stitched up the original stars and stripes had any individual American been even remotely tied to the flag. It was a sweet moment for Ralph Lauren, American fashion's first billionaire, to give back to the land that had given him so many opportunities. The designer's Polo Ralph Lauren Corp. had donated the millions to restore the gigantic 185-year-old star-spangled banner—the very flag that inspired national anthem writer Francis Scott Key—which was hanging, tattered and threadbare, on a wall of the Smithsonian's National Museum. With the stroke of a pen, Lauren, the marketer of stars-and-stripes sweaters and "Betsy" coffee mugs, had catapulted himself into the league of America's great benefactors.

And what must have made it all the more sweet was that Lauren had one-upped Tommy Hilfiger at the same time. Lauren couldn't get over the fact that Hilfiger, his archrival and the hippest designer of the 1990s, had snatched *his* symbol, the American flag, and was waving it all over his advertising, which further validated Tommy's own red-white-and-blue logo. The Gap had ripped off Ralph as well, with its own flag sweaters, but it was Hilfiger who had stolen much of Lauren's thunder in the 1990s. So Ralph had a burning desire to get the flag back from Tommy. A once-in-a-lifetime opportunity came along in 1998. During his January State of the Union message, President Bill Clinton made a public appeal to recruit donors to save America's historical treasures. Lauren heard about the speech and made his move.

On July 13, at a ceremony to officially present his gift, Lauren looked every bit the statesman in his Purple Label pinstripes, standing onstage at the National Museum next to President Clinton and Hillary Rodham Clinton, pledging allegiance to the flag, *his* flag. The designer beamed broadly when President Clinton declared in his speech: "You know, most of us have, maybe not most of us, but a lot of us, including Hillary and me, have these great Polo sweaters with the American flag on it."

To dispel any notion that Old Glory was for sale to the highest bidder, the Polo organization had promised not to parlay its deed into a public relations bonanza. "We've been assured that this is a philanthropic gift and not a marketing gift," said A. Michael Heyman, a Smithsonian spokesman.

But the media quickly connected the dots. *The Washington Times* ran an editorial cartoon of an American flag with a Polo logo in the corner. *New York Times* columnist Frank Rich observed: "A shopper at a Ralph Lauren Polo outlet store should only get such a bargain as Ralph Lauren got in Washington. . . . an avalanche of publicity that would cost more in the open market, even if you could get it wholesale."

Ironically, at the same time, Congress was considering a law to safeguard the sanctity of the American flag that would bar its use in paintings and other flag motif merchandise flooding the market in recent years. If enforced, such a law would put Lauren in the precarious position of being both a savior and a desecrater of the flag. Lauren "[risked] being thrown in jail for body scrub with a flag logo," Rich ventured, then added: "Is this American justice? Tommy Hilfiger, who's given not a dime to flag preservation and whose own red, white, and blue flag logo knocks off Old Glory without reproducing it, will escape scot free."

Indeed, Hilfiger had been making out like a bandit by copying the style of Lauren, who himself was fashion's most flagrant usurper. For more than thirty years, Lauren had splendidly co-opted the props of the establishment—the polo shirt, the English country look, and even the Ivy League's L.L. Bean—imparting them with his own pedigree and a Waspy snob appeal that millions of people loved.

Without Ralph Lauren, there would be no Tommy Hilfiger Corp., which was for all intents and purposes a clone of Polo Ralph Lauren. Opening his business some seventeen years after Lauren, Hilfiger imitated Lauren's business model to perfection, having hired a number of Polo executives and alumni to help pull off his coup. Hilfiger had been a quick study and even an innovator. He was the first designer who dared to identify with the inner-city street style that was pure melting-pot America—a move that paid off quite handsomely. For both Lauren and Hilfiger, it was Old Glory that had been the most effective marketing tool and a blatant symbol of their redefinition of fashion the American way.

BY THE LATE 1990s, fashion had come to this: a tug-of-war over marketing. In Paris, Bernard Arnault's LVMH empire had its hands full, attempting to revive classic French brands while chasing Gucci, Armani, and other fashionable American trademarks that looked promising. Meanwhile, the last of the great couturiers, Emanuel Ungaro, was stuck on a slow boat, trying to market his way into the millennium. But on the other side of the Atlantic, Ralph Lauren and Tommy Hilfiger were living proof that the end of fashion was already here.

Both men had captured the hearts and minds—and the money—of millions of consumers by being *out* of fashion. Designers without portfolios, neither had apprenticed in Paris, nor studied fashion in school or anywhere else. They didn't sketch; they didn't sew; they hardly *designed*, so to speak. Their clothes weren't so original. Still, they remained ahead of the fashion curve by largely ignoring it. Each stayed grounded in the classics: the khakis, blazers, shirts, and sweaters which they recycled every season in new colors and fabrics, adding a little new detail here and there, all cleverly packaged with arresting, resonating images. They were the haute couturiers of marketing.

All you had to say was Ralph or Tommy. Like Madonna. They were the masters of the fashion universe, galloping lengths ahead of the rest of the fashion pack. Founded in 1967, Polo Ralph Lauren had sales of $1.7 billion in the fiscal year ending April 1999—translating into more than $5 billion at retail—turning out apparel for men, women, and children, sheets, towels, furniture, cosmetics, china, crystal, and even designer paint in hues of denim, suede, and thirty-two shades of white. Likewise, Tommy Hilfiger tallied $1.7 billion in sales in the fiscal year ending March 1999—or nearly $4 billion at retail. He was destined to overtake Polo sooner, rather than later, since Hilfiger had only just begun to diversify from menswear and cosmetics into women's apparel, home furnishings, and the rest. The surefooted Hilfiger had already beat Lauren to the New York Stock Exchange by five years, and his stock consistently rode high above the other apparel stocks. Hilfiger's stock had traded as high as $70 a share during all of 1998—or more than twice the price of Polo's shares. Although Lauren didn't make it to Wall Street first, he got there in time to run with the bulls. Polo's 1997 stock offering allowed Ralph to hang on to 90 percent voting control of Polo, while yielding him a $440 million jackpot, turning him into a billionaire.

Welcome to the era of designer as powerful brand name, with the clothes as the expression of the designer's personality. Lauren and Hilfiger both enjoyed pole positioning, front and center in America's malls, where they drew shoppers into more than 1,500 department stores such as Macy's, Bloomingdale's, and Dillard's, where they each had in-store boutiques, as well as to their own chains of specialty stores and discount outlet stores.

As menswear designers from the start, both figured out early on just what it took to sell clothes. Neither Hilfiger nor Lauren veered off into fashion land, the avant-garde styles that women's-wear designers created to tantalize the fashion press. It was pointless to try to sell men on high-fashion novelties. Menswear designers had no choice but to flex their creativity in the way they packaged the familiar—pants, shirts, and jackets—to make them more desirable than the anonymous store brands offered on the main floor. And by the late 1990s, when women's-wear fashions gravitated to more classic styling, fashion in general turned entirely on marketing. "It's not the jeans or the shirt but the image," said Terry Lundgren, vice chairman of Federated Department Stores, owner of Macy's, Bloomingdale's, and Rich's. "Customers want to be like Ralph and Tommy; those brands relate to the image of what [consumers] are. Marketing is more important today than it has ever been."

In fashion, as in baseball, there's nothing quite like fast company. Ralph Lauren and Tommy Hilfiger were like Mark McGwire of the St. Louis Cardinals and Sammy Sosa of the Chicago Cubs. As they traded homers during the 1998 season, the dueling sluggers lifted each other to peak performances, leading both of them to break Roger Maris's thirty-seven-year-old record—thus elevating the overall tenor of Major League Baseball. Driven to win, Lauren and Hilfiger stole each other's best moves as they took the lead in ushering American fashion into a modern era.

The triumph of Tommy and Ralph was made possible when fashion washed up on America's shores in waves of blue denim, that all-American staple that Calvin Klein and Gloria Vanderbilt recast as designer jeans, starting in the late 1970s. At the same time, Seventh Avenue's Liz Claiborne stepped up to offer career women a spread of affordable mix-and-match sportswear options, imparting a new respect for the American look that would gather even more steam over the next decade, culminating in the 1990s with the advent of the Gap.

Ralph Lauren, who had always preached "the appropriateness of American sportswear," believed that fashion would someday catch up with him. "The American sensibility has become a very important international sensibility," he explained. "We created sportswear. Ours is a more modern culture because of the way people live. We travel, we're athletic, we move. Americans are the leaders because we know how to do sportswear better here than anywhere else."

So just how did these two middle-aged white men capture the imagination and the wallets of people of all ages from every walk of life around the world? The secret was their ability to fulfill a deep-seated desire among all consumers: to belong. Traditionally, fashion had derived much of its power and allure from being original, unique, and exclusive—from the fact that no two women will own the same piece of couture. But that fashion is over. The new fashion is about inclusion, belonging to a world or lifestyle that feels good, looks good, and above all else, is accessible. Like the American dream, the new fashion has to appear available to all—regardless of the economic reality most people live. Perhaps more than any other designers, Ralph and Tommy intimately understood this desire to be an insider, rather than an outsider. And a look at their careers, how they mirror and how they differ, reveals why their fashions reign supreme. Not surprisingly, their business practices are methodical and painstaking, not to mention very similar.

RALPH LIFSHITZ WAS born in 1939, the youngest of four children and the son of Russian Jewish immigrants. His father, Frank, painted murals and houses for a living, raising his family in a two-bedroom apartment in the Bronx. Young Ralph set his aspirations high, having gotten his first close look at America's upper classes during the summers when he worked as a waiter and camp counselor at Camp Roosevelt in the Catskills during the 1950s.

A devoted movie buff, Ralph soaked up the dapper, insouciant style of matinee idols like Fred Astaire and Cary Grant and aimed to dress just like them. Ralph stood out at Dewitt Clinton High School as the prince of preppy, dressed in tweeds, corduroys, and sweaters tied around his shoulders, "as Brooksy as you can get," he later recalled. This was around the time that Frank Lifshitz was said to have changed the family surname—which the kids were always teased about—to the smooth, patrician-sounding Lauren. The name change marked the beginning of Ralph's social climb from Bronx striver to Fifth Avenue baron. Next to his senior picture in the 1957 *Clintonian* yearbook, Ralph Lauren listed his ambition in life: "millionaire."

After high school, Lauren began taking classes at night at City College of New York, but soon dropped out to begin his first stint in the rag trade: selling suits at Brooks Brothers. During the early 1960s, he would ply the pavements in the scrappy world of wholesaling, peddling ladies' gloves and men's ties, and became known as the nattiest road man in the garment district. On his modest salary, he still managed to tool around

Manhattan in a Morgan, a jaunty English convertible, and to buy his wardrobe at the posh Paul Stuart on Madison Avenue. "Nobody was interested in style as much as Ralph," remarked Clifford Grodd, Paul Stuart's chairman, to Jeffrey Trachtenberg, Lauren's biographer, who concluded: "Ralph didn't fantasize about becoming a fashion designer, he became a designer to fulfill his fantasies."

And so finally, in 1967, Lauren's fantasy came to life as he became a designer—of neckties—opening a modest showroom in the Empire State Building. He named his brand "Polo," which he figured evoked just the right amount of snob appeal. Bloomingdale's sold "Polo by Ralph Lauren" ties for $15—which was twice the price of other fine ties—and promoted them as status symbols, with ad copy like: "The age of elegance inspires the unique design of our 'Regency' tie by Polo." Lauren's tony ties flew off the counters and soon he was well on his way to making shirts and suits to go with his ties, buoyed by a $50,000 investment from Norman Hilton, the suit manufacturer that became Lauren's first financial partner.

Lauren will go down in fashion history for introducing the concept of "lifestyle merchandising" in department stores, where each fashion brand was segregated in its own appetizing ambiance. In 1970, Lauren convinced Bloomingdale's to put all his ties, suits, dress shirts, and raincoats together in his own special little boutique. Lauren designed this outpost to feel like a gentlemen's club, with mahogany paneling and brass fixtures. Once enveloped in the Polo lifestyle, shoppers who intended only to pick out a shirt would instead browse around and buy an entire outfit.

Through the years, Lauren festooned his in-store shops with walking sticks, antique alligator luggage, and other slick props, which went a long way to weave a spell around Ralph's rich man's look and stirred all kinds of longings in people, the dream that the upwardly mobile shared for prestige, wealth, and exotic adventure. Whether it was a $200 Fair Isle sweater or a $7,000 mahogany highboy with tartan-lined drawers, Polo's dream merchandise seemed to belong to aristocrats, Ivy Leaguers, and adventurers, who rode horses on ranches, took safaris in Kenya, and yachted in Newport.

"I elevated the taste level of America," Lauren often observed, reflecting on the nuances and the fine details he used to rework fashion's old standards. Polo's tweed hacking jacket, for example, came in richer-looking wool with real horn buttons and grazed a man's body with soft, natural shoulders. His knit shirts with a discreet polo-player logo embroidered on the chest had a faded patina that made them more comfortable, as if you'd worn them for ages. Lauren's ersatz old-money look was more expensive than usual, but still within reach of those who lusted for a piece of the good life. And millions of Americans did.

More than anything, Lauren burnished his fantasy world in the evocative imagery of his advertising, shot by Bruce Weber, the fashion photographer who also created some of Calvin Klein's most memorable ads. In blocks of as many as twenty pages in *Vanity Fair* and *The New York Times Magazine* and *W*, the advertising spreads were seductive movie sets that showcased Polo's extensive lines of apparel, accessories, and home furnishings in the most appetizing way: in stately mansions with roaring fireplaces, replete with distinguished gentlemen and lithe brunettes, all outfitted in character. Much of his elegant staging rang true. "I would be hard pressed to find any photo from my boarding school or summer days that placed side by side with a Polo ad would show its artifice," wrote Lang Philips in an article headlined "Confessions of a Young Wasp" in *New York*.

But not everybody could abide Polo's packaged affectation. "The only difference between a parvenu in a sharkskin suit and a parvenu in a Lauren blazer is that the latter has pretensions," wrote Jonathan Yardley in *The Washington Post* in 1986.

The underside of such resentment against Lauren was a mix of old-fashioned snobbery and jealousy. The hard-line Wasps wore their pedigree in boxy Brooks Brothers suits, cashmere sweaters, faded rugby shirts, and Top-Siders, which represented quality and tradition, but never fashion. So when Ralph came along, he was an easy target for Waspy curmudgeons. Here was this Jew from the Bronx who had co-opted their town-and-country style and had turned it into fashion. He did such a good job that the British royal family—the ultimate Wasps—loved to wear Polo too.

Certain members of fashion's old guard in Paris were naturally contemptuous of Lauren's stunning success. In an effort to bring him down, Yves Saint Laurent sued Lauren, alleging that he copied one of his couture gowns, and a French court found Lauren guilty as charged.

While Lauren would develop a thick skin against his detractors, he would never be defensive about his important contribution to fashion: "I don't put myself in with Saint Laurent or Ungaro," he later reflected. "But I am doing something they aren't doing that is original, and I am proud of that." (LVMH's Bernard Arnault would later pay Lauren the ultimate compliment in declaring that Polo was the American fashion house that he admired the most.)

IN THE MID-1980s, Tommy Hilfiger was just getting his feet wet on Seventh Avenue when Ralph Lauren had already set the agenda as the most successful designer in America. He had pulled off this feat with the assistance of his longtime business partner, Peter Strom, a former executive at Norman Hilton. By 1986, the year Lauren was ready to pull out the stops to make a historic footprint in the world of retailing, Polo's licensees generated about $400 million in annual sales.

In the tradition of America's nineteenth-century department store founders like Marshall Field in Chicago and John Wanamaker of Philadelphia, Ralph Lauren opened his own retail palace on the corner of Madison Avenue and Seventy-second Street in the former Rhinelander mansion. In 1894, the wealthy Gertrude Rhinelander Waldo had ordered up the five-story limestone French-style château, which took five years and more than $500,000 to build, complete with bowling alley and billiard room.

Ralph Lauren took on a long-term lease on the fabled Rhinelander, where he spent an estimated $33 million to create retail's most sumptuous *mise en scène*—an investment that paid off, not for the profits the store generated, but for the fabulous way it depicted Lauren's posh imagery so completely. Even the most jaded shoppers couldn't help but be bowled over by all the mahogany, the magnificent floral arrangements, the vintage paintings of noble gentry on horseback. With Cole Porter tunes filling the air, it was easy to get carried away, as many dazzled American shoppers and foreign tourists did, trooping home with armloads of navy Polo shopping bags.

Most shoppers would never get to see where all this merchandise was created—which since 1991 was inside another palatial setting farther south on Madison at Sixty-first Street, at Polo's headquarters inside a steel high-rise. A swift elevator ride to the fourth floor delivered visitors to Polo's reception area, known as the Reading Room. As regal as any library inside an English country estate, the high-ceilinged, mahogany-paneled Reading Room was replete with an exposed balcony, a majestic staircase, and lush appointments all around: cushy sofas, a well-worn leather wing chair, and a hassock covered in zebra skin. Down the hallway of this "Upstairs Downstairs" facade was a stark contrast: white-walled cubicles with computers and file cabinets, where the serious work got done.

Amid the stuffy grandeur of the Reading Room was an unexpected, whimsical note: a pile of M&M's in a huge oriental bowl. All day, employees and visitors scooped up handfuls of candy. "Everyone loves M&M's," explained Lauren. "For twenty years I've always had bowls of M&M's around. This is a happy place."

M&M's might have sweetened the ambiance, but Ralph's definition of a happy place needed further elaboration. Happy, as in fat and happy and prosperous—well, he was certainly right about that. But happy, as in kicky and happy-go-lucky—that interpretation wouldn't fly. The house of Lauren was buttoned up and dead serious—full of tightly wound people with a Moonie-like devotion to the man whose name was on the door. Polo Ralph Lauren didn't get to be the mightiest oak in American fashion by taking it easy.

In an industry where high-strung personalities, creative tension, and second-guessing are par for the course, Polo was renowned as being the most complicated, the most obsessive of all. "Ralph is demanding and the politics are difficult," explained one former design assistant. "Everybody is scared to question Ralph."

Another former staffer shared his view about what went on behind the walls of the Reading Room: "Ralph was always telling us that we're the standard, that everybody is always imitating everything we do, that everybody wants to be like us. There was always this arrogance about who we were and that bred an elitism among everybody who worked there. People at Polo just thought they were just better than anybody else."

So it was easy to understand how an $8-an-hour sales associate working behind the polished counters at Polo, outfitted in a $1,500 suede safari jacket and $300 jodhpurs, could slip into the role of a country squire, thanks to Polo's generous employee discount. "The salespeople were totally sucked in. We were romanced by it all," recalled a former salesman, who waxed wistfully about the late 1980s, the years when Polo employees were treated to gourmet catered lunches of dilled chicken salad and couscous, free of charge. "The chitchat in the afternoon wasn't about the *Dallas* episode last night. All we talked about were clothes, like Ralph's latest $600 crocodile moccasins which had just arrived and that everyone wanted to buy."

The Reading Room, just like Polo's in-store displays, makes for that all-important first impression, which is the essence of Ralph Lauren, the quintessential, keep-up-appearances man. The man, the merchandise, the company are one seamless facade maintained by his troops with dogged devotion.

The people at Polo often spoke in Hollywood metaphors. "Think of this as a movie," a Polo executive once told the salespeople at the Madison Avenue store. "Ralph is the director and you are the actors, and we are here to make a movie."

And indeed, Lauren once fancied himself as a leading man. "I always see a movie running in my head," he once told the *Los Angeles Times*. "I'm the star of the movie and it's a vision of what a particular world represents to me."

So it stood to reason that he would star in his own fashion ads. For years, his handsome, perpetually tanned face set off by wiry gray hair jumped from the pages of magazines. Once, in the 1980s, he portrayed a leathery Steve McQueen, in a T-shirt, beat-up jeans, and cowboy hat, slugging a bottle of beer. After his hair grew whiter in the 1990s, he turned into a suave Cary Grant, as the role model for his top-drawer Purple Label suits, made in England.

Cary Grant was a Ralph obsession. One New York evening when Lauren presented an award to Audrey Hepburn, he stood onstage wearing oversized Cary Grant spectacles. The dapper actor himself never had it so good. "Now I think my life is so much better than what I wanted," Lauren told the *Los Angeles Times*. "A few years before he died, Cary Grant came to my house for lunch with his wife. [Grant] said that my life is a real example of what people think *his* was. The interesting thing is, I'm more Cary Grant than Cary Grant."

But more people likened Lauren to the self-made mogul and master of reinvention, Jay Gatsby, from F. Scott Fitzgerald's novel *The Great Gatsby*. (Coincidentally, perhaps, Lauren designed the costumes for the 1972 movie of the same name, starring Robert Redford, another actor whom Lauren had idolized.)

Over the years, Lauren invited the world to ogle his lush life in a number of glossy magazine profiles. Those upbeat stories always depicted him as larger-than-life, no doubt because he wielded a big stick, as one of the most formidable advertisers in fashion. With his immense ad budget, Lauren didn't have to bother with wooing the press with free lunches and clothes. Only a few editors were treated to his special gift: "designer" steaks from the steers raised on his Colorado ranch that arrived in a wooden box with an RRL brand on it.

It is little wonder that so many people insist on calling him Ralph Lo-REN—the affected pronunciation just sounded more exclusive and otherworldly. In the pages of *W* and *Town & Country*, Ralph lived large in residences that resembled the dreamscapes in his ads. His homes included beach-front spreads on Long Island and in Jamaica, a Fifth Avenue duplex apartment, a baronial estate in Bedford, New York, and— the place where those steaks come from—a fourteen-thousand-acre cattle ranch near Telluride, Colorado, named Double RL (for Ralph and Ricky Lauren). The ranch even had a teepee, a rustic hideaway furnished with log furniture, a bearskin throw, cowboy hats, and Navajo blankets—"stuff inside there an Indian never dreamed of," one of the ranch hands told *W*.

"It's a Wonderful Life" was the cover line for the December 1996 issue of *Town & Country*, where Ralph, clad in a black turtleneck, military-style navy blazer, and weathered jeans, strolled hand in hand with his fetching blond wife, Ricky, who wore Polo's flag sweater over her jeans. Inside *Town & Country*, the Laurens canvased their leafy Bedford estate alongside their three Polo-perfect offspring, all in their twenties: David and Dylan, both graduates of Duke University, and Andrew, an alum of Skidmore College. The kids hadn't gravitated to fashion, but the eldest, Andrew, had pursued his father's fantasy, as he struggled to be an actor.

Meanwhile, inside Lauren's Hollywood workplace, he starred in the role of *working* designer. His PR people bent over backwards to convince inquiring reporters that yes, it was Ralph who designed every sock, every sheet pattern, every napkin ring that bore his label. Once, when a reporter sought to speak to Ralph, a PR woman crisply begged off: "Ralph is busy *designing*."

Reporters obligingly listened to this storybook spiel—and rolled their eyes. Everybody knew that though Ralph Lauren stood alone on the runway to take his bow, he was running a design machine, like so many others, where dozens of assistants and licensees performed much of the creating. All that mattered was the outcome. And the Polo machine— ever-rigorous in its standards and practices—churned out a slew of fine merchandise at many price levels, better than anyone else in fashion.

The French couture houses, which paid a steep price for having ignored their licensees in the 1980s, could have learned a lot from Ralph Lauren. He was never careless with the merchandise that bore his label. Every shirt, every bathrobe, every armchair had to uphold the Polo image. "We work with them as though they are part of our company," Lauren said of his twenty-odd licensees. "We design everything including the ads. We retain as much control as we can without owning the company."

And under Lauren's vaunted control, "Every year the bar goes up," said one person who formerly worked for Westpoint Stevens, maker of the sheets and towels for Lauren's home collection. "[Lauren's people] say they want everything to be perfect. But all they really want to do is to please Ralph. But sometimes they don't even know what he wants. So we're always paranoid. Small mistakes get magnified. The people at Polo are the best in the business, but they can be difficult to work with."

Ralph Lauren had arrived at a pinnacle of consistency in a creative process that people who have worked with him have described as painstaking and plodding. Lauren was always more verbal than visual, and he liked to recite his concepts to his design team. Lauren would often begin by describing a little vignette of his idealized customer, such as a sophisticated woman with a casual, elegant style, who loved to travel to Europe. Lauren's design staff returned weeks later with prototypes of actual sample garments, which were placed in meeting rooms, along with sketches and storyboards, with antique books, fabric swatches, pictures, and other props. The staffers prepared their samples, taking inspiration from the closets of vintage clothing and furnishings Polo had collected over the years.

Lauren himself would get most involved when it was time to review the sample garments, when he rejected, tinkered, and asked many, many questions. Such meetings dragged on for days, turning into a game of office politics as everyone jockeyed to impress the boss. "Ralph is the king of meetings," said one of his former high-ranking assistants. "He's always running late and when he walks in, there are twenty people in the room, his staff and some people from the licensee. Then somebody would start sucking up and would say, 'Ralph, what you are wearing today is brilliant, those boots are terrific.' Everyone else would join in. So, before the meeting starts, Ralph then spends another twenty minutes talking about his woven belt or whatever he's wearing."

This assistant said: "Ralph is a great editor, but he can't draw it. You have to design a dozen samples. You have to present the right alternatives and you must give him enough of them so that he can pick from the group. But still, he can't make a decision. He chews over the location of every ad, of every possibility, of every concept. Then he comes back the next day and changes his mind."

Was it indecisiveness or an obsession for perfection? his staff often wondered. They watched him waffle when he decorated his homes or when he dickered over whether he needed a haircut. Once, when Lauren decided to repaint his prized antique Mercedes, one of the eight vintage cars in his collection, he polled everybody in the office. The former staffer explained: "He had six gray cards and he called me in his office and asked me what color did I like. I swear that they all looked the same. No difference between them. He held them up to the light. Then he walked over to the window. Then he had to show them to everybody, even the receptionist, to get her idea."

People with money and power have always gone to extraordinary lengths to get what they want. So how did his assistants get inside the head of the man whose ideas are so innate and full of nuance, who only knows what he wants when he sees it? Lauren surrounded himself with like-minded people who shared his taste level and his Waspy sensibilities—such as Kelly Rector, a stunning brunette and accomplished horsewoman who grew up in Connecticut, who later worked for Calvin Klein, whom she married in 1986.

So when Lauren told his charges to make a tartan that was "more Scottish" or to redo a raincoat that wasn't "army surplus enough," they had a pretty good idea of what he wanted. And perhaps one of their hardest tasks was helping him choose a scent for his fragrances, after he lost his sense of smell following a brain tumor operation in 1987. "Do I need a focus group? No," he once explained. "My talent and the company's talent is the ability to have instincts and sophistication. To travel, to feel, to get a sense of the public and a sense of visual things. We are constantly feeding off of each other."

The most loyal of Lauren's staffers, who learned to put up with his precarious ways, stayed on for years and became indispensable acolytes, known in house as the "Ralphettes." The queen of this sorority came with a Polo-esque name: Buffy Birritella, who served as Polo's senior vice president of women's wear. Birritella joined the company in 1971, leaving her job as fashion editor for *DNR* (*Daily News Record*), the menswear version of *WWD*.

Birritella even looked like Ricky Lauren, with her straight blonde mane, slender figure, angular face, and outdoorsy flair for fashion. She instinctively knew what was "very Ralph" and what was "not Ralph enough." For Polo's Madison Avenue emporium, it was Birritella who picked out the styles that would go on one hundred brass doorknobs, which took a year to make. She also climbed the scaffolding to supervise the workmen cleaning the mansion's limestone facade. "Ralph wanted the patina left in certain spots, so I pointed them out," she told *Avenue* magazine.

For Ralph Lauren to engender so much loyalty and dedication in so many people reflects the charisma of this complex, low-key man. "When you see him in meetings, he has an enormous presence. You never thought of him as short," said one employee about Lauren, who looks to be about five four. In 1992, *The Washington Post*'s Cathy Horyn wrote about the effect he had on his employees: "There probably isn't a man or a woman on his staff who hasn't felt the soft stroke of his voice, fallen for the tenderness of his gaze and suddenly found themselves wanting to turn cartwheels for him just because he happened to stop them in the hallway or at a design meeting and say, 'Tell me what you like. Tell me what you're going to wear tomorrow, Saturday night.'"

Ralph Lauren entered the 1990s in terrific shape. The fashion house that he and Strom had built was now generating sales at retail in the billions, rock solid and in for the long haul. As Strom prepared to retire in 1995, his succession would be as orderly as the changing of the guard, for waiting in the wings was Michael Newman, the financial chief and fifteen-year Polo veteran who would become vice chairman and chief operating officer—responsible for much of the heavy lifting for Ralph, who served as Polo's chairman and CEO.

AS OTHER DESIGNERS jealously looked at his long string of incredible hits, they had to admit: Ralph was *the man*. Lauren had stayed true to his classic design aesthetic, which virtually insulated him from fashion's changing whims. But being on top was never as comfortable as it appeared. Lauren worried about becoming too complacent, losing focus, and going right out of style. As worthy competitors such as Hilfiger, Gap, and J. Crew took on Polo in the mid-1990s, Lauren was forced to raise the bar. Every season, he once reflected, designers are "gobbled up and spit out every two seconds. To be a classic in this day and age is a real challenge."

Lauren couldn't help but be haunted by what had happened to his contemporary, Calvin Klein, Seventh Avenue's other Bronx sensation, who had launched his fashion house around the same time Lauren did in 1967. Throughout the seventies and most of the eighties, Calvin and Ralph played out Seventh Avenue's most spirited rivalry. Klein had built a mighty empire, fortified by his fragrances, jeans, and underwear that were cherished by consumers the world over, thanks to his sexy, cutting-edge advertising. But for reasons other than fashion, the house of Klein, in 1991, was on the verge of coming undone.

Having successfully bounced back from drug rehabilitation in the late 1980s, Klein was fighting demons in his own business. In 1990, Calvin Klein Inc. reported revenue of $200 million, with $4.3 million in net losses—the third time in the previous five years the company had been unprofitable. The house of Klein was being dragged down by its core jeanswear division, which accounted for 80 percent of Klein's revenue—and $14 million in operating losses in 1990. The problem was fundamental: Klein's famous jeans were stone cold at retail because he had lost his magic touch with the youth market. The jeans division was also the culprit of a bigger distraction: the huge junk-bond debt the company had accrued in the 1980s when it bought Puritan Fashions, its former jeans licensee. In 1991, Calvin Klein Inc. still owed a staggering $55 million in junk-bond debt—and had only three years to pay it all off.

As Klein appeared to be headed toward bankruptcy, his day of reckoning never came. The next year, Klein got an unusual reprieve: a helping hand from his buddy, David Geffen, the billionaire Hollywood mogul and founder of Geffen Records. Geffen paid off all $62 million of Klein's debt securities—effectively providing the company with a generous loan. Then Geffen jumped in to assist Klein and his longtime business partner, Barry Schwartz, to restructure their company away from manufacturing into a house of licensees. From then on, nothing came between Calvin and his Calvins. The designer threw himself into making over his jeanswear division to recapture America's youth.

Klein's reversal of misfortune was swift. By 1994, the company's turnaround was right on track, and Klein was able to dig out of his hole and repay Geffen. Klein bolstered his management by hiring a new president, Gabriella Forte, a plum executive he lured away from Giorgio Armani. Then he began his push into home furnishings and retail boutiques around the world. Klein's experience was a close call—and a textbook lesson—that fashion, even in the major leagues, was always a slippery slope.

———

SO LAUREN WASN'T about to rest on his laurels through the company's midlife years. Throughout the 1990s, he would be consumed with making over the house of Polo, skillfully repositioning the business to make it more populist by adding lots of lower-priced lines to be in step with the Gap generation—*and* more attractive to Wall Street. Like a plastic surgeon performing a face-lift, Lauren left no visible scars of demarcation, in a balancing act to turn on young, urban shoppers without turning off his maturing, elite fans. After years of spotting Tommy Hilfiger in the rearview mirror, Ralph now faced his rival in the passing lane. From then on, the designers would bob and weave around each other—sometimes colliding head-on.

WHILE RALPH LAUREN prevailed as the merchant prince of Madison Avenue, Tommy Hilfiger was busily monitoring Polo's every move. Not surprisingly, Hilfiger—the second in a family of nine children, whose father, Richard, was a jeweler and watchmaker in upstate Elmira, New York—got his start on the sales floor. He was a toothy, mop-topped high school senior in 1969 when he and two friends scraped together $450 and opened "People's Place," the only boutique in Elmira specializing in bell-bottomed jeans. People's Place flourished for a few years before going bankrupt in 1977. Three years later, Hilfiger moved to Manhattan, where he landed a freelance assignment designing Jordache jeans. Then he was discovered by Mohan Murjani, head of Murjani International, maker of the hot-selling Gloria Vanderbilt jeans and Coca-Cola sportswear, which launched him as a menswear designer in 1985.

Born in India, Mohan Murjani was a flashy, ambitious scion of a Hong Kong apparel contractor, who had come to New York with an agenda: to leapfrog into the forefront of America's burgeoning designer fashion boom. He saw the squeaky-clean Hilfiger as the ideal marketing vehicle to introduce what was essentially Polo at popular prices, what Tommy liked to call "preppy classics with a twist." Murjani's Polo-lite debuted with a $40 "public" pant in khaki ("made to fit the public"), a $25 "Harvard" button-down shirt, and a $30 "Newport" polo knit shirt. Tommy's answer to Ralph's embroidered polo pony insignia was a Bavarian crest which he found in the public library.

Hilfiger had only been on the market for a short time when Murjani went for the gusto when he made Hilfiger the centerpiece of a controversial campaign created by the famous adman George Lois. In the summer of 1985, a huge billboard high above Times Square telegraphed: "The Four Great American designers for men are R—L—, P—E—, C—K—and T—H—." Another print ad brazenly declared: "Every decade someone with talent and a sense of the times takes a good look at the great classics and makes them better. That's what Tommy Hilfiger did when he redesigned the button-down shirt, the polo shirt, the sweater, the classic chino and everything else modern men and women wear. Style marches on."

Fashion insiders were taken aback. They considered Hilfiger's bravado as crass—and a lie. Hilfiger hadn't paid his dues on Seventh Avenue and was clearly a fake. "He may have well-styled, well-made products, but I don't like the connotation that he is a creative designer," sniffed Jack Hyde, a longtime men's fashion writer and professor at the Fashion Institute of Technology in New York.

But there was no denying that Hilfiger's cart-before-the-horse approach was catchy and original. It was also working. Shoppers began asking for that new designer they often called "Hil-finger"—because the sportswear looked great and didn't cost too much. Paul Cavaco, a fashion industry stylist, noted in 1990, "To the consumer, Tommy is a classic. . . . The ad campaign—as much as I don't like it—is brilliant."

Hilfiger would never live down his public relations pole vault into fashion's major leagues. As Lauren's most visible facsimile, he was branded with the scarlet letter as fashion's great pretender. In those early years, the forces on Seventh Avenue often likened him to the Monkees, the prefabricated rock group who starred in the hit TV series of the 1960s and were modeled explicitly after the Beatles. The more popular Hilfiger became, the more fashion cognoscenti snubbed him. No doubt it unnerved many struggling designers that Hilfiger was living proof that deft packaging and deep pockets could turn any ambitious nobody into a fashion sensation. Years later, when Hilfiger said that he was ready to introduce an expensive women's collection, Amy Spindler, *The New York Times* fashion critic, pounced: "By setting his sights on fashion, as opposed to clothing which has earned him his good name and fortune, he runs the risk of revealing in larger-than-life runway proportions the undeniable banality that informs his esthetic . . . the wizard could just be a small man with a megaphone."

In reality, Hilfiger was hardly a swaggering braggart. He was reserved and somewhat square. He looked downright foolish when he starred in his own ads in the late 1980s. There he was, grinning, leaning against a vintage convertible above the caption: "Tommy and His T-bird," or astride a motorbike, "Tommy and His Harley." He looked stiff instead of hip. To his credit, he had the good sense to quit.

Tommy finally changed his tune starting in the early 1990s, with the help of adman Michael Toth, who helped him fashion a more believable persona. From then on, Hilfiger left the modeling to groups of grinning, well-scrubbed young models, who captured the feel-good side of the American dream, of Fourth of July picnics and downtown parades—a niche that hadn't been filled in designer imagery. Lauren had cornered the Wasp aesthetic while Klein had cornered the market for sex. So that left a wide-open field for Hilfiger. "Tommy came down the middle and said, 'Here's Norman Rockwell, you can aspire to being fun and having fun in your life.' And more people identified with that," Toth said.

Tommy clearly was having lots of fun when he pressed the flesh with his customers. He made in-store appearances his trademark, clocking in at least a dozen appearances every year at department stores such as Belk's, Dillard's, and Macy's. Most designers rose above such grassroots stumping after they hit the big time. "I haven't done a store appearance in maybe twenty years," Ralph Lauren remarked in 1997. "I lead a quiet life. People buy Ralph Lauren because they love the product. They don't care that I'm in the press every day. I'm happy that I'm not."

But when Tommy hit the retail hustings, he became a natural politician, with the earnest appeal of *American Bandstand*'s Dick Clark. Tommy turned on like a TV—flashing his perfect set of teeth, set off by dimples. He was one of those gee-whiz guys who just hadn't gotten over the fact that he had really made it—and his very presence could create a scene. Once, a crowd of about a thousand turned out at Macy's in New York, when Hilfiger stood at the end of the runway and ripped off his windbreaker and sunglasses, tossing them to the squealing spectators, just like a rock star. The young, delighted fans—a rare blend of white, black, and Latinos—roared. Later, Tommy planted himself at a table and stayed for more than an hour to sign autographs and pose for pictures.

Such retail road shows served another purpose as well—the chance for Tommy to check out first-hand what the coolest kids in Atlanta and Dallas were wearing. He chatted up shoppers to learn how he could make his collections more appealing and then he took that information back to his staffers in New York.

Hilfiger's reputation as an affable, approachable designer even resonated with celebrities, who were just as star-struck upon meeting Hilfiger. *GQ*'s creative director, Jim Moore, was present during a photo shoot with former New York Knicks coach Don Nelson in the locker room at Madison Square Garden. When Knicks players John Starks, Patrick Ewing, and others heard that Hilfiger was on his way over to be photographed, "They couldn't believe it," Moore remembered. "They were all running around grabbing basketballs for him to autograph. It was a funny dynamic. It was like, *who is the celebrity?*"

AS "HONORARY CHAIRMAN" and principal designer for his namesake house, Tommy Hilfiger was the face man, an effective image-maker, with seemingly boundless energy to spare. Hilfiger attended key meetings where he put forth his opinions, but he rarely talked to the press about designing or even managing his company. In showroom presentations to retailers, he could be commanding—unfolding sweaters, pointing out fabric details, and even reciting wholesale prices. But mainly, he put his trust in company management and dozens of staff designers who kept all the plates spinning at his headquarters, an eleven-story brick building at 25 West Thirty-ninth Street in the heart of New York's garment district.

The house of Hilfiger was built with a number of executives who were once associated with Polo Ralph Lauren, notably its three principals: Silas Chou, chairman; Joel Horowitz, chief executive officer; and Lawrence Stroll, vice chairman. Through the years, these three had poached many valuable players from Polo, including Edwin Lewis, Hilfiger's former CEO who retired in 1994, and at least a dozen other key executives.

At the top of Hilfiger's Polo alums was Silas Chou, the man who was credited with masterminding the Tommy revolution. Born in 1950 in Hong Kong, Chou was also the chairman of Novel Enterprises, a publicly traded apparel manufacturing business founded by his family, which was a key knitwear supplier to companies such as Murjani, Liz Claiborne Inc., Limited Inc., and Polo. Chou had been a partner with Lawrence Stroll in running Polo's Canadian and European licensees in the 1980s.

In 1989, Chou and Stroll stepped in to rescue Hilfiger when he was sinking under the weight of the financially troubled Murjani, which was heading toward collapse. Chou wanted to build his own stable of designer brands for Novel and he believed that Hilfiger could be his first. Having already produced Hilfiger's knitwear for Murjani, Chou always had been impressed with the Hilfiger look. "I saw products I liked," he said. "Tommy's clothes had a personality, a traditional American look but with a modern touch—that 'twist,' as he calls it. I liked the oversized, relaxed fit which was different from Polo shirts, which were tight to the body. Our European customers always thought Polo was too tight."

After Chou negotiated with Murjani to take over Hilfiger, he made it clear that he had big plans. "I told Tommy, 'I don't want to be just a licensee; I want to be with you all the time so we can row in the same direction,'" Chou reminisced. Having incorporated Tommy Hilfiger Corp. in Hong Kong, Chou and Stroll provided the initial financing, and each took a 35 percent stake, while Hilfiger got 22.5 percent, and Horowitz received 7.5 percent. Months later, Chou and Stroll sold their interests in Polo's European and Canadian operations.

As chairman of the venture, Chou remained in Hong Kong, but he knew just where to find the perfect chief executive to work in New York. Chou had his sights set on Edwin Lewis, a fifteen-year veteran of Bidermann Industries, Polo's women's-wear licensee at the time. Prying Lewis away from Polo was a feat, because Lewis was rumored to be the heir apparent to Ralph's business partner, Peter Strom. But Chou won

Lewis over by giving him equity in Hilfiger and free rein to run the show. Tapping into his retail connections, Lewis gave Hilfiger instant credibility with department stores.

Watching from the sidelines over the years, Ralph Lauren resisted the urge to criticize his rival. But privately, his associates said he seethed, dismissing Tommy as a copycat, a Polo markdown, a designer who subsisted only by leaching so many top talents from Polo. Hilfiger "only took off after he hired Ed Lewis," Ralph later reflected privately to a reporter.

While Tommy's role model was Ralph, Chou's corporate model was the venerable Liz Claiborne Inc., one of the most professionally run fashion companies on Seventh Avenue—and a public company since 1981. "From the beginning, Silas set it up with all the proper reporting documents for tracking the business—the types of things that Wall Street would be asking for," said Horowitz. "It made it easy for us when the time came for us to go public."

Tommy Hilfiger Corp. filed for its listing on the New York Stock Exchange in 1992, becoming one of the first fashion houses to jump into the bull run of the 1990s. The company's balance sheet revealed its impressive climb. Between 1990 and 1992, sales had quadrupled to $107 million, with a net income of $9 million. Hilfiger's initial public offering raised $46.9 million, of which $11.3 million was earmarked to develop more than 1,000 in-store shops in department stores. The fashion house would go on to perform splendidly on Wall Street, exceeding analysts' earnings projections every quarter, and impressing institutional investors, who made millions on the stock. Unwittingly, Tommy had repaid his debt to Ralph in the most tangible way. The respect Hilfiger earned on Wall Street made it far safer for Polo to go public on the New York Stock Exchange five years later.

"We are just the luckiest sons of bitches around," Chou reminisced one afternoon at Hilfiger's headquarters in 1997. "We did the right thing in the right place. The right thing was casual wear, the right place was the U.S. in the late eighties and nineties, when America moved into the information age. Ralph was really the pioneer in casual wear, but with our experience, we saw that with Tommy, we could use our expertise to deliver the same product, but at a better price."

The Polo alum with the closest ties to Lauren was Joel Horowitz, who became Hilfiger's CEO after Ed Lewis retired. Joel Horowitz's father, Sidney Horowitz, a close friend of Ricky Lauren's parents, was a veteran apparel production manager who was one of Ralph Lauren's first employees in 1968. After Joel dropped out of Miami (Ohio) University in his sophomore year in 1968, Sidney Horowitz talked his nineteen-year-old son into coming over to Polo, where Joel joined as a production assistant for Polo's new dress-shirt business. Over the years, Horowitz helped manage Polo's first store in Beverly Hills and ran Polo's short-lived jeans division in the 1970s. Horowitz joined Murjani in 1983, where he met Hilfiger.

Horowitz said his experiences during the struggling early years at Polo and later at the freewheeling Murjani taught him that delivering merchandise to stores on time was tantamount to success. "Now I'm not knocking Ralph, because he was successful anyway," Horowitz said. "But the fact is that you have to execute. You have to get all the products into the stores at the same time, which is what we did at Hilfiger. And that's why we were able to skyrocket the way we did."

IN THE LATE 1990s, Hilfiger and Polo were on parallel tracks, having peddled their products across America's malls as well as operating their own boutiques, mainly in Europe and Asia. Both produced merchandise through hundreds of contractors around the world and thus were saddled with the mind-boggling minutiae and logistics of multinational commerce. Thus, they planned out the bulk of their collections about a year before the merchandise reached the stores.

Four times a year, the Hilfiger organization held planning sessions called "adoption meetings," where its designers put the finishing touches on its collections before they went into production. On one hot Friday afternoon in August 1997, Tommy showed up just after lunch to review certain styles that would arrive in stores in the fall of 1998. Tommy was the vision of Pat Boone that day, in a blue seersucker suit, a white pique shirt, and white bucks. Michael Sondag, the company's senior vice president of design, led the way to the meetings.

Two scruffy boys carrying shopping bags got on the same elevator as Hilfiger and Sondag. "Do you want to buy some candy?" they asked in unison. Hilfiger grinned and directed them through glass doors to a receptionist. "Tell them that Tommy sent you." The kids shrugged in disbelief. One of them said, "Awww, you ain't Tommy. Tommy isn't even *here.*"

Hilfiger held the elevator door open to watch their reaction as the receptionist pointed, confirming who he was. Incredulous, one kid extended his leg into the air to show off the Hilfiger sneakers he was wearing. Hilfiger cracked up and waved to them as the elevator doors closed.

A crowd of young assistants was sitting on the floor waiting when Sondag and Hilfiger walked into the first of a series of design rooms set up like little vignettes with clothing samples, fabric swatches, and storyboards. There were basketballs, a pair of wooden skis, old ice skates, picture postcards, and ski posters. All in all, a scene very similar to what the people at Polo had described as Ralph's method.

"Okay, here we go again, holiday 1998," said Sondag as everybody settled down. Hilfiger sat on the carpet and rolled up his shirt sleeves, as all eyes were watching him.

Sondag stood next to a display called Athletics and started his spiel: "What we want to do is give everything a real active feel, the basketball shirts, the soccer shirts, and the jerseys. We want to go upscale and go upmarket and come up with more sophisticated athletics. Spectator athletics, that are as good-looking to wear on the streets as they are to work out in." Unfolding a stack of sweaters in gray, black, and white, he said, "Here's that icy look in woven. Tommy, you seemed to have liked this when we were showing it to you last week?"

Hilfiger nodded approvingly, then he piped up to mutter some fashion-speak: "Modern high-tech outerwear fabrics. Texture into the knits . . . That's what we wanna all wear, isn't it? It's much cleaner."

Hilfiger interrupted Sondag to question why there was so much ivory, gray, and black. "If the customer is walking the aisle and sees so much black and gray in one month and comes back another month and sees the same, it may not be different enough. So we need an infusion of color." Sondag agreed, then led everyone to another room.

Standing next to Sondag was Craig Reynolds, senior vice president of merchandising, whom Hilfiger calls his "chief of police." Reynolds's job was "to make sure the licensees don't do anything to conflict. We don't want the same shirts in our jeans line that are in our sportswear line. They all have to be different. But there still has to be a continuity between all categories."

Next were more meetings with licensees: Oxford Industries, for dress shirts, and Hartmarx, for suits and tailored clothing. Hilfiger examined samples for his new dress shirt with a double button under the collar— the extra button allowed a man to wear a tie with a bigger knot. After a model tussled with closing the top button, Hilfiger concluded: "We need to work on the collar."

The next order of business was coming up with a new suit label to distinguish Hilfiger's $750 Italian-made suits from his $395 models. Hilfiger mused: "When the salesmen tell men this is our bridge line, they have to identify it with something else other than just saying it's a better make and better fabric. I think we need to re-color the label, maybe white with navy lettering. Silver? But silver isn't as expensive, it doesn't have the value platinum has . . . call it the platinum collection? Armani has a black and white label but he doesn't advertise it. Ralph does Purple Label. Calvin has white at Saks. Donna does a black and gold label. Can we make up some labels in silver on the midnight background? I want to see what they look like."

It seemed tedious that six people would spend a good half hour dickering over the color of a label that would be hidden inside a suit jacket. But for a fashion image-maker like Hilfiger, the color of the label is a key marketing tool—and just as important as the way the suits looked.

LABELS ON THE inside, logos on the outside. Hilfiger knew the importance of symbols and insignias that would connect with shoppers. Initially, Hilfiger used logos as a merchandising magnet, a clever way to draw attention to his department store displays during his early years when he didn't have in-store shops. There was no way that shoppers could miss the shirts with "Tommy Hilfiger" in letters as big as the E on an eye chart, adorning the mannequins facing the aisles.

But logos would serve another purpose in the 1990s as Hilfiger would update his image into something younger and more textured when he aligned his brand with rap culture, the seminal movement that won over the MTV generation. Hilfiger was one of the first designers to plaster his name on rugby shirts and tops that fit right in with such status logos as Puma, Adidas, and Gucci that rappers loved to wear in music videos.

"We always bought into logos," Russell Simmons, founder of Def Jam records and his own fashion label, Phat Farm, told *Vogue* in 1996. "The reason for it is that it represents all the shit we don't have. We're not ripped-dungarees-rock-n-roll-alternative-culture people. We want to buy into the shit we see on television but we want to put our own twist on it. Part of the fantasy of fashion is about being successful. It's aspirational. I put this on, I'm getting laid. Not because I'm cool and raggedy but because I'm cool and clean. Because I want to buy into this culture."

Hilfiger certainly understood the power of rap culture, a genre to which the forces in the fashion industry couldn't (or wouldn't) relate. The homeboy look had crept onto the runways in the early 1990s when Chanel's Karl Lagerfeld put his runway models in droopy pants and huge CC logos, which made for riveting, drive-by flirtation with street style. But since most fashion houses, including Polo, either feared or didn't know exactly what to make of the hip-hop crowd, they steered clear of any association with the rappers. This was uncharted territory. It was already established that black consumers followed the white mainstream. But fashion wasn't at all prepared for black youths to lead white consumers.

Timberland, the maker of hiking boots and rugged outdoor gear, was caught by surprise when it learned that inner-city kids were buying its $150 hiking boots three and four pairs at a time. When Timberland's sales spiked 46 percent to $295 million in the first nine months of 1993, Jeffrey Swartz, Timberland's executive vice president, gave *The New York Times* a reason: Timberland was just selling more to its core customers, whom he described as "honest working people" who liked Timberland's functional, outdoorsy clothes. Swartz estimated that no more than 5 percent of Timberland's sales came from "urban" shoppers. Of course, Timberland was happy to get the additional business, but Swartz emphasized that Timberland had no intention of courting its swelling number of inner-city fans. "We are not going to build this business on smoke. We are not able to execute trendy," Swartz maintained.

But Tommy Hilfiger saw things differently. Once the rappers started buying his colorful, logo-filled clothes, Tommy saw an opening to broaden his reach to America's youth, black and white, who all liked hip-hop music. It was easy for Hilfiger to get it, because he had always been a pop music buff. As teenagers, Tommy and his younger brother, Andy, played bass guitar in a family rock group called Hippo, which was their father's nickname. In the late 1980s, Hilfiger began wooing the rock world, having provided blazers and polo shirts to British rocker Pete Townshend for a concert tour.

Around the same time, Andy Hilfiger was steeped in the hip-hop world, residing in an apartment in East Harlem and working as a lighting man for rock bands and music videos. Andy always arrived on the set with a bag full of his brother's polo shirts and Tommy Hilfiger logo duffel bags, which he passed out to concert promoters and rap stars who had already seen L.L. Cool J on stage sporting Hilfiger's red, white, and blue jumpsuits, originally designed for the Lotus Formula One auto racing team. Andy knew that dropping a few duds on the right folks could pay off down the road: "I never pushed for them to wear Tommy onstage, but you know, when you give away clothes, somebody's going to wear them *somewhere* where they will be noticed."

Tommy's rap-culture moment finally happened one Saturday evening in 1994 after Andy stopped by the Macklowe Hotel to drop off a few shirts for rapper Snoop Dogg. A smart move. That night, Snoop wore a striped rugby shirt with "Tommy" across the front and "Hilfiger" on the back on *Saturday Night Live*.

The next week, retailers, stylists, and shoppers lit up the phone lines at Hilfiger's showroom, clamoring to get their hands on that rugby shirt. On the cover of his hit CD *Grand Puba 2000*, Grand Puba leaned against his black Lamborghini convertible in a dark-green Tommy jacket over a white Tommy T-shirt. Once Hilfiger became the designer of choice among the rappers and urban youths, the suburban white kids followed, so they could be as "down" as the black kids.

Tommy, who started as a Ralph copycat, was now a fat cat doing his own thing—a hybrid mix of preppy and urban street styles. And Hilfiger was serious about emphasizing multiculturalism. Hilfiger's West Thirty-ninth Street headquarters was unique on Seventh Avenue as its creative ranks swelled with a number of twenty-something African Americans, Latinos, Asians, and foreign expatriates on staff. The company's mission statement sounded as if it came from the United Nations: "By respecting one another, we can reach all cultures and communities."

It remained to be seen whether Hilfiger's reach would someday lift those minorities into the executive suite—which would surely be a first on Seventh Avenue. One of the most promising talents was Lloyd Boston, the company's creative director, an African American who since 1993 had been in charge of designing all of Hilfiger's shopping bags, merchandise hang tags, and other packaging. Hilfiger met Boston in 1990 after a fashion show at Rich's department store in Atlanta, when Boston took him to task. "He didn't use any models of color in his fashion show," Boston recalled. "I told him, 'I love your clothes, but I don't see myself represented.'" Tommy apologized, noting that he always included black models in his shows, but Rich's had chosen the models before he arrived.

Boston, a sophomore art major at Morehouse College, told Hilfiger he wanted to be a graphic designer. Tommy took down his phone number and called him a few days later, offering him a one-year internship in New York. Boston transferred to Rutgers University in New Jersey, where he completed his degree at night school while working for Hilfiger during the day. Hilfiger paid for his final semester at Rutgers and offered him a job after graduation.

Hilfiger's multicultural mosaic was more than just progressive; it was very strategic. After all, Tommy was in his forties, married with four young children and living in Greenwich, Connecticut. He would always need a window into the world's fast-paced pop culture. Kidada Jones—the daughter of *Vibe* founder Quincy Jones—who helped style his fashion ads, kept Hilfiger in check. "Kidada speaks her mind," said Andy Hilfiger. "She will say, 'Tommy, this baby blue isn't happening anymore,' or 'Andy, those pants are *whack*' [out of style].'"

Hip-hop star Coolio once modeled in a Hilfiger fashion show and then joined Tommy onstage for his runway finale. Many fashion editors in the audience shook their heads as the grinning white guy from Elmira became an honorary homeboy.

Rap group Mobb Deep rhymed his praises: "Tommy Hill was my nigga/ and others couldn't figure/How me and Hilfiger used to move through with vigor." Tommy was knocked out. "I thought it was cool— he called me his nigga!" he told *Playboy*.

Unlike the executives at Timberland, the honchos at Tommy Hilfiger Corp. weren't tentative about embracing the rap crowd. "I feel proud that we're able to appeal to such a wide, diverse audience out there," said Horowitz. "That is something I don't think anyone has ever achieved. And I think it is really a tribute to Tommy and how he respects his position and what he's done with it." As for the white people who dissed Hilfiger, claiming that he was nothing more than a "ghetto" brand, Horowitz was unfazed: "You know, I really don't care what *they* think."

Unbeknownst to *them*, Hilfiger had his bases covered—and loaded. White New Yorkers, in particular, couldn't see Hilfiger beyond all those black bike messengers and roughnecks riding the subways who uniformly sported his logo. But Hilfiger was far more than a logo man. In 1997, the number one designer dress shirt in many department stores belonged to Tommy. His $400 business suits were top-sellers at Dillard's, Burdines, Parisian, and Macy's.

"Tommy is a sportswear designer who brought a new life to what was stodgy and expected in tailored clothing," said Ned Allie, an executive at Hartmarx, which made the suits. "Tommy's charcoal gray suit has a beaded stripe that would be bright white or even red. These subtle nuances are what make it so fresh. The market is already flooded with European labels; we don't need another Armani out there. With Tommy, the whole design world in the U.S. started looking at him, and American people are gravitating to him."

And so did establishment types like Britain's Prince Charles, President Bill Clinton, and former U.S. Senator Bill Bradley. Golf sensation David Duval donned Hilfiger's sportswear on the pro tour, and hundreds of middle-aged white men in the suburbs followed.

IN AUGUST 1997 at Macy's in New York, Polo Sport and Tommy Hilfiger were across the aisle from each other on the second floor, bisected by Nautica, another popular menswear brand. These three brands comprised more than 40 percent of all men's sportswear sold in department stores. The Polo Sport outpost resembled a pro shop, with a video wall flashing images of men in flashy Polo Sport togs hang gliding, skiing, and cycling. Across the aisle, Hilfiger's shop was all sunshine and swagger, with a poster featuring three guys strolling on the beach and a corner alcove labeled "Tommy Surf."

The symmetry begged the question: Were they separated at birth? Hardly, declared Lauren. "There are people in this business who are leaders and people who are followers," he expounded in a 1997 interview at his office. "Tommy Hilfiger hasn't anything new to say. His goal was to do Ralph Lauren at a lower price and that's what put Tommy on the map. He's for the younger customer who couldn't afford Polo." Hilfiger's ascent simply meant "There is room in department stores for both McDonald's and Burger King."

Nevertheless, the flame-broiled upstart made him testy. "Tommy gives Ralph the hives," insisted one of Lauren's former publicists. "He is obsessed with all the press Tommy is getting. When *Vanity Fair* published its profile on Tommy in 1996, Ralph was livid. The photos [of Hilfiger's Greenwich, Connecticut, home] included all of Ralph's props, the flags, the boots, the country stuff. Ralph was beside himself."

But Hilfiger, growing more confident and richer by the year—his salary would climb to $13 million in 1996—was now a cult figure in his own right. He relished the horse race. He told *Playboy* in 1997, "Ralph and I are engaged in something like the Pepsi-Coke war, or the BMW-Mercedes war. We're moving fast and forward and we're each conscious of what the other is doing."

Hilfiger was feeling mighty secure in 1996, when he was on the verge of crossing an important threshold—to finally be validated by the fashion establishment. The industry's most prestigious trade group, the Council of Fashion Designers of America, voted Hilfiger the best menswear designer of 1996. As fate would draw him closer to his rival, Tommy picked up his award at the black-tie ceremony at Lincoln Center, sharing the stage with Ralph, who won the CFDA award for women's wear, his third trophy from the CFDA.

————

FROM 1995 ONWARD, Hilfiger watched with fascination as the tables turned: Lauren, fashion's great interpreter, began to copy his copycat. Polo backed off its elitist stance by introducing new collections for men and women at "accessible" prices. Lauren permanently marked down his core product—polo shirts—from $55 to $49; Hilfiger's sold for $44. Lauren's Polo Sport collection was foundering until 1995, when Lauren showed perfect hip-hop pitch when he signed the exotic African American model Tyson Beckford as his poster boy under an exclusive contract that was reportedly valued at a million dollars a year. As many writers applauded Ralph's move, Tommy shrugged it off, noting that it was he who had put Tyson on the runway, years ahead of Ralph, the man who had initially ignored the hip-hop movement and hardly ever used blacks in his ads. As Tyson's buff, dark-skinned torso jumped from the packages of Polo Sport underwear, the brand's street credibility soared, putting it on par with Tommy.

Lauren explained that his new emphasis on Polo Sport in the late 1990s had nothing to do with Hilfiger or anybody else. "I sensed that people were into health and fitness more than they were into clothes. I am one of them. I've been running and biking for years. Polo Sport is part of that future, for the young and old."

But the ever-image-conscious Lauren wasn't about to bend over too far in the direction of hip. Tempering his mass market push a bit—and trumping Hilfiger's popular suits—Lauren introduced his top-of-the-line Purple Label collection of $1,800 suits in 1995 with a blitz of print ads. "Purple Label just started. It isn't a big business yet," Lauren said two years later. "But what Purple Label is doing is leading a trend. The market is starting to say, 'Wait a minute, even though the masses are wearing jeans on casual Fridays, suits can be sold at high prices.' Purple Label invigorates a company. It shows that you are leading."

Purple Label, Polo Sport, and a mainstream women's collection called Lauren by Lauren all lifted Polo's profile and sales as the fashion house prepared to go public. In 1996, *Fortune* began working on a major profile of Ralph, who invited writer Susan Caminiti to his Colorado ranch where Ricky Lauren and Buffy Birritella were also on hand.

The designer got bossy when *Fortune*'s photographer started taking pictures. "Ralph knows the lighting; he knows his best angle; he knows how a picture should look," she recalled. Lauren loved the shots of him in weathered jeans and a denim shirt, at home on the range—he wanted that image for the cover shot. But the November 11, 1996, cover of *Fortune* featured the distinguished designer as a captain of industry in navy pinstripes, white shirt, and black-and-white-patterned tie, with the caption: "Ralph Lauren: a $5 billion empire built on the fashionably correct."

(Months later, when Caminiti was researching a story on Hilfiger—which was never published—an anxious Tommy Hilfiger kept quizzing her. "Is this going to be on the cover of *Fortune*? Is this going to be like Ralph? His article was six or seven pages. Is it going to be like that?" he kept asking her.)

Tommy seemed obsessed with Ralph who, conversely, seemed obsessed with Tommy. Hilfiger even had the nerve to use Clemente Di Monda, the old-school Italian-born barber who had tended Lauren's hair for years. When Clemente's barbershop lease expired in 1991, Lauren invited him to open a new shop in one of the empty spaces on the eighth floor at Polo's headquarters at 650 Madison Avenue. So, whenever Tommy wanted a haircut, he had to troop over to Ralph's digs.

(And on one such occasion in the spring of 1999, Polo staffers were taken aback when Tommy Hilfiger walked down the hall from the barbershop only to wander inside one of Polo's showroom offices, where sample merchandise was sitting out in full view. He looked around for a moment, but nobody had the nerve to ask him to leave. Hilfiger later explained that he had taken a wrong turn on his way to the men's room.)

RALPH AND TOMMY were running neck and neck in the fall of 1996 when both launched jeans collections. Each designer planned to spend as much as $20 million to advertise his jeans. In coming out with Polo Jeans, Ralph had more on his mind than just outdoing Tommy. He wanted desperately to make a big splash with jeans, a category in which he had failed twice before. It had been downright embarrassing that Lauren had yet to get a handle on jeans—which he practically lived in and which were part of the romantic imagery of his Southwestern and country look over the years. While he kept striking out, Calvin Klein had reigned as the designer-jeans king throughout the 1980s.

Lauren's first jeans licensing venture, Polo Westernwear, was with Gap back in 1978, when Gap's three hundred stores were peddling Levi's and searching for some designer sizzle. Lauren had hoped to stake his claim on the western-wear market, as a designer alternative to jeans such as Wrangler and Lee. But Polo Westernwear didn't lasso enough consumers, primarily due to fit problems. Ralph designed his jeans to be tight, which looked terrific on lithe models, but were too snug for most women and men. "As a matter of fact, even Ralph himself began to wear Levi's," Trachtenberg wrote in his biography of Lauren. Polo Westernwear only sold a paltry $12 million in its first year, riding off into the sunset in a hurry as Gap pulled out of the venture.

It would be nearly ten years before Lauren would dive back into the jeans pool with Double RL jeans, named after his ranch. This time, Lauren's dream client was an upscale bohemian who knocked around in beat-up jeans. The company rolled out Double RL jeans in a store-on-wheels—a $1 million, customized Peterbilt eighteen-wheeler, decorated with a mural of thundering horses. On September 22, 1993, the designer truck pulled onto campuses like New York University and Wesleyan.

The college kids who wandered inside found prices that were insane: $150 for faded flannel shirts and $70 for preweathered jeans—the same kind they could find at vintage clothing shops for a third of that price. After a few months, Double RL stopped trucking.

But Ralph's third attempt, Polo Jeans, was the charm. At $48, the jeans were priced right and they sported Lauren's favorite symbol, the American flag. This time Ralph reclaimed Old Glory with his own personal fillip that Tommy couldn't knock off: Polo Jeans sported a tiny flag insignia, with RL initials in white to replace the stars. In ads, Tyson wore Polo Jeans against a backdrop of a flag with beige and red stripes, reminiscent of Jasper Johns' famous *Flag* painting. A couple of years later, Ralph would sit on top of the flagpole when Polo made its $13 million donation to the Smithsonian.

Polo Jeans sauntered into Macy's in New York in August 1996, unveiled by supermodels Bridget Hall and Tyson Beckford, who, along with fifty Harley-Davidson bikers, came roaring down Broadway into Herald Square in front of Macy's. The models stayed to sign autographs, and the event received a smattering of local press.

Weeks later, Tommy Jeans, which featured a number of baggy styles favored by the hip-hop set, came on board with a familiar stroke of marketing-on-wheels: a Tommy Jeans tour bus. Wrapped in a gigantic Hilfiger ad, the bus cruised its way through twelve more cities for in-store fashion shows and parties, showering fans with freebies like jeans, CDs, and guitars. The bus entourage included Andy Hilfiger and the kids of celebrities: Kidada, Quincy Jones's daughter; Kate Hudson, Goldie Hawn's daughter; and Kentaro Seagal, Steven Seagal's son. "By the time we got to Denver, the crowds were huge," Andy recalled. "People kept telling us that they saw us on CNN when we were in Atlanta and Dallas."

In the battle of the jeans, both designers had impressive first-year sales of more than $100 million. But retailers agreed that Tommy Jeans, by measures of sales and buzz, had outpaced Polo Jeans, winning the first round of the jeans war.

IRONICALLY, WHILE TOMMY AND Ralph had been preoccupied with polishing their images to perfection, they failed to realize that despite all that slick marketing, most young shoppers could hardly tell them apart.

Such were the fashion prerogatives evident on the evening of November 17, 1997, in New York at the Barnes & Noble store in Union Square, where Tommy Hilfiger was appearing in person to sign his new coffee-table book, *American Style*. Barnes & Noble was draped in full Tommy regalia that night, as the soundtrack blared Hilfiger's theme song, "Young Americans" by David Bowie, and while the salesclerks scurried about in Tommy khakis and pinstripe shirts. What was most striking was the way the young people came dressed—in either Tommy or Polo or a bit of both.

Damani Davy and two of his Long Island high school buddies were the first to arrive at Barnes & Noble, displaying their addiction to their main man. Davy, a lanky seventeen-year-old, wore Hilfiger's puffy vest and baggy corduroys sliding down to his hips, revealing "Tommy Hilfiger" on the waistband of his underwear. "Tommy captured street kids 'cause that is mostly who supported him," Davy said. "He gave us what we want to wear, like baggy clothes, lots of color, and reflectors on the back of the jackets." Next to him stood Errol Sanders, in a Polo Sport baseball cap, who chimed in, "Tommy isn't gassed up. He *remembers* who put him there."

Further back in line was Matt Spiro, a thirteen-year-old squirt of a kid with Buster Brown bangs, whose baggy pants, sweater, and jacket all had "Polo Sport" or "Ralph Lauren" logos. Spiro spoke up: "I want to be a designer so I study all the fashion stuff. Ralph Lauren is my favorite. I'm not *really* a big Tommy Hilfiger fan. I have Polo everything—shoes, pants, and underwear"—and one hundred shares of Polo Ralph Lauren Corp. stock. "I bought it the first day it came out at $26," he bragged coolly. "I think it's up around $28 now."

So why had little Mr. Polo bothered to show up for Tommy Night? "I like Tommy, too. He seems more down to earth than Ralph Lauren," Spiro said. "The great thing about Tommy is that he knows what people want."

Behind Spiro stood a handsome guy in a black turtleneck with an RL logo who looked just like Tyson, the Polo Sport model. Tyson's twin, whose name was Edmond, had this to say: "I like Tommy, but I gotta support my boy Tyson, who is the first black person who ever modeled for Ralph Lauren. Tommy uses more black models; I'd rather support him than Ralph. And I do have on Tommy Hilfiger underwear tonight."

So Edmond, like the others, was an equal-opportunity consumer. Nevertheless, he wasn't swallowing all the hype. "The best jeans are still Levi's," he insisted.

IT WAS INEVITABLE that the like-minded designers would finally collide. In the summer of 1997, Hilfiger and Polo ran virtually the same magazine ad with the same model, Letitia, on the beach. In Hilfiger's version, Letitia wore red, white, and blue men's underwear while Polo's ad featured her in a red, white, and blue swimsuit. "I don't know how it happened, but I freaked when I saw it," said Toth, whose agency created Hilfiger's ad. "And I bet that Ralph did, too."

TOMMY HILFIGER WAS in high-fashion heaven in November 1997. He finally had his answer to Ralph's Madison Avenue flagship—his own little White House in Beverly Hills. At the corner of swank Rodeo Drive and Santa Monica Boulevard, Hilfiger built from the ground up a two-story federalist-style fortress with columns and a rotunda dome, in spanking white limestone, at a cost of $20 million. With flags flying on top, it jumped out on the block with Chanel, Giorgio Armani—and Polo, which was located just two doors away.

With its pale pearwood fixtures, enameled "Tommy White" walls, and a grand, winding staircase, the store was an inviting place to shop—and to dine, in the upstairs café run by restaurateur Wolfgang Puck. Hanging on the walls were Andy Warhol originals from Hilfiger's private collection, including a portrait of Mick Jagger, Tommy's neighbor on Mustique island. A glimmering, custom-made Harley-Davidson, parked on the first floor, was for sale for $40,000.

The shop was loaded with apparel for men, women, children, and infants—not to mention Tommy's new, top-drawer $1,200 cashmere sportcoats called Hilfiger, which were made in Italy.

To celebrate his Beverly Hills moment, Hilfiger went for the full-court press. The buzz began on Sunday, November 9, when the *Los Angeles Times Magazine* put Tommy's toothy mug on the cover, with the headline: "Tommy Hilfiger 90210." On Tuesday night, Tommy chatted it up with Sinbad, the host of *Vibe*, the late-night TV talk show. *USA Today*'s cover story on Thursday proclaimed: "It's the Tommy life everyone seems to clamor for now."

Friday night was the curtain-raiser for the Sunday store opening. Hilfiger co-chaired a black-tie benefit and auction at the Century Plaza Hotel, where 1,500 guests, including Dustin Hoffman, Sidney Poitier,

Sean Penn, and Russell Simmons, were entertained by Sheryl Crow and Natalie Cole. Before dinner, there was a fashion show with celebrity models who wore Hilfiger's madras shorts and "huge fit" jeans.

Tommy emceed the show: "Here comes Emily Marcus from *Moesha*! Here's Aleca Donna from *Clueless*. We have Peter Paul, one of my top models in New York, who is an upcoming rap star. Show it to them! Allll-right!" Finally, Hilfiger hit the runway himself, on the arm of supermodel Naomi Campbell. The event was taped and aired later on VH-1, the cable TV music station.

The next morning, Hilfiger, in a crisp navy blazer and chinos, took the press on a tour of his new Beverly Hills digs. Checking out the parked limos and all the hubbub on the corner were the salespeople at Polo, who were naturally quite curious. Ralph had never deigned to put himself and Tommy in the same league, let alone on the same block. But on Rodeo Drive, Tommy was looking good. "People around here were a little worried about Tommy coming here at first," a pretty brunette saleswoman in Polo's shoe department said. "I told the store manager that we need to stock more boots and lug-sole shoes, you know, for all the urban customers who will now be shopping on our block."

After a full week of seducing L.A., Tommy headed back to New York, planning to cram more into his schedule now that he was a client of the William Morris Agency, which was developing movie, music, and publishing projects for him.

The Hilfiger organization was right on track in its growth strategy, which was built around a twenty-five-year plan. Horowitz explained in 1997, "It's a generational thing. It's inevitable. The next generation doesn't want to wear what their parents did and that's how we've planned it. Everybody compares us to Ralph. Well, that's fine because we went into this saying, 'We're the next generation Ralph Lauren, because what better model to follow?'

"We're now about halfway there, so we're starting to see how this all works," Horowitz continued. "Ralph has confronted that. He had to look in the mirror. He did some great things reinventing himself with Polo Sport. Not many people are able to do that. But he built such a solid foundation that even with some jolts along the way, he was able to withstand that and come back strong. We're not in that league yet. But that's where we want to be."

Style marches on, indeed.

AS INGENIOUS MARKETERS backed with solid businesses, Lauren and Hilfiger have designed fashion machines that hum to the pace of modern times. Nevertheless, they will always be challenged to stay on their toes. In 2000 and beyond, Lauren will have to find more ways to captivate Generation X shoppers, while Hilfiger will be pressed to grow along with the young consumers he won over in the 1990s.

Silas Chou is nonetheless convinced that Hilfiger has real staying power. "Maybe we can break this tableau of apparel companies lasting for no more than two generations," he observes. "All the brand names of the past history always stick with a snobbish image. We never built our image on snob appeal and people don't wear Tommy for snobbish reasons. They wear Tommy to have individuality. And luckily, that has coincided with the whole society's transformation."

Truly, society had been transformed, as more people no longer felt compelled to choose between one designer and another. Inevitably, the most formidable competition for Tommy and Ralph was coming from the Gap, and its sister stores Banana Republic and Old Navy, which had brilliantly staked their claim on the American look at lower prices. The Gap divisions had proven that they could have the same clout and cachet with consumers that designer names once had.

What is now critical is the force of personality driving the Tommy and Ralph brands. Can these one-time outsiders continue to cast their spell of insiderness, making the American dream of belonging that much more real and accessible to their followers? If consumers believe in the power of Old Glory, the answer is incredibly clear.

WHAT BECOMES A LEGEND MOST? WHEN GIORGIO ARMANI TAKES HOLLYWOOD

The press gives the readers a distorted image of fashion. They portray it as a world full of mad people who dress imaginary women and men. This is the antithesis of my way of presenting fashion.

GIORGIO ARMANI, July 30, 1998

*T*he Emporio Armani concert on September 12, 1996, was some enchanted evening, even by New York standards. The heat began to rise after 9 P.M., when Lauryn Hill and the Fugees were rocking the stage with their hip-hop version of "Killing Me Softly," the Roberta Flack ballad. The trio was pumping to a groove that sparked a spontaneous eruption in the audience. One by one, spectators sprang to their feet, singing along and bopping in the aisles.

Before leaving the stage, the Fugees gathered at the microphone to give a "shout out" to their fashionable host for the evening: "We just wanna thank Armani for giving a few kids from the ghetto some great suits."

Amid the partying people, about four rows back, stood Giorgio Armani, roaring with glee and blowing kisses toward the stage. The concert was crackling with energy, coming together just the way he had intended. The unscripted plug from the Fugees was sublime, as were the compliments that came later from actress Mira Sorvino. Those kudos telegraphed a powerful message: A lot of very cool people dig Giorgio Armani. And the veteran fashion warrior could look forward to getting even more pop from the event, which would replay to millions on VH-1, the cable network that bought the rights to televise the concert.

The night was another big score for the Milanese maestro of fashion. Armani had come to Manhattan that fall to christen two new flagships on Madison Avenue. The champagne started to flow on September 10, when Armani invited the press for cocktails, and a hundred celebrity friends for supper at his sleek, eponymous boutique at Sixty-fifth Street, where affluent boomers could get their fill of $2,500 "black label" Armani suits.

A couple of days later came the big moment to celebrate the opening of Emporio Armani, at Fifty-eighth and Madison, a sort of "Armani-lite," where thirty-somethings could cop Italian style in an $800 suit. Emporio was Armani's bridge to the future, and he went all out to create a memorable night that would generate lots of buzz.

The Emporio Armani concert was billed as a "high-energy, high-volume celebration of style." Manhattan's legendary florist and party-planner, Robert Isabell, and the Armani people had turned the cavernous, Twenty-sixth Street Armory on Lexington Avenue into a swank cocktail lounge. Cantilevered tiers were carpeted to create a cozy theater where guests sat on thick pillows across from small tables lit with votive candles. A platoon of gorgeous hunks in black T-shirts delivered drinks, and circulated trays of dim sum and skewered chicken.

The sixty-two-year-old Armani, dashing with his deep tan, snowy hair, and true-blue eyes, brimmed with vitality. He showed off his trim, disco body in a snug navy T-shirt and flat-front pants. Starting at 7:30 P.M., the fashion host with the most stood guard at the entrance, where he reached out to shake each and every hand of his thousand invited guests: the downtown club kids, the fashion industry crowd, and enough famous faces to give the paparazzi whiplash, including Arnold Schwarzenegger, Mike Tyson, Robert De Niro, Lauren Bacall, Quincy Jones, Michael Keaton, Spike Lee, Pat Riley, Winona Ryder, Caroline Kennedy and her brother, John F. Kennedy Jr., and Sarah Ferguson, Duchess of York.

The program served up an eclectic mix from pop music's cutting edge: Hill and the Fugees, Jakob Dylan and the Wallflowers, D'Angelo, Me'Shell Ndegéocello, along with guitarist Eric Clapton, an Armani buddy and walking billboard for the designer. Rounding out the evening was a fashion show, of course, and a wacky video starring Jennifer Tilly as a big-haired mall rat who suddenly turned chic, thanks to the fashion wizardry of "Salvation Armani." After a pasta buffet, everyone moved onto the dance floor, where Armani was still working up a sweat around 2 A.M.

Armani was most definitely in The Zone. He stayed up late to play the evening for all it was worth, an estimated $2 million. A *major* splurge. And a huge shot in the arm at a critical juncture. The triumph proved once more that Giorgio Armani, the man and the brand, was still kicking, amid the onslaught of Gucci, Prada, and Dolce & Gabbana, the latest fashion flavors of the season.

The party was also a testament to Armani's ability to enliven his persona without the direction of Gabriella Forte, the steely executrix who had been the custodian of the Armani image and his conduit to the press for more than fifteen years. In the spring of 1994, Forte had shocked her boss when she bolted for a bigger job: president of Calvin Klein Inc. Armani was livid when he found out she was leaving. "He recruits my people, my collections," Armani snapped to *Women's Wear Daily*. "Next he will be calling me up to head his design studio!"

Forte's sudden resignation stung Armani badly, but a decade before he had recovered from a blow far greater. In 1985, Sergio Galleoti, Armani's dynamic co-founder and intimate friend, died after a long illness. It was Galleoti, a former architectural draftsman, who had encouraged Armani to go out on his own. Together they had pooled a $10,000 investment to open Giorgio Armani SpA, in 1975.

Armani called his relationship with Galleoti one of "great complicity." Each partner resided in his own apartment at the company's Milan headquarters, a magnificent seventeenth-century palazzo on Via Borgunuovo. Pushy and outgoing, Galleoti deftly handled the company's business side, freeing up the serious and reserved Armani to design in his studio.

Galleoti's death was a defining passage in Armani's life. Compelled to tend to the business matters of his burgeoning fashion house from then on, Armani plotted for the long term, positioning the company to be a trademark that didn't depend on the talents of any one individual.

Armani, who would turn sixty-five in 1999, had begun to make the difficult transition of letting go, of delegating more responsibilities to his younger staffers and giving them more credit in public. "For the moment, they still count on me," he said in March 1997. "But I think it is dangerous to depend on the health of one person and that is why I want to depersonalize the house." Armani made such a gesture later that year when, for the first time, he took his runway bow alongside the members of his menswear design team.

And after all those uptight years, Armani was finally ready to loosen up. "I had an image that was too serious—like I was on a pedestal," he reflected in March 1997. "I now feel more at ease, without having a filter, a barrier. I have changed a lot . . . I now take the opportunity to smile."

To be sure, Armani's personal makeover made him more daring. His decision to elevate his profile with the Emporio concert in 1996 was a gamble, especially since the Armani image was about a mature, timeless style. He was way outside of his box in his quest to cultivate a younger, downtown image. But Armani had managed to pull off a glamorous, laid-back event where he came across as effortless and clever—and not as some old fool trying too hard. The party, he revealed months later, "felt very young and it was great fun. There were all the celebrities and it had the *feeling* of Armani. This was one of those influential events that people remember for a long time."

The payoff was both psychic and tangible—the TV coverage, scads of press, and an overflow of goodwill. Clearly, the Italian master who spoke hardly any English was fluent in the language of high-fashion marketing.

Since the early eighties, Giorgio Armani had been one of the world's best-selling designers, a creator who was equal parts steak and sizzle—fashion and marketing. But long before he created a fashion empire and became an icon to the stars, Armani could claim the title of fashion revolutionary. In 1975, he opened his fashion house with a radically chic look: the unconstructed suit, whose slouchy jacket with sloping lapels hung like a sweater. Armani's signature style blurred the distinction between sportswear and business suits by taking linings and shoulder pads out of jackets, the creases out of trousers, and the starch out of shirt collars. His suits came in featherweight wools, cashmeres, and linens, all textured and patterned in shades of taupe and gray. Those supple materials draped and rumpled gracefully, giving men a comfortable, effortless sophistication. And setting himself apart from the rest of high fashion, Armani consistently manufactured high-quality tailored garments on an industrial scale. Nobody did it better, retailers agreed.

Barneys New York was the first American retailer to take a flier on

Armani. In 1976, Barneys' owner, Fred Pressman, ordered a shipment of the rumpled suits, confident that Barneys' progressive clientele would go for Armani, which they did. Barneys' success goaded Saks Fifth Avenue, Bloomingdale's, and swank haberdashers, including Louis of Boston, to do the same. But the most powerful magnet for the designer turned out to be Hollywood. In the 1980 movie *American Gigolo*, actor Richard Gere, playing a swaggering Beverly Hills stud, was a walking Armani fashion show. Best fashion moment: the scene where Gere lovingly tossed a rainbow of folded shirts across a bed. The close-up revealed the Giorgio Armani label inside the neck.

Gigolo put Armani on the public's radar. The next year, Armani's annual sales were an impressive $90 million. From Hollywood to Wall Street to the regular Joe on the street, men of all pinstripes got into the Armani habit. It was amusing to hear men get so worked up over clothes. Mark Girman, an owner of two car washes in Pittsburgh, told *The Wall Street Journal* that Armani had changed his life. After seeing Gere in *Gigolo*, Girman took a new fashion turn. Nine years later, the car-wash connoisseur had collected twenty-five suits, many shirts and ties, an overcoat, and eight pairs of shoes—all by Armani.

Armani had cast the same spell over a new generation of executive women who were unimpressed with the fussy, figure-molding haute couture that was coming out of Paris. Armani's soft, comfortable tailoring went over big in a feminist age; a lady in Armani was sophisticated, and breathing easy—even after a heavy meal. Armani's pantsuits were the pinnacle of power dressing, a conservative yet polished look that CNN anchorwoman Willow Bay liked to wear on camera. "Armani is safe," Bay told *Harper's Bazaar*. Most women appreciated that Armani didn't startle them with unusual new styles every year. "Change has to be subtle," Armani once said. "When a woman alters her look too much from season to season, she becomes a fashion victim."

All you had to say was "Armani"—as generic as Kleenex—and the name instantly conjured the image of modern élan. "Giorgio Armani changed the whole notion of the way the world dresses," said Patrick McCarthy of *Women's Wear Daily*. Italian knitwear designer Rosita Missoni, whose own colorful sweaters were also fashion classics, gushed succinctly: "Armani put women in men's clothes. He is a *genius*."

ARMANI MAY HAVE invented the unconstructed suit, but he didn't own it for long. In fashion, imitation has always been the fastest path to popularity, and Armani knockoffs popped up faster than dandelions in a backyard. Since the 1980s, scores of Seventh Avenue apparel makers had come out with their versions, which they invariably touted as "*our* Armani jacket." Macy's coattailed the trend with an Italian-style brand whose name rang a bell: "Alfani." And fashionable women on a budget knew where to go shopping: the Calvin Klein department, where high-quality Armani-like suits were priced at least 20 percent lower than the real thing.

Knockoffs would always be a source of validation—and irritation—for Armani. The designer grew more exasperated as others kept taking his ideas to the bank. Armani got so fed up by the fall of 1982 that he abruptly called off his October fashion show. He was incensed because the press refused to play *his* way. In order to get a running start on the knockoffs, Armani tried to convince fashion writers attending his show to hold off writing their reviews until his merchandise had safely arrived at stores months later. No way, the fashion press balked, calling his worries a case of "Armanoia."

But Armani's tantrum was just another melodrama for the gossip columns that soon blew over. The next year he was back to his runway ritual and on July 19, 1983, *The New York Times* reported: "The news was from Europe and most of it had to do with Giorgio Armani, the Italian designer who said he would never stage a fashion show ever again in his life. Well, Mr. Armani did have a fashion show and his collection looks like a winner."

So Armani got real and focused on his designing. A decade later, no longer fretting about knockoffs, he had the gumption to knock himself off. At the suggestion of Colombe Nicholas, who was president of Armani's U.S. division at the time, Armani hired a relatively inexperienced talent, a twenty-three-year-old black American named Patrick Robinson, to design the copies. Nicholas auditioned several job candidates by requisitioning sketches of an imaginary Armani collection. Robinson's sketches were by far the best, in the true spirit of Armani, she said. Gabriella Forte agreed, and told a euphoric Robinson, "I know that Giorgio will just *love* you."

Robinson, a Californian who graduated from Parsons School of Design in New York, moved to Milan in February 1992 to take the $80,000-a-year position as design director for Le Collezioni, Armani's second-tier women's label, priced a notch below his top collection, which everybody in the know referred to simply as "black label," because the label inside was black with white lettering. Armani's black label became the gold standard that none other than Ralph Lauren would imitate when he came out with his "Purple Label" top-drawer suits tailored in England.

"The years I spent at Armani were the best training that a designer could ever have," explained Robinson, who spent his first month in Milan meeting with Armani every day. After that, the boss left him on his own. Yet Armani insisted that Robinson do what Armani himself had done in the 1960s: learn the craft first and the design second. So Robinson commuted regularly to nearby Turin to study how the clothes were made inside the factories owned by Gruppo GFT, the manufacturer licensed to make Le Collezioni.

"Armani taught me that the technical people in the factories aren't always so good at fitting clothes," Robinson reminisced. "Armani knows the way a jacket is supposed to look. He doesn't say, 'It should be twenty-three inches.' He can just look at something on a hanger and tell you that it should fall *this way*."

From the outset, sales of Le Collezioni "went through the roof," Nicholas remembered. Soon, Le Collezioni surpassed black label to become the core of Armani's women's-wear business. "Patrick understood the Armani look completely and they were in perfect synch. But then again, Patrick *did* have a great master to interpret."

Robinson characterized Armani as the consummate perfectionist, who didn't mince words. "We had our yelling fits. Did he *yell*!" he remembered, laughing. "But Armani was pretty cool and pretty amazing. He's running this huge empire all in his head. He knows everything, what every little string is doing. He's in *complete* control." (Robinson resigned from Armani in 1994 to design the Anne Klein collection in New York.)

Successful as Le Collezioni was, Armani would always be wary of his competitors. "I pay attention to what's being copied because I always need to keep a distance," Armani explained.

And to Armani, distance—in terms of design—meant centimeters and not miles. Never one to jump onto the latest runway trends, Armani preferred to stay put, to recycle his core silhouettes, with only a few modifications each season. It didn't hurt, of course, that Armani kept designing plenty of good looks worth repeating.

While Armani's approach seemed pretty logical, this wasn't the usual way high fashion worked. In the 1990s, more designers fell into the habit of shock therapy: runway collections that were provocative, outlandish—and thrilling—to fashion editors who lauded them for moving fashion "forward."

But not Armani. Like Lauren and Hilfiger, Armani knew his customers depended on his surefooted styles, which they continued to buy, knockoffs notwithstanding. His business kept growing steadily, and during most of the 1990s Armani reigned as *the* top-selling designer brand at Saks Fifth Avenue and Neiman Marcus.

As he flaunted fashion's conventions, Armani epitomized the end of fashion. Sophisticated people no longer cared if fashion moved forward or backward; they just wanted fashion to provide them with attractive clothes suited for modern living. Armani's uncontrived, antifashion stance dovetailed with the zeitgeist of casual dressing. People now wore fashion *their* way, like journalist Carl Bernstein, who told *The Wall Street Journal* that he liked to pair his $1,500 Armani jackets with beat-up jeans.

"Fashion is finished, for me the *diktat* is finished," Armani declared to *New York* in September 1997. "That is, 'this is fashion and you must dress this way'—it's finished. Fashion is what a woman makes. She puts on an Armani jacket, a skirt by Gigli. This is fashion."

But the irony of this antifashion philosophy was that it took so long to take hold. While Armani's unconstructed suits were new and original in 1975, variations of his look continued to remain in style for two decades. What's more, he built his billion-dollar empire largely through the sales of expensive clothes—and not perfumes, jeans, and underwear, the way Calvin Klein did.

Firmly established as a high-fashion clothing brand from the start, Armani basked in that heady intangible known as mystique. Among top designers, mystique is usually fast and fleeting. But Armani had a secret weapon: celebrities, who are by far today's most powerful fashion role models to the masses. The whole world associated Armani with the rich and famous. When real estate agents and advertising executives saw how chic and sharp Glenn Close or Lauren Hutton looked in Armani, they went for Armani too.

From *Gigolo* to the Oscars, Armani benefited from a long-standing tradition of dressing the stars, a practice that over the years effectively transformed him and other designers into stars in their own right.

THE SYMBIOTIC RELATIONSHIP between fashion designers and Hollywood dated back to the 1950s, when couturier Hubert de Givenchy began his heady association with Audrey Hepburn, the world's most famous fashion role model of all time. By the late 1990s, many designers could brag that they dressed Sharon Stone, Gwyneth Paltrow, or some other ingenue of the moment. But "gilt by association" was only meaningful when such luminaries delivered the shoppers to the stores. And not many designers, or stars, could make that claim.

Armani could. He was the first designer to milk his celebrity connections by developing a publicity machine to get his clothes on the backs of Hollywood's most influential and most visible A-list of actors, directors, producers, and agents. Such headliners became an integral component of his master marketing plan to keep his trademark in lights.

The centerpiece of Armani's celebrity strategy was the Academy Awards, the biggest photo op of the year. After Armani opened a Beverly Hills boutique in 1988, the designer set out to become *the* designer of choice on Oscar night. By 1991, *WWD* called the Oscars "The Armani Awards," by virtue of the fact that everybody who was anybody was wearing Armani. After his Oscar coup, Armani developed a relationship with dozens of famous people who lived in his clothes and graced the events he hosted. At the October 1990 dinner he gave at New York's Museum of Modern Art to celebrate *Made in Milan,* a documentary on Armani directed by Martin Scorsese, there was a famous face everywhere you turned: Scorsese, Richard Gere, Cindy Crawford, John F. Kennedy Jr., Robert De Niro, and more. Such glitterati assured Armani of getting many mentions in the press and on TV, since his guests were exactly the people the public loved to see.

WHY DOES A celebrity endorsement have so much pull with consumers? "Celebrities work on another level because people think of them as real people more than models," said Martha Nelson, editor of *In Style*. "People have a history with them. With Demi Moore we think, 'I remember when she had that little haircut in *Ghost* and wasn't that amazing she got so buff for *Striptease*?' We feel that we have known her over a long period of time and there is an emotional connection."

In Style, which debuted in September 1994 with Annette Bening—wearing a navy Armani—on the cover, brilliantly tapped into the public's adulation of the style of celebrities. Publisher Time Inc. took a page from its winning formula at *People* and came up with a more fashionable hybrid. *In Style* featured celebrities in full-length shots, out on the town, behind the velvet rope at movie premieres, inside their fabulous homes—and of course, at awards shows like the Oscars. In a record three years, *In Style* had turned a profit, and by the end of 1997, the magazine had a paid circulation of more than 1 million.

As more affluent consumers got hooked on reading *In Style*, more fashion houses flocked to become advertisers in the magazine, led by Gianni Versace, who was one of the first designers to understand its powerful attraction.

"Versace loved the approach of *In Style*," noted Hal Rubenstein, veteran fashion reporter and Versace observer. "Versace thought that people were tired of looking at models. He understood that, oddly enough, movie stars look like real people. Their breasts aren't perfect, their hips are wide, they are more approachable and people relate to them."

Like Armani, Gianni Versace was early to beat a path to celebrities. Versace's association came quite naturally since so many of his signature items, such as shiny print silk shirts for men and skintight gowns for women, were made for the stage. Versace's main man was his close friend, singer Elton John, who sat in the front row of his fashion shows and showed up to knock out a few tunes to launch Versace's boutique on Fifth Avenue in the fall of 1996. Versace also put the stars to work as models for his advertising, including Madonna, the artist formerly known as Prince, and Courtney Love.

In the spirit of Armani, Versace had courted the flashiest of the famous, the likes of Sylvester Stallone, Tina Turner, and actress Elizabeth Hurley. And Versace was just as often linked to the infamous, such as Mike Tyson, who often wore Versace in public. Gianni Versace himself once bragged to a reporter that rapper Tupac Shakur "wore Versace on the day he walked into prison *and* on the day he walked out of prison." Fashion insiders liked to say that a rich man's wife wore Armani, while his mistress favored Versace.

In the aftermath of the murder of Gianni Versace in July 1997, the platinum-haired Donatella Versace, who took over designing for the eponymous house, continued to draw her late brother's celebrity mascots at fashion shows. Turning out for Donatella's first Paris couture show in July 1998 were Sean Puffy Combs, Melanie Griffith, and Jennifer Lopez, all decked out in Versace. Such stardust gilded the Versace trademark, as the fashion house claimed annual sales of more than $500 million in 1997.

So first it was Armani, followed by Versace, who set a new standard by using star power to achieve fashion horsepower, and the rest of the industry followed. The fact that Armani—who never spent much time in America and didn't speak English—managed to captivate all those celebrities, years ahead of such canny marketers as Calvin Klein, was the result not only of keen instincts about modern culture, but also of Italian sensibilities.

"The Italian designers have always been sharp in finding ways to reach the American public," said Sara Forden, a Milan-based reporter for *Women's Wear Daily*. "Italians are grounded in the American mentality and American habits. They are quick to spot what is hot, whether it's a business trend or a lifestyle trend."

Culturally, Italian fashion designers have gravitated toward Hollywood for a long time. Perhaps that is because Italy has always had its own homegrown film industry to promote. The 1950s and 1960s were the golden years of Cinecittà, the famous Rome studio that turned out a slew of international hits like *La Dolce Vita* and *L'Aventura*. Actors Sophia Loren, Gina Lollobrigida, and Marcello Mastroianni became world-class stars. "In Italy, we have no royalty like in France," observed Armando Branchini, a Milanese management consultant. "Movie stars are our royalty."

But inside the haughty Paris couture salons in the 1950s, movie stars weren't shining so brightly. In 1955, Christian Dior refused to provide a wedding gown for a movie starring Brigitte Bardot, who was a fast-rising star at the time. "There was no way Dior would risk incurring the displeasure of some of his most elegant clients by allowing his dresses to be put on vulgar display on the screen," wrote Marie-France Pochna, a Dior biographer. "Dior was a snob. He ranked living, breathing aristocrats far higher aesthetically than their pale imitations on stage and screen."

So while the couturiers staked their claim on European aristocracy and American socialites, the Italians looked up to the stars. When Italian high fashion was centered in Rome in the 1960s, Valentino Garavani, known simply as Valentino, became a favorite of the Hollywood jet set.

Besides being a talented couturier, the darkly handsome and heavy-lidded Valentino prevailed as fashion's most glamorous bon vivant—and the personification of *la dolce vita*. Amid the lush trappings of his yacht and palatial homes, Valentino loved to entertain on a grand scale, surrounded by such Hollywood legends as Elizabeth Taylor and Joan Collins, who were among his favorite clients. Valentino zeroed in on Sharon Stone, Hollywood's fashion plate of the 1990s. Sophia Loren was also among the galaxy of stars Valentino invited to his black-and-white ball to celebrate his thirtieth anniversary in business, where his clients Aretha Franklin and Bette Midler belted out a soulful "Happy Birthday." The 1992 gala was a reprise from a year earlier, when Valentino first celebrated his thirtieth anniversary at his magnificent villa in Rome, with an A-list of stars and European royalty in attendance.

VALENTINO SET A powerful example of Hollywood marketing for Armani, but it was Nino Cerruti, another charismatic Italian designer, who would first expose Armani to the world of movie stars. Armani worked as a design assistant for Cerruti from 1964 to 1970, during the time the house of Cerruti began dressing European actors on the screen.

Nino Cerruti was thirty years old in 1960 when he became the third-generation leader of Cerruti 1881, the Italian textile manufacturer famous for its fine wool fabrics. The young textile heir was all about style. At six two, he was a debonair Cary Grant type whose stunning wife, Chantall, was a former model for Balenciaga. Nino Cerruti relished his role as a menswear designer, in the forefront of the peacock revolution led by Pierre Cardin, whose sculpted suits were the rage of the sixties. Cerruti opened a posh menswear boutique in Paris in the 1960s that became his springboard for penetrating the movie studios in Rome, Paris, and Hollywood.

Cerruti had a penchant for theatrics. In the summer of 1958, he dreamed up a publicity stunt involving Anita Ekberg, the blonde bombshell who was riding high from her role in *La Dolce Vita*, the famous film satire about jet-set decadence starring Marcello Mastroianni. Cerruti hired Ekberg to help him introduce a new color called *battalion*, a greenish or petrol blue, in menswear.

First, Cerruti convinced Italian automaker Lancia to customize forty of its sleek "America" convertibles in the same shade. Cerruti remembered how easy this was: "Lancia charged us absolutely nothing. They did it just for the publicity. Imagine today going to a car manufacturer and telling him, 'Please paint me forty cars!'"

On the day of Cerruti's fashion show, a caravan of Lancias—each with a pretty model in a blue dress—cruised the streets of Rome, then rolled onto the Via Veneto, the famous trolling ground of local playboys and starlets, which had been blocked off to traffic for the occasion.

One Lancia was left on display inside the nearby Excelsior Hotel, where Cerruti 1881 was holding a menswear fashion show. Down the runway came the petrol blue suits, followed by Ekberg in a slinky blue number designed by Cerruti. She broke a bottle of champagne against the hood of the Lancia, as the paparazzi fired away. "That's how we launched the new color. It was very crazy. Very *Dolce Vita*," Cerruti recalled. And the strategy worked, he maintained, recalling that many of the most fashionable men across Europe turned on to Cerruti blue that year.

Cerruti's Paris boutique, located on the bustling Place de Madelaine in the heart of the Right Bank shopping district, became famous for its exquisite tailoring, and drew actors Terence Stamp, Michael Caine, and Jean-Paul Belmondo, who became regulars. Orson Welles ordered his hats from Cerruti. Before long, Cerruti was dressing his famous clients in front of the camera as well. In 1965, Cerruti outfitted Belmondo and Alain Delon in sharp double-breasted suits for the French production *Borsalino.* Throughout the 1970s, Cerruti's clothes appeared in several French and Italian movies, worn by actors Yves Montand, Catherine Deneuve, and Liv Ullmann.

Giorgio Armani entered the picture in 1964, when Cerruti hired him to design a new menswear line called Hitman. The son of a transport company manager from Piacenza, not far from Milan, Armani arrived at Cerruti 1881 after first dropping out of medical school. He shifted into the world of fashion, spending six years as a window dresser and buyer at the Rinascente department store. Cerruti remembered being impressed by Armani's serious, professional demeanor and his drive to succeed. "What I could spot was that he had all the right sensibilities," Cerruti recalled.

At Cerruti 1881, Armani learned all about fabrics and manufacturing inside the company's factories. Armani said that his six years at Cerruti 1881 were "fruitful years. My experience with the firm's tradition definitely influenced the forging of my own career."

Having exited Cerruti 1881 in 1970 to lay the foundation for opening his own fashion house, Armani wasn't closely involved in Cerruti's movie projects, most of which occurred after he departed. But his seasoning at Cerruti 1881 obviously rubbed off, since Armani moved precipitously to cultivate Hollywood soon after he opened his own house. It came as no surprise to Cerruti to learn that Armani had been in his own business for barely three years when he designed the wardrobe for *American Gigolo.*

Armani flashed back to the time when John Travolta, who was originally cast to play the lead in *Gigolo,* came to Milan to be fitted for his film wardrobe. At the time, Armani didn't realize that Travolta was such a big deal. But one hot July afternoon when the two were kicking back at an outdoor café in the Piazza San Babila, Armani watched the Milanese on the street go crazy for the star of *Saturday Night Fever*. "People were all the way across the street yelling 'Travolta!' " Armani remembered.

Cerruti contended that his former charge was ambitious and a quick study. "Armani had already left when we began doing a lot of movies. But he has a way of knowing and of learning. Armani's approach to movies and his approach to celebrities were exactly the kinds of things we were doing when he was here."

Well, not exactly. From the beginning, Armani made the stars integral to his overall marketing game plan, whereas Cerruti didn't. While Cerruti basked in the reflected glory of the stars he dressed, Cerruti still remained largely anonymous to the American public. Nevertheless, Cerruti 1881 was a solid establishment and had grown into a $350 million-a-year business by the mid-1990s.

After *Gigolo*, Armani enjoyed another windfall of publicity for something he had nothing to do with: rumpled linen jackets with the sleeves pushed up, worn by Don Johnson and Philip-Michael Thomas, who played detectives in the eighties hit TV series *Miami Vice*. The show attracted millions of viewers who tuned in just to check out the clothes. Meanwhile, menswear retailers cashed in on the *Miami Vice* style of unconstructed blazers and pleated pants. The show's costume designers used many sources to outfit the actors. But most people outside the fashion industry weren't aware that it was Nino Cerruti who created *Miami Vice*'s original look. (Cerruti even won a Cutty Sark menswear fashion award for *Miami Vice*.) Most people associated the detective duo's continental élan with Armani, who dined off all the free publicity he was raking in from the series.

Taking a few cues from his famous protégé, Cerruti set out to win over Hollywood starting in 1986, when he hired a full-time publicist in Los Angeles. Cerruti's first movie assignment in America was outfitting

Michael Douglas and Kathleen Turner in *The Jewel of the Nile*. He had designed clothes for Turner in several other films and for her own personal wardrobe. She returned the favor by attending his fashion shows in Paris, becoming his first American muse. "Kathleen was very kind and very helpful to me," he said.

Cerruti thus became one of Hollywood's busiest tailors, commissioned to provide on-screen wardrobes for Jack Nicholson, Jeremy Irons, Clint Eastwood, and Harrison Ford, as well as Richard Gere in *Pretty Woman*. But Cerruti said he was also expected to give, in return for the privilege of dressing Hollywood's leading men. By the early 1990s, there was no shortage of fashion houses willing to bend over backward, ready to pay big bucks to get their styles on the likes of Harrison Ford. Film production companies, taking advantage of an oversupply of designers and an undersupply of big stars, became more demanding. "Hollywood is like a Turkish bazaar where they expect you to give 1,000 percent," Cerruti explained. "The productions used to pay for the clothes we made for the movie, but now we get a credit [at the end of the movie] in exchange for supplying the clothes for free."

But Armani still managed to drive a harder bargain because he had become almost as famous as the actors he outfitted. Armani didn't need to give away his clothes just to see his name roll by in type in the end credits, when moviegoers were filing out of the theater. Still, Armani obliged by giving a discount when his clothes were used in movies, such as *48 Hours* and *The Untouchables*, where his name was prominently featured—in the *opening* credits.

Armani was able to negotiate such visible plugs because by the mid-1980s, he was well on his way to becoming a household name. In addition to his movie projects, Armani had appeared on the cover of *Time* magazine in 1982. His PR people in Milan had already outfitted a number of stars like Glenn Close and Robert De Niro. So the Armani machine was up to speed when the designer opened his first boutique in Beverly Hills on Rodeo Drive in 1988. Armani dispatched Gabriella Forte to America to prepare for his West Coast coming out.

Forte was born in Italy but grew up in New York, where she used to run her own fashion PR firm, which made her the perfect go-between for Armani. She certainly lived up to her surname, which means "hard" or "strong." A dictatorial taskmaster, Forte was known to terrorize employees with her profanity-laced tirades. A petite, broad-faced woman who wore her long black hair in a severe center part, Forte was the *voice* of Armani. She fielded most press calls, furnishing pithy quotes which she attributed to Armani. Steeped in the world of Armani, she wound up marrying Eddie Glantz, a New Yorker who had been a member of Armani's menswear design team in Milan since 1979, the same year Forte joined the company.

Forte was indispensable in bringing Hollywood to Armani. She had become chummy with Jay Cocks, a former film critic who covered Armani for *Time*, who introduced her to many movie people whom she steered into Armani's world. "Gabriella is a true movie buff, and she loved to work with the stars," recalled Pier Filipo Pieri, a publicist who worked for Forte from 1984 to 1989. After Pieri handled the arrangements to send Glenn Close an Armani gown to wear for a big event in Washington, she sent him a huge bowl of red tulips and a gracious note of thanks.

In searching for a West Coast representative, Forte knew Armani was more impressed with pedigree than an impressive résumé. First and foremost, high fashion had always been a business of relationships. The famous houses in Paris and Milan were great believers in hiring fancy foot soldiers to link them to the upper reaches of the upper crust. More often than not, the Europeans recruited countesses or marquesses, or other outgoing ladies who were already entrenched in the international social whirl. At Yves Saint Laurent, for example, the position of *couture direc-trice* went to Baroness Hélène de Ludinghausen, a descendant of the Russian Stroganoff family, who gave the culinary world its famous beef Stroganoff.

In 1981, Armani enlisted Lee Radziwill, the former princess and sister of Jacqueline Kennedy Onassis, to be his "special events" coor-dinator on the East Coast, and it would be Radziwill who would suggest a candidate for the Beverly Hills position. Radziwill had mentioned the job to her niece Maria Shriver, who told her close friend, Wanda McDaniel, a former society columnist for the *Los Angeles Herald Exam-iner* and one of Shriver's bridesmaids when she married Arnold Schwar-zenegger.

Blond and fetching, McDaniel, the wife of Al Ruddy, a Hollywood producer whose credits included *The Godfather,* was pretty much the ideal candidate. A graduate of the top-ranked University of Missouri School of Journalism, she had the instincts of a reporter, and she was already hooked into Hollywood. After Forte met with McDaniel, she sent her to Milan to get Armani's final approval. McDaniel then returned to Beverly Hills, where she got down to business.

Forte told her to feel free to pick any title she wanted. But McDaniel preferred not to use a title. She explained to the *Los Angeles Times*, "It'll be a real hands-on job. I'll hostess lunches for the new Armani shop opening on Rodeo, help get Armani clothes in films and generally be a sort of ambassadress."

When Giorgio Armani on Rodeo Drive opened in August 1988, McDaniel got off to a fast start. The first "shopping party" she organized for the boutique was covered by Marylouise Oates, a columnist at the *Los Angeles Times*. One of the first to arrive was producer Dawn Steel, an Armani devotee who just happened to be one of the most powerful women in Hollywood. The day's heavy hitter was Barbara Sinatra, who, Oates reported, "bought up a storm, at least fifteen pieces," while Shriver dropped by with Schwarzenegger and purchased a rose-colored suit.

Given Armani's strength in menswear, McDaniel concentrated on finding a high-profile man to become a billboard for Armani. Choosing the right person wasn't so easy. In 1985, Armani reportedly tried to woo up-and-comer Kevin Costner for one of his advertising campaigns, but Costner turned him down. Actors were accustomed to being hounded by publicists to hawk all kinds of products, and the most serious, intellectual actors weren't interested in being flacks for fashion. Those were the most difficult ones, and they were precisely the types whom Armani wanted to wear his clothes—the actors who seemed to be above it all, yet were still highly visible. As it turned out, the first celebrity Armani would sign up wouldn't even come from Hollywood.

McDaniel set her sights on Pat Riley, the Los Angeles Lakers basketball coach, who had already been wearing Armani for years. Riley was a prime catch who had everything going for him. The National Basketball Association was making a resurgence, and the Lakers, led by its famous center, Magic Johnson, were a hot, winning team. Riley's public profile soared with the Lakers' five NBA championships, and, as luck would have it, Riley moved on to coach the New York Knicks, another popular team that always made it to the playoffs, and whose hometown just happened to be America's fashion and media capital. (Riley would remain in the spotlight after he left New York in 1995 to coach the Miami Heat.)

The rugged-handsome Riley was a fashion role model right out of central casting, a real man's man. Riley's coat-and-tie years in Catholic schools had left him with perfect carriage and impeccable grooming habits. With his slicked-back hair and manly swagger, Riley, at six-four, was a sharp dresser with an innate sense of style. "My players always called

Emanuel Ungaro, with a model in one of his signature couture gowns, in his Paris studio in 1988. PHOTO BY DERRY MOORE

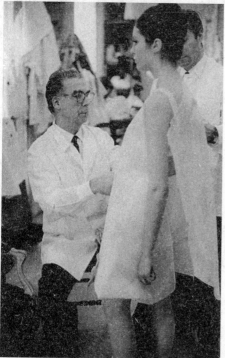

Cristobal Balenciaga, the world's most revered couturier and mentor to Emanuel Ungaro, at his Paris atelier, 1960. "One never knew what one was going to see at a Balenciaga opening. One fainted. It was possible to blow up and die," gushed Diana Vreeland in her 1984 memoir D.V. PHOTO BY HENRI CARTIER-BRESSON, MAGNUM PHOTOS

Now that's Italian! Giorgio Armani with Sophia Loren at the September 12, 1996, concert extravaganza he threw to celebrate the opening of Emporio Armani in New York. The cost of the party: $2 million. PHOTO BY KEVIN MAZUR, COURTESY OF GIORGIO ARMANI

At the 1996 Emporio party, Giorgio Armani and Pat Reilly, the National Basketball Association's most valuable fashion plate who inspired American men to get into the Armani habit. PHOTO BY KEVIN MAZUR, COURTESY OF GIORGIO ARMANI

Giorgio Armani and Glenn Close, one of his earliest celebrity role models on September 12, 1996. Armani's clothes "go with my philosophy of simple, unadorned elegance," Close said. PHOTO BY KEVIN MAZUR, COURTESY OF GIORGIO ARMANI

Nino Cerruti staged a paparazzi moment with La Dolce Vita *star Anita Ekberg, who modeled "battalion" blue at his menswear fashion show in Rome, 1958. Cerruti was one of the first designers to recruit movie stars to promote his name.* COURTESY OF NINO CERRUTI

President Bill Clinton, Ralph Lauren, and Hillary Rodham Clinton in front of the
Star-Spangled Banner, at the National Museum of American History in July 1998.
Lauren's fashion house donated $13 million to restore the 185-year-old flag.
PHOTO BY JEFF TINSLEY, COURTESY OF THE NATIONAL MUSEUM OF AMERICAN HISTORY,
SMITHSONIAN INSTITUTION

Rapper Snoop Dogg with Tommy Hilfiger inside his New York showroom in 1994.
Snoop wore a Hilfiger rugby shirt on Saturday Night Live, which did the trick to
inspire youth all across America to go shopping for their own Tommys.
PHOTO BY MARTHA SWOPE, MARTHA SWOPE ASSOCIATES CAROL ROSEGG, COURTESY OF
TOMMY HILFIGER CORP.

Swaddled in silk. Lauren Hutton, Zoran, and Isabella Rossellini, 1992.
PHOTO BY ERIC BOMAN

Saks Fifth Avenue newspaper ad for Zoran, fall 1998.
PHOTO BY SKREBNESKI, COURTESY OF SAKS FIFTH AVENUE

LVMH chairman Bernard Arnault and his wife, Hélène, congratulate Michael Kors backstage after his fashion show for Celine, in Paris on October 17, 1998. With Kors, Arnault finally found a designer who craved commercial success—and not just artistic acclaim. "Fashion is creativity, with the goal of having as many customers as possible," Arnault said. PHOTO BY BERTRAND RINDOFF-PETROFF, COURTESY OF CELINE

In a New York state of mind: Donna Karan and Barbra Streisand, 1993.
PHOTO BY JORN BARRETT, COURTESY OF GLOBE PHOTOS, INC.

After his 1988 debut collection, a star was born. Isaac Mizrahi reclined at the feet of supermodel Dalma, who wears his jumpsuit on the May 2, 1988, cover of W. PHOTO BY GEORGE CHINSEE, *W/*FAIRCHILD PUBLICATIONS

Body double: Ralph Lauren and Tommy Hilfiger party in pinstripes at the Fresh Air Fund benefit on June 9, 1995, in New York. PHOTO BY GEORGE CHINSEE, *WOMEN'S WEAR DAILY/*FAIRCHILD PUBLICATIONS

Fashion with wit and a sense of irony. Advertisements for Target Stores and Marshall Field's in Chicago, which are both owned by Dayton Hudson Corp.
COURTESY OF DAYTON HUDSON CORP.

me *GQ*," he said, laughing, referring to the men's fashion magazine. Riley was already wearing Armani in the early 1980s when he and his wife were passing through Milan and decided to pay a visit to Armani's showroom. "I always liked his clothes," he said. Riley didn't get to meet the designer on that trip, but soon he would get to know him quite well.

In January 1990, *GQ* put Riley in Armani on its cover—which was around the time when McDaniel and Forte first sat down with him and made a proposition: Armani wanted Riley to be on his team. The relationship started out slowly. Armani initially provided the coach with a couple of customized suits in 56 Long (Italian size), and then everyone waited to see what would happen.

The reaction was swift, as Riley turned out to be a slam-dunk. The NBA season stretched out over many months and Riley was constantly on the radar. Whenever the Lakers played, the TV cameras planted at courtside captured Riley pacing up and down, so spiffy in those suits with the sloping lapels. Sports commentators began to pepper their play-by-play banter with asides about Riley's wardrobe. Before long, every coach and player in the NBA began to spruce up. They all wanted to be like Riley, the NBA's most valuable fashion plate. And so did thousands of basketball fans, who started filling their closets with Armani suits.

The natty coach, who described himself as a conservative dresser, preferred Armani's classic one-button navy suits, with Armani's white shirts and subtly patterned ties. Armani's tailors, he said, "made an adjustment in the jacket because I like the button stance right below the buckle."

He emphasized that he wasn't on Armani's payroll, that he was more like an "unofficial spokesman." Each year, both Riley and his wife, Chris, received a free Armani wardrobe, and the coach gladly obliged to show up for Armani-sponsored charity events and store openings. Armani also flew Riley to Milan to sit in the front row at his fashion shows. That was hardly a chore; Riley admitted that he loved to study the clothes Armani sent down the runway.

And indeed, Armani's runway presentations were like no other in fashion. Armani never hired supermodels nor did he use jazzy theatrics, both of which would detract from his low-key designs. Every Armani fashion show, whether in Milan or on the road, required the installation of a special runway—*la pedana*—a long path of frosted tiles that are lit from underneath in order to fully illuminate the textured fabrics, details, and muted shades.

In the 1990s, Armani's fashion presentations became chockablock with the famous—Martin Scorsese, Robert De Niro, Sophia Loren, Isabella Rossellini, and Lauren Hutton—sitting ducks posing to be shot by the paparazzi. Armani flew his VIPs over first class and put them up at one of Milan's top hotels, usually the Principe e Savoia, a few minutes from Armani's headquarters. Then Armani's public relations staffers coddled his special guests, squiring them around Milan to go sightseeing, shopping, and nightclubbing.

Meanwhile, the workaholic designer remained sequestered in his studio, unavailable to meet with his invitees until after his show, when he usually hosted a dinner in his apartment at his headquarters. Armani rarely vacationed with his clients like Versace or Valentino did. Only a few—Michelle Pfeiffer, Eric Clapton, and Lauren Hutton—have visited his beachfront vacation hideaway in Pantelleria, Italy.

It would always be difficult really to get close to Armani if you didn't speak Italian or French, the two languages he spoke fluently. Armani always had an interpreter by his side when he was among Americans, although he appeared to understand more English than he let on. Oddly enough, his ignorance of English worked in his favor, in creating yet another layer of inaccessibility to fuel his already larger-than-life persona.

Over the years, as many designers tried to emulate Armani's stellar front row, they succeeded in recruiting Isabella Rossellini and Tom Cruise, who began as Armani devotees but turned into free agents who flitted from one designer to another. The Armani people usually shrugged off such defections, but not always. Once, a flap ensued over who would dress Anjelica Huston when she picked up her award at the 1992 Council of Fashion Designers of America gala in New York. When the Armani staffers heard that Huston—typically an Armani devotee—would be wearing a white beaded dress by Calvin Klein that night, they didn't like it. Rumors flew that the house of Armani might even cancel its table at the benefit. Lee Radziwill called to pressure the CFDA, as did Forte. After a CFDA official told Forte that the event was "for American designers and American clothes," Forte retorted to *WWD:* "So maybe they shouldn't ask Armani, Chanel and all the rest to buy tables."

But Armani could rest assured that Riley, who had turned down many offers through the years, wouldn't be tempted to try out another designer. Riley said: "I'd almost feel like a traitor. Anyway, I'm not interested in endorsements, even if somebody would pay me. I enjoy wearing Armani."

Eric Clapton also relished wearing Armani after he backed off from Versace in 1992. Gianni Versace used Clapton's departure to take a swipe at his Milanese archrival. When Clapton wears Armani, he "looks like an accountant," Gianni Versace cracked to *WWD*. Clapton fired back: "I had a business deal with Versace and now I have a business deal with Armani. The Versace clothes don't cater to me anymore. I appreciate what he does, but I think his clothes are more for the southern Italian male or for Sylvester Stallone types."

GLAMOROUS AS THEY are, fashion shows are fairly low-voltage to the general public, who will probably never see a tape of an Armani runway show to get a glimpse of Pat Riley or Claudia Cardinale. However, billions of ordinary folks around the world are guaranteed to star-gaze for three long hours on Oscar night. As the luminaries paraded into the Dorothy Chandler Pavilion, celebrity interviewer Joan Rivers usually greeted them with the same question, "Who are you wearing?" And more often than not, they responded: "Armani." The designer would forever be remembered as the first designer who swept the Oscars without taking home a single trophy.

The ripple effect of Armani's movieland coup has spread far and wide. After Armani threw down the gauntlet, the Oscars turned into fashion Olympics, as houses from around the world jockeyed for months to get their clothes exposed at the big show. Armani's subdued elegance sent Hollywood fashion victims running for cover, compelling image-conscious actors to find a designer they could call their own, or to hire one of fashion's newest and busiest professionals: freelance stylists.

Long before Armani, the Academy Awards used to be a no-brainer. Back in the years when the Hollywood studios ruled, the contract stars were hemmed into the formulas of musicals, historical spectacles, and plots with happy endings. And when the actors got dressed for the big night, they stayed right on the studio lot, turning themselves over to the professionals, such as costume designers as Jean-Louis at Columbia, Edith Head at Paramount, and Adrian at MGM, the designer who put Joan Crawford in shoulder pads.

"The stars were so used to having stuff made especially for them— the clothes that showed their best features, their best colors, to fit their image on screen," recalled Bob Mackie, a costume designer who formerly worked for Edith Head and Jean-Louis. For the Oscars, "you dressed them as sexpots or grand actresses, or the way the studios wanted them to be perceived by the public."

Back then, all eyes were on the stars, and not the costume designers, who were largely unknown to the public anyway. Mackie was a sketcher for Jean-Louis, who made one of the most memorable gowns of the sixties, the flesh-toned, skintight confection worn by Marilyn Monroe when she sang "Happy Birthday" to President John F. Kennedy at Madison Square Garden in 1962. "That dress was so impressive, but nobody knew who made it," Mackie remembered. "Jean-Louis never got any pop from designing that dress."

But by the 1970s, there was no more studio system to lord over the stars, and the professional costumers began buying more film wardrobes from established fashion houses instead of whipping up original creations. So on Oscar night, Hollywood players were left to their own fashion devices. Staged glamour gave way to individual expression. The men were tucked safely in black tie, while the women, if they were stumped, had a Plan B: Beverly Hills retailer Fred Hayman, who became the Oscars' official fashion coordinator. Hayman served as a clearinghouse, rounding up gowns from a number of designers. And he steered business his way too, for Hayman's Rodeo Drive shop was stocked with fabulous gowns every spring.

Without the old studio standards, the Oscars turned into a showcase of the good, the bad, and the ugly. TV viewers tuned in to scoff at the inevitable Oscar faux pas. In 1990, Demi Moore showed up in sequined biking shorts and Kim Basinger wore a one-sleeved, bouffant Cinderella number. And Cher. Only Cher could get away with wearing feather headdresses and baring her navel in some outrageous getup, compliments of

Bob Mackie. That was the heyday of "Mr. Blackwell," the chief of fashion police, who used to find plenty of Oscar fashion victims for his "worst-dressed list" at the end of the year.

But the Oscars' airbrushed glamour would make a stunning comeback by the mid-1990s. In the age of celebrity worship and TV shows like *Entertainment Tonight,* stars felt as if they were onstage every time they went out in public. As more actors became concerned with their off-screen images, which could enhance—or sabotage—their on-screen careers, they were less willing to experiment with fashion, especially on Oscar night.

"It's not so much about insecurity of the stars but the fact that society is driven so much by clothing, style, taste and beauty," said Wayne Scot Lukas, a freelance stylist who has dressed clients like Janet Jackson, Melanie Griffith, and Tina Turner. "The public nowadays is judging actresses by every facet of their lives. If you smoke, how you sit, who you went out with that night and what you were doing. They have no private lives. We as a public have put them on the pedestal as these fabulous, amazing creatures and now they become the media target. We create these gods and then we make fun of them. We knock them down."

As a few stylists became bosom buddies with the stars, the designers began to court them too. Armani flew Philip Bloch, one of the most influential stylists based in Los Angeles, to Milan to attend one of his fashion shows. For a fee, roughly between $500 to $1,500 a day—or higher—such stylists could be enlisted as fashion fixers. The stylists combed designer showrooms in Los Angeles, New York, Paris, and Milan as well as the racks at Saks Fifth Avenue and Barneys in Beverly Hills, to make their famous clients look at all times, in the words of Lukas, "hip, cool and pulled together."

Lukas contended that he tended to gravitate to the designers who were eager—and equipped—to work with celebrities: "The people at

Armani are selfless. They give you the accessories, the alterations, anything you need. And the same thing goes for Versace."

After his all-stars took over the Oscars in 1990 and 1991, Armani became the fashion standard by which all of Hollywood would be judged. Armani even got listed for a wardrobe credit at the end of the show for dressing Billy Crystal, the 1991 Oscar host. Millions of television viewers got used to hearing Armani's name again and again. When Whoopi Goldberg hosted the ceremony in 1992, she twirled around onstage during her opening monologue to show off her velvet Armani gown. The Armani impact lingered weeks after the fact when *People, In Style*, and *W* came out with their Oscar fashion spreads, which were always full of Armani sightings. Invariably, Team Armani—Jodie Foster, Annette Bening, Michelle Pfeiffer, Anjelica Houston, Winona Ryder, Sigourney Weaver, Faye Dunaway, and Salma Hayek—hogged the spotlight in getting the most complimentary mentions in the press.

The celebrities regarded Armani as a sure thing—the safest option on a night when even the most seasoned veterans can suffer a bit of stage fright. "On a night like the Oscars, you're in gobs of makeup, instead of blue jeans, and everybody's looking at you," said Glenn Close. "I lead a very laid-back life: I don't spend a lot of time on myself. Armani makes me feel comfortable. If I'm in a beautiful Armani outfit for a formal occasion, it goes with my philosophy of simple unadorned elegance. I don't need any jewelry."

Armani stitched up a very full, beaded, strapless gown for the very pregnant Glenn Close when she was nominated for best actress for *Fatal Attraction*. Always on Oscar night, Close says she wants to feel as natural as possible—and not look as if she were outfitted for a movie role. "When I'm in Armani I don't feel that I am somebody else. It's important that his clothes make me look better but enhance who I am. The clothes focus on *you*."

Armani got to see all of this for himself when he attended the 1991 ceremonies at which his friend Martin Scorsese was nominated for best director for *Goodfellas*. Amid the movie-star gridlock, Armani still managed to draw a crowd as everyone came over to meet him. He was so overwhelmed by all the attention that he skipped all the after-parties and retreated to the Regent Beverly Wilshire Hotel with his staffers for a quiet dinner.

Even though Armani usually had a long list to dress for the Oscars, the designer managed to take the time to study each individual. He said: "I like to keep a direct rapport with the performers who like what I stand for. In forming my relationship with them I ask them, 'What do you have in mind?' And then, we spend a whole week working on something for them to wear."

As for the men: "My approach to menswear has never been *fashion*. I never put them in things that are too showy. I have to slow them down. When they are handsome or famous, they don't need very much or they look overdone."

While Armani designed in Milan, McDaniel and her Beverly Hills staff of four, along with a few freelancers, toiled all year to make the night come together. Whenever they located new faces to bring into the fold, they knew who to focus on: those young stars who exuded a classic elegance. Armani's understated look meant: You wear the clothes, the clothes don't wear you. So in 1992, when Warren Beatty's *Bugsy* was nominated, his wife, actress Annette Bening, wore a simple black wool crepe gown with cap sleeves and brilliant earrings. The critics in the press agreed; she was a "perfect 10."

The young screenwriting duo Ben Affleck and Matt Damon looked dapper and all grown-up in classic Armani tuxedos when they came to pick up their 1998 award for *Good Will Hunting*. On his way into the ceremony, Damon began the evening with an acceptance speech, telling

Joan Rivers: "We really want to thank Molly over at Armani for giving us these great tuxedos."

According to its official policy, the house of Armani doesn't pay its famous billboards for the night. The nominees and certain regulars, of course, received free gowns and tuxedos, altered to fit them at the Beverly Hills store. Another tier of celebrities was granted a gown or tuxedo on loan. All the trimmings—shoes, handbags, and sunglasses—are part of the package.

Membership in Armani's exclusive club has its privileges. A select list of celebrities are said to receive a year-round discount of as much as 50 percent at his boutiques. And for a few of his favorite clients like Jodie Foster, Armani has furnished wardrobes for movie promotional tours.

In the late 1980s, when dressing the stars was still a novelty, the actors were quite easy to please, bowled over as they were that a famous designer actually wanted to dress *them*. McDaniel explained: "It started out as, 'Oh my god, Armani is going to let me wear something!' It was like a privilege coming into the inner sanctum, it had a mystique."

But by the late 1990s, as more designers relentlessly chased the stars, the tables turned. Designers wooed nominees and presenters with boxes of evening clothes—without any obligation to wear them. In 1997, the record appeared to belong to Lauren Holly, who was married to comedian Jim Carrey at the time, when she received, unsolicited, fifty-six free gowns from thirteen different designers.

The designers' publicists cajoled and begged, and the rumors flew, as the most imperious stars played gimme-gimme, requesting cash payments or free wardrobes in exchange for wearing a designer gown on Oscar night. Joining the scramble were jewelers like Harry Winston, which provided millions of dollars worth of precious gems as loaners for the night.

The Oscar fashion sweepstakes went into full swing on the day the nominees were announced. On Valentine's Day in 1995, Angela Bassett wore a red Escada pantsuit to read the names of the nominees at the official press conference. After the Escada publicists worked the phones, that fashion factoid got at least six media mentions.

Nineteen ninety-five was the year of *Forrest Gump* fashion. The maker of Hush Puppies had crafted a special pair of size 9½D shoes for Tom Hanks (he wore Hush Puppies in the movie) and promised to make a donation to his favorite charity if he wore them on Oscar night. (He didn't. But Hanks did wear the tuxedo Calvin Klein sent over.) *Gump* producer Steve Tisch received a 0.4 carat diamond stick pin, a gift from the International Diamond Council trade group. Donna Karan showered Tisch with two tuxedos and two gowns for his girlfriend for the Golden Globe Awards and the Oscars. "I'm trying to get up the courage to ask Donna for a suit for my niece's bat mitzvah," Tisch joked at the time.

Sharon Stone, the most coveted fashion diva of them all, was "confirmed" to wear a Valentino but pulled a fast one and changed her mind at the last minute. She came out onstage, with co-presenter Quincy Jones, in a $22 Gap turtleneck and a black skirt. Gap sold thousands of what became known in-house as "the Sharon Stone shirt" in the months to follow.

Armani, who had started this horse race, would get his just deserts at the 1995 Oscars, when his tribe included Foster, Pfeiffer, Uma Thurman, and David Letterman, the show's host. But much of the thrill was gone for Armani, who was fed up. *Basta.* An Armani spokesman said in 1995: "Mr. Armani is very much against the idea of buying stars." And in 1997: "We're cutting back. We don't need forty-five names on a press release. Mr. Armani has now made the Oscars a second priority." Freshening his celebrity roster with luminaries outside Hollywood, Armani mined golden names like golfer Tiger Woods, boxer Oscar de la Hoya, and hip-hop diva Lauryn Hill.

Meanwhile, the rest of high fashion pressed on to hustle Hollywood. The house of Christian Dior, aiming to revive interest in its couture collections by John Galliano, went for Nicole Kidman in 1997, who came with her husband, Tom Cruise, in a lime-green embroidered Dior gown. Everyone agreed Kidman looked smashing, but Dior's brief shining moment at the Oscars quickly evaporated, failing to do the trick to induce women to go shopping for Dior suits and gowns—the way Armani had done.

HAVING SCALED BACK his Hollywood pursuits, Armani redirected his energy to his time-tested formula. Consistency, after all, was money in the bank. The Armani mystique had worked its way through the fashion cognoscenti to the celebrities and, finally, to the masses. Giorgio Armani SpA had blanketed the world with 250 boutiques selling everything from $60 A/X jeans to $10,000 beaded gowns. The company's wholesale volume in 1998 reached about $1.2 billion (more than $3 billion at retail), with about a third of sales from the U.S. and Canada.

Even though he stood at fashion's most enviable pole position, Armani still wasn't off the hook. Having established his beachhead long before the rest, he had done the hard part. Now what was left for him to do was to stay focused and continue to make fabulous clothes, while the other designers played catch-up. Still, Armani had to be aware that he was about to hit a generational wall. He had to keep finding ways to keep his trademark young and vital, through advertising, celebrities, and other types of marketing. And as good as he was, even Armani had his limitations. To date, his Armani A/X jeanswear chain—his version of Gap—

has yet to turn on lots of people. Lucky for him that A/X accounts for less than 15 percent of his business.

As for the other designers who played celebrity roulette, they would also need some serendipity: the right stars at the right time—and the hope that their picks would do justice to the clothes. Cutting through the clutter would also be tougher, as there were few opportunities for designers to hog the big screen as Armani had in *Gigolo*. In 1998, several new movies each featured a slew of designer labels, such as Woody Allen's *Celebrity*, starring Leonardo DiCaprio, Gretchen Mol, and Melanie Griffith—who dressed in Karl Lagerfeld, Badgley Mischka, Dolce & Gabbana, and Hervé Leger. And what goes around comes around: Armani and Cerruti would be together again—hanging in wardrobe in *Hurly Burly*, starring Kevin Spacey, Robin Wright Penn, and Sean Penn.

So in the end, what would most fashion designers get from all this exposure? Perhaps not as much as they hoped for. In most cases, designers would find that all that groveling to celebrities turned out to be an expensive distraction keeping them from doing what they needed to do: figuring out what bona fide—paying—customers wanted to wear.

Designers "can overhype the influences of celebrities," observed *In Style*'s editor Martha Nelson. "In the end, it doesn't matter what celebrities wear. People are not willing to be led around by their noses either by some anonymous fashion editor, some designer or even by celebrities, if the clothes don't work for them."

And that summed up Armani's edge: making his designs work for his fans whether they were Broadway ingenues or bank vice presidents in Minneapolis. "Armani is synonymous with fashion at every level," said Sara Forden, the *Women's Wear Daily* reporter based in Milan. "At weddings even in small villages throughout Italy, it's not unusual to find the mother of the bride or members of the wedding party wearing Armani."

Most likely, those wedding guests felt that it was worth splurging for designer finery that was comfortable and flattering, with the added value of feeling like stars when they got dressed. Conversely, Glenn Close favored Armani because she wanted low-key elegance that would let her shine through, as a normal person. Armani had accomplished what seemed impossible. He made ordinary people feel like stars and made stars feel like regular folks. And everybody looked good.

GIVING THE LADY WHAT SHE WANTS:

THE NEW MARSHALL FIELD'S

The consumer is king. His preference is law and his whim makes and unmakes merchants, jobbers and manufacturers. Whoever wins his confidence controls the mercantile situation; whoever loses it, is lost.

CHARLES COOLIDGE PARLIN, market researcher

*T*he Windy City skyline, in striking origami relief, adorned the invitation to Chicago's smart set to save the date of September 4, 1988.

On that night, Marshall Field's would kick off the city's fall social season with its most spectacular black-tie benefit in years. The site was the Water Tower Place mall on North Michigan Avenue, along the tony retail stretch known as the "Magnificent Mile," where Field's had just completed a $10 million renovation of its seven-story branch store.

The gala, benefiting Chicago's Lyric Opera, was a bold stroke of bravado for Marshall Field's—a maneuver calculated to underscore position as Chicago's favorite department store now that Bloomingdale's had come to town. The trendy New York emporium had just big-footed into Chicago, landing a bit too close for comfort for Field's, right across the street from Water Tower Place, in a gleaming new six-story building. To commemorate its Chicago debut, Bloomie's had scheduled its own glitzy gala, a September 23rd benefit for the Chicago Symphony.

The festivities took place during the end of that heady era when department stores had plenty to celebrate. Starting in the late 1970s, designer fashions and perfumes were on a roll, accompanying the breakneck expansion of department stores into suburban malls. In 1978, when America was teeming with more than 20,000 shopping malls, Lord & Taylor swept through suburban Detroit, inaugurating three new branches on three successive nights, with glossy benefits at each location. Each black-tie opening featured a designer headliner: Bill Blass, Oscar de la Renta, and Mary McFadden. Such spectacles were integral to Lord & Taylor's marketing strategy to come out swinging, positioning each of its new branches as the "happening" places to shop. And where there was buzz, hordes of shoppers were bound to follow.

Inevitably, the 1988 autumn face-off between Field's and Bloomingdale's played as a swaggering rivalry between Chicago and New York. Bloomingdale's aimed to be the more exclusive—the tickets to its soiree went for $225 apiece, compared to the $175 admission to the throw-down at Field's. Bloomie's also planned to regale Chicago with a French twist: Karl Lagerfeld was jetting in from Paris to show off his latest Chanel couture collection during the gala.

But Field's was astute in throwing the first party of the season, the better to impress Chicago socialites when they would be fresh and expectant, just like back-to-school students. Even though Chicagoans dearly loved *their* Marshall Field's, the home team still needed to score big points. "This was a moment to take a stand, to be the superior store," recalled Michael Francis, who was a Field's marketing executive at the time. "We tried to find out, point by point, what Bloomingdale's was doing and our goal was to do it better. No expense was spared to put on a big show." (Even though local vendors donated thousands of dollars in refreshments and discounted services for both affairs, Bloomingdale's and Field's spent an estimated $250,000 apiece on their fall parties.)

As Chicago suddenly became retail's liveliest battleground, *Vanity Fair* fanned the flames, predicting that "store wars" between Field's and Bloomie's were shaping up to be "the noisiest confrontation in retail history." Philip Miller, Field's dashing fifty-year-old chairman, was ready to rock and roll. "It'll be fun to test our mettle," he said.

The confrontation between the retailers came at a critical juncture in the history of department stores. America's oldest retailing format had been growing stale and unexciting, losing ground to a new generation of discounters, specialty stores, and catalog merchants. By the early 1990s, a number of venerable local chains had either gone out of business or merged with their former rivals. Those who survived the wave of consolidation that started in the mid-1980s were focused on streamlining their operations and filling their floors with more affordable merchandise.

Less than two years after Bloomie's moved to Chicago, Marshall Field's would meet a similar fate. In 1990, Field's was sold to Dayton Hudson Corp., the Minneapolis retail concern best known for its fast-growing Target Stores discount division.

Dayton Hudson proceeded to take Field's down a new path. Under Phil Miller, the high-toned Marshall Field's had shunned the so-called moderate merchandise category. But Dayton Hudson, preoccupied with generating profits, did just the opposite. By adding more moderate goods, Field's could draw many more shoppers, which it sorely needed in the 1990s after so many out-of-town competitors had been closing in. By the early 1990s, Chicagoland was bustling with branches of Bloomingdale's, Nordstrom, Henri Bendel, Lord & Taylor, and an aggressive discounter called Kohl's. Even Carson Pirie Scott, the moderate-priced department store that was Field's State Street neighbor, was showing new signs of life. "Marshall Field's and a little of Carson's used to be the only game in town. But eventually Chicago became a market for everybody," said Gary Witkin, who was Field's chairman from 1990 to 1992.

Under Dayton Hudson's stewardship, Field's shifted more and more of its merchandise from class to mass. The glitzy "store wars" of the eighties were finished. Retailers of every stripe now waged "markdown wars." During its "Field's Days" and "13 Hour" sales, Marshall Field's was filled with such signs as "Look at this bargain."

Gloria Bacon, a Chicago physician and Field's charge-card customer since 1963, didn't like this new agenda. She longed for the return of the Field's of the 1970s, when the ever-obliging sales associates steered her to the unusual and exclusive, like the fabulous Italian wool knitwear that she couldn't find anywhere else in town. Bacon was turned off by the way Field's had practically rolled out the red carpet to welcome the hordes of bargain hunters who pawed through the store's ubiquitous markdown racks. "The ambiance is gone," she lamented in 1997. "Field's isn't special anymore, it's just another generic Midwest department store."

Her sentiments were shared by many Chicago shoppers who, having grown up on the upscale Marshall Field's, had shifted their loyalties to Saks Fifth Avenue and Nordstrom, which felt more like the great Field's they once revered. "Customers [were] telling us we're not what we used to be," Dan Skoda, Field's president, said in July 1997. "We lost the image of what we stood for."

The $64,000 question was: Would Field's ever be able to get it back? It was hard to be optimistic. Field's predicament reflected the decline in department store retailing that coincided with the mass merchandising of fashion that began in the 1990s. In order to survive, department stores were forced to merge with stores they used to compete with, to form national chains, positioning themselves to compete more effectively.

"When you go national, it's an incredible task to tailor your goods by city or market," said Witkin. "This is the reality of running a bigger business." Moreover, he noted, department store buyers were no longer the tastemakers who picked out special merchandise for every branch location. Buyers in the 1990s were loath to experiment like they used to. They couldn't afford to gamble with avante-garde fashions that might catch on with only a handful of the most discriminating shoppers. It was safer to concentrate their business with a few key vendors.

Therein lies the great retail conundrum. Field's had to abandon its white-glove heritage in order to compete in a modern era. But without its distinctive image, Field's was hard-pressed to stand out in a crowd of look-alike department stores.

So just how do department stores create an identity nowadays? It isn't easy. Even the label "department store" is a misnomer, because there are fewer and fewer departments inside them. Most chains have stopped carrying electronics, toys, books, appliances, and furniture. What's left standing are the goods that generate the highest profits—primarily apparel and cosmetics.

"Establishing an identity is much harder today for department stores," observed Arnold Aronson, a New York retail consultant. "The typical customer isn't loyal to any one store; she's looking for the best values on her favorite brands." Furthermore, he added, harried shoppers "have changed their perception of what they value nowadays. They are starved for time; they want a store that's efficient, has decent service, and gets the job done."

Traditionally, department stores have built their reputations by being exciting and glitzy—and now all of that is history. In today's economics, department stores are all about being affordable and predictable—and often dull, which is the safest and surest way to profits.

FOR GENERATIONS, AMERICANS had a love affair with their local department stores. In the mid-nineteenth century, when the first merchant pioneers founded department stores, most towns were just starting to build their central business districts. Retailers, including Marshall Field's, John Wanamaker in Philadelphia, Rich's in Atlanta, and Neiman Marcus in Dallas, exposed their communities to the finest of merchandise. In the process, the locals became sophisticated consumers, as well as members of a big retail family.

At Christmastime, for instance, many families from around the Midwest made a special trip to downtown Chicago to enjoy the storybook window displays at Marshall Field's. They worked their way up to the eighth floor, where Santa was stationed in front of the magnificent seventy-foot Christmas tree in Field's Walnut Room restaurant. For decades, people put their trust in institutions like Field's, whose palatial downtown stores and sleek mall branches were symbols of civic pride, just like the Chicago Cubs and the White Sox. Every town had a JCPenney's and a Sears, which were reliable for kitchen curtains, electric drills, and washing machines. But only department stores delivered style on a grand scale to big cities. Field's took the lead in Chicago as the arbiter of good taste and high quality, and thus became the premier fashion authority of the Midwest.

By the time "designer" became the merchandising hook starting in the late 1970s, Bloomingdale's had become among the most tantalizing of New York retailers, introducing shoppers to Pierre Cardin, Yves Saint Laurent, and a kicky new tie designer named Ralph Lauren. Bloomie's became the quintessential "retailing theater," especially during its famous international promotions, when the entire store brimmed with exotic merchandise from whatever country Bloomie's was promoting that year. In 1978 the theme was "India: The Ultimate Fantasy," while in 1981 it was "China: Heralding the Dawn of a New Era." Shoppers were treated to folk dancers, cooking demonstrations, and commemorative shopping bags. The foreign promotions didn't do much to enhance the bottom line, but they worked wonders to polish Bloomie's mystique. They were the trademark of Marvin Traub, the store's legendary chairman from 1970 to 1991, who transplanted Bloomie's chichi to Washington, D.C., and Boston with stunning success.

In coming to Chicago, Bloomie's took on its stiffest competition outside New York. Marshall Field's was no longer coasting on its fabled carriage-trade laurels. Field's had become flashy and very popular after 1982, when the chain was purchased by BAT Industries PLC, the giant tobacco and retail concern from London. BAT had emerged as a white knight to rescue Field's from the clutches of Wall Street corporate raider Carl Icahn. Flush with cash from its core tobacco business, BAT was determined to fix up Field's, as well as Saks Fifth Avenue, the other stellar-but-dusty department store chain it had purchased a year earlier. Accordingly, BAT spent freely to upgrade Field's—about $70 million in the first two years. "We had an obligation not just to purchase Marshall Field's, but to put our blood and guts and investment into it," said Arnold Aronson, who presided over BAT's retailing division at the time. The British conglomerate even committed itself to a five-year, $110 million renovation of Field's seventy-five-year-old downtown flagship, a questionable indulgence given that State Street was no longer Chicago's shopping mecca. Chicago's business leaders were delighted at the possibilities that a spruced-up Marshall Field's could deliver—the "new" Field's could be just the magnet to pull affluent shoppers back into Chicago's downtown Loop.

In 1983, BAT recruited a seasoned veteran, Phil Miller, the president of Neiman Marcus and a Bloomingdale's alum, to become chairman of Field's. Outgoing and boyishly handsome, the blond, blue-eyed Miller dressed in snappy double-breasted pinstripes and was often referred to as "the Robert Redford of retailing." Miller served on local boards with Chicago's Gold Coast society, and he lured them downtown to posh events in the Walnut Room, such as the 1986 Oakbrook Polo Ball, which Prince Charles attended. Miller also courted the masses, when he invited the stars from the hit TV series *Miami Vice* to make an in-store appearance in 1985. Field's visibility surged, as did Miller's. "People would stop Phil on the street. He was like Mr. Chicago," recalled Phyllis Collins, Field's veteran high-fashion buyer.

Miller's biggest challenge was clarifying Field's merchandise mix. When he arrived, the store was a hodgepodge that ran the gamut from expensive to budget. Miller's ultimate goal: to dominate the Chicago market in what he called the "better-best" category of high-end merchandise—about one-fourth of Field's business—while bolstering the store's core "upper-middle" business. Miller converted Field's bargain basement into "Down Under," a section devoted to Cuisinart food processors, housewares, and electronics that beckoned yuppie homeowners. At the same time, Miller turned Field's into the designer headquarters of the Midwest with brands that included Fendi, Bottega Veneta, Christian Lacroix, Emanuel Ungaro, and Donna Karan. "You can't get some designers' trunk [fashion preview] shows because Marshall Field's has them all sewn up," observed Larry Gore in 1986, as the representative for several Chicago specialty stores. "The designers want Marshall Field's; they want *that* name in Chicago."

Miller's strategy worked wonders. As Field's market share and fortunes climbed, analysts projected that by 1990, Field's annual sales would reach $1 billion—up from $750 million in 1984—with a healthy 10 percent to 12 percent operating profit margin, about double the profit levels at the time of BAT's acquisition.

Moreover, Miller *knew* what it took to wow Chicago. For the Lyric Opera benefit in 1988, all seven floors at Marshall Field's Water Tower Place store were transformed into what the *Chicago Tribune* described as a "Disneyland of party areas." For 1,200 guests, the fantasy began as soon as they walked in and onto a "stage" facing an audience sipping champagne—an effect designed to "make stars out of the guests," a Field's publicist explained.

Chicago had always been Field's kind of town, but on that glorious night, Field's was steeped in "New York, New York." Seventh Avenue's most glamorous designers—Bill Blass, Carolina Herrera, and Carolyne Roehm—were on hand. So was cabaret crooner Bobby Short, who took his act to the seventh floor. There was even a replica of Harlem's famous speakeasy, the Cotton Club. And circulating through the gourmet spread of lobster tails, caviar, and six-foot-tall chocolate bombe cakes (served by waiters on ladders), was Chicago's own talk-show queen Oprah Winfrey, svelte in brocade and black velvet. She told the *Chicago Tribune*, "I'm not eating and I still think this party is great."

Departing guests carried home champagne memories—and little gift bags filled with $165 worth of goodies: a split of Veuve Clicquot champagne, a silk bow tie from Charvet of Paris, Blass and Herrera perfumes, and a box of Field's famous Frango mints. Miller was jubilant: "I hope this will be known as the best party Chicago has seen in a long time. It's to remind Chicago that Marshall Field's and Chicago are synonymous and we can have the most fun together."

Two weeks later, Oprah dolled up again, in 6.5-carat canary yellow diamond earrings, and headed for Bloomingdale's. The requisite red carpet, klieg lights, and blaring trumpets welcomed 3,500 partygoers, including Italian fashion magnates Carla Fendi and Massimo Ferragamo. Ten bands blasted on all six floors, where guests downed flutes of "Bloomie's Blush," a champagne cocktail invented for the occasion. At the end of his Chanel fashion show, Karl Lagerfeld, sporting sunglasses, ponytail, and Japanese fan, sauntered down the runway to take a bow. Amid hundreds of white orchids and roses, Marvin Traub exulted, "This is the most spectacular store we've ever done. Chicago is a marvelous city and we wanted to do it marvelously."

Fred Jackson, publisher of *Town & Country,* was duly impressed. He told the *Chicago Tribune*: "If it's done by Bloomie's, it's on a New York scale. They don't spare a thing."

All in all, an unforgettable evening, made all the more unforgettable by the strange speech made by Robert Campeau, the Canadian real estate developer and owner of Bloomie's through his recent $4 billion purchase of Federated Department Stores. Traub graciously introduced Campeau, who stepped up to the mike and proceeded to ramble on about America's Wild West, the early days of radio, switching back and forth from English to French. Mortified, the guests tittered, and wondered what was going on.

About a year later, they found out. Campeau, the mogul who had piled up mountains of debt to buy Federated, was fast running out of cash. On January 15, 1990, Campeau's retail empire collapsed and filed for Chapter 11 bankruptcy protection. Campeau Corp.'s $7.5 billion filing was the largest retail bankruptcy in U.S. history to date. (Divorced from Campeau, Federated came out of bankruptcy in 1992, when it acquired Macy's and then reorganized to become a healthy, well-run chain of more than 420 stores with annual sales of $15 billion by 1996.)

By the end of 1989, the party was also over for Field's—but not because of Bloomie's. Right before Christmas, BAT had put Field's and

Saks up for sale to thwart a hostile takeover bid from billionaire raider Sir James Goldsmith. Phil Miller countered with his own pitch to rescue his retail empire, by putting together an investor group that made a run on Field's—but with no luck. The winning bid—a stunning $1.4 billion—came instead from Dayton Hudson Corp.

After having failed to acquire Field's a decade earlier, the Minneapolis retailer was thrilled to have at last captured Chicago's crown jewel. Dayton Hudson called the acquisition an "ideal marriage" between likeminded Midwesterners, mainly because its own Dayton's in Minneapolis so closely resembled Field's.

But to Chicagoans, Marshall Field's was far more than a department store. Field's *was* Chicago. Founder Marshall Field and his heirs were among the city's most prominent philanthropists, through their investments in such local landmarks as the Merchandise Mart, the University of Chicago, and the Field Museum of Natural History. Dorothy Fuller, a former Field's fashion director, explained: "Marshall Field's is a Chicago institution and the people of Chicago think it belongs to *them*."

IN THE MIDST of America's industrial revolution, when railroads and factories went up after Reconstruction, Chicago was a bustling, dusty frontier town where the locals hungered for both basic merchandise and pointers on how to live and to dress well. In 1868, a hard-driving wholesale clerk named Marshall Field and his business partner, Levi Z. Leiter, opened their first store, Field and Leiter. In a six-story building on the corner of Washington and State streets, Field and Leiter delighted their community with a dazzling array of the finest goods available. A "marble palace, with enough merchandise to turn almost every female head," reported the *Chicago Tribune*, which marveled at the counters lined with bolts of silk, $1,000 lace tablecloths, horsehair sofas, and

Staffordshire china imported from England. In the first year, the store's sales reached an impressive $8 million, with a $300,000 profit. In 1881, Marshall Field, at age forty-seven, bought out his partner and renamed the store Marshall Field & Co.

A prescient merchant, Field zeroed in on fashion-conscious ladies. Early on, he hired a "style expert" to travel to Europe by sea to bring back "special Parisian frocks" to America's heartland. During the 1880s, when women wore cumbersome hoop skirts, Field & Co. was the first in Chicago to offer the radical "bustle" dress, from the Parisian couture house of Worth. In a move to encourage women to spend the entire day shopping, Field's installed a tea salon and restaurant, which became famous for chicken pot pie and its signature Field's Rose Punch. There was even an "Evening Room" for ladies to see how their gowns looked under artificial light. The wife of U.S. President-elect William McKinley called on Field's to create her inaugural gown. *"Give the lady what she wants,"* Marshall Field reportedly declared in a fit, after observing one haughty salesclerk in action. His legendary command became the store's motto, and the gold standard that Field's would maintain for decades to come.

Even though other department stores, such as Carson Pirie Scott, sprang up around Chicago, Marshall Field didn't worry about out-of-town stores invading his turf. According to a Field biographer, Philadelphia merchant John Wanamaker once dropped into the store and told Marshall Field: "I like this city. I think you could use another store here." Field responded coolly: "Probably. But I've been thinking of expanding. You come here and I think we'll open in Philadelphia." Wanamaker reportedly "smiled weakly and shook hands, promptly forgetting about his idea of competing with Field's."

Rebuilt twice after devastating fires, Marshall Field & Co. moved in 1907 into an eleven-story limestone and granite monument—

crowned with a magnificent Tiffany-glass dome—that took up an entire block on State Street. As the dry-goods anchor of Chicago's burgeoning downtown Loop, Field's served every need. Along with a dizzying spread of apparel, furniture, and housewares, the store offered eleven restaurants, workrooms to repair antique furniture and clocks, a dry cleaner, an ice cream kitchen, and more. On Saturdays, parents dropped their children off at Field's for charm school and handicraft classes. Chicago gangster Al Capone bought his $35 silk shirts by the dozen at Field's Men's Store annex, which specialized in shotguns and hunting paraphernalia. Field's reputation for style soared to new heights in 1914, with the publishing of *Fashions of the Hour*, a bi-monthly magazine mailed free of charge to Field's customers. It featured photographs of Chicago socialites in the latest fashions and articles on art, travel, and gardening.

In 1941, Marshall Field pulled out all the stops when it designed a special dress salon called "the 28 Shop." During World War II, when the pace-setting Paris fashion houses were shuttered, the 28 Shop filled the void by showcasing America's up-and-coming designers like Adrian, Norman Norrell, and Hattie Carnegie. The marketing of designers by name was a bold new step for Field's, where merchandise had only carried the Marshall Field & Co. store label. Chicago's wealthiest matrons headed to Field's entrance at 28 East Washington Street, where they boarded a private elevator lined with velvet benches. Arriving on the sixth floor into a rotunda foyer, clients were greeted by a butler and a hostess who led them into a lovely pink salon with twenty-eight dressing rooms, designed by Joseph Platt, the former Hollywood set designer for *Gone With the Wind*. Saleswomen whisked gowns out from the stockroom and stood guard to wait on each client. The 28 Shop was an immediate hit and became the fashion headquarters for the most stylish women in the Midwest.

Although the 28 Shop was the place where the elite met at Field's, the salon imparted cachet to everything else in the store. Starting in the 1950s, Kathleen Catlin, Field's legendary fashion director and head buyer for the 28 Shop, prevailed as Field's most influential tastemaker. Catlin dressed the displays for Field's windows, staged fashion shows, and schooled local fashion writers about the latest trends from Paris. Her fame spread far beyond Chicago. "Kathleen was so well-received in Paris because Field's bought more couture than any other retailer back then," recalled Dorothy Fuller, who formerly worked under Catlin.

At the Paris house of Balenciaga in the early 1950s, for instance, Catlin was thoroughly enchanted by the grand couturier's chemise or "sack" dress. She followed her instincts and, unlike the other American buyers, ordered several Balenciagas. Without bust or seam darts, the dresses were so unusual that "we put them on backwards at every fashion show . . . we only discovered that later on," recalled Fuller. Carmel Snow, the editor of *Harper's Bazaar*, wired Catlin to commend her on the Balenciagas: "My dear, how courageous!" And perspicacious. By the late 1950s, every smartly dressed woman in America donned a chemise, and the style lasted throughout the 1960s.

Catlin's sharp instincts made her an invaluable consultant to the leading dress houses on Seventh Avenue. "Kathleen knew that we had to create a desire," Fuller recalled. "The manufacturers flew in from New York, laid the (couture) clothes out on a table, and measured each seam. They went back to New York to copy the dresses and then Field's bought the copies."

In effect, Field's leadership led to the democratization of high fashion. Knockoffs came out of the 28 Shop and trickled all the way down to the budget floor, another Field's invention in 1885. The bargain basement concept was hatched by Harry Selfridge, one of Field's most colorful merchants, "who swept through the store with the dash of a circus promoter and the fervor of a revolutionist [sic]." Selfridge was confident that Field's would attract more working-class clientele by creating a special area for goods that were "trustworthy or less expensive, but reliable." Marshall Field wasn't keen on the idea at first, and he fretted that too many newspaper ads shouting "specially attractive bargains" would tarnish Field's uptown gloss.

But Field's bargain basement worked like magic and became a clever merchandising tactic that other stores across America soon copied. Shoppers who once wistfully window-shopped at Field's reportedly "came by the thousands in the first week to grab the cheaper silks, dress goods, hosiery, handkerchiefs, cloaks, ribbons and shawls." (Selfridge later moved on to London to create his own retail empire, Selfridge's, the first American-style department store in England. He frequently sent his buyers to Chicago to walk the floors at Field's.)

With more than one hundred years of such astute merchants as Catlin and Selfridge, Field's established its authority at opposite ends of the shopping spectrum. The receptionist who bagged a $19.95 budget coat and the Gold Coast socialite who selected a $3,000 original were both loyal clientele, confident that the fashions inside their hunter green Marshall Field's shopping bags represented the best of everything. (Marshall Field & Co. became known as Marshall Field's after 1982.)

IN 1990, FIELD'S was basking in the glow from its years under the charismatic Miller, who moved on after the acquisition by Dayton Hudson to become vice chairman of Saks Fifth Avenue. Having paid dearly for Field's, Dayton Hudson was keen to prune the fat from the store's operations, so the new owner folded Field's right into its existing department store division, in order to reap the advantages of shared expenses and economies of scale. Hundreds of Field's employees were let go. Many Chicagoans feared the worst when they heard that most of Field's buyers would be transferred to Minneapolis headquarters.

Phyllis Collins, the high-fashion buyer whose husband had an established law practice in Chicago, was one of the few Field's merchants allowed to stay. She didn't view the Dayton Hudson people as the enemy. "Never in their minds was this a takeover. They didn't want to fire people; they didn't have a superiority attitude. Everyone was on a first-name basis. They made an effort not to rip us apart."

Nevertheless, Collins believed that Dayton Hudson officials had underestimated what they were taking on. "They thought they were buying another Dayton's—and Dayton's wasn't used to competition in Minneapolis. They thought that with Field's, it was Frango mints and a Christmas tree in the Walnut Room and you've got them [customers]. But this is Chicago, this is a sophisticated city where you've gotta do it better, you've gotta sing and dance."

And just as many locals had feared, Field's began to lose its luster under Dayton Hudson. Gloria Bacon, a Field's aficionado, was appalled when she discovered $19.99 Nine West shoes displayed right next to the $350 Chanels. Field's solicitous saleswomen had disappeared, and almost every month there was a storewide sale.

Furthermore, Field's, the once-proud independent, had been forced into group therapy. Every price tag in Field's read "Dayton's, Hudson's and Marshall Field's." Advertisements for designer fashions in *Vogue* were labeled "Dayton's Oval Room *and* Field's 28 Shop." Even Field's exclusive Frangos were now available at Dayton's, Hudson's—even Target. Finally, when Field's came out with a new, "environmentally friendly" brown shopping bag, shoppers revolted. Field's backed off, and brought back its signature hunter green tote.

In making such moves, management wasn't prepared for such a backlash. "The Chicago customers hated these changes," recalled Gary Witkin, Field's president succeeding Miller. "There was this psychological perception that Field's was no longer Chicago-owned. It created a sensitivity for people to look for differences that they hadn't seen. The customer said, 'You are messing with my Marshall Field's.'"

As more Chicagoans became aware that Field's was being run from Minneapolis, Nordstrom saw an opportunity to win them over. In radio commercials, Nordstrom underscored its unwavering commitment to Chicago with the tagline: "Our buyers are your neighbors."

But whether the buyers were next door or a few hundred miles away in Minneapolis was beside the point. Department store retailing was no longer a buyer's market. Gone was the ritual of the 1970s, when buyers spent half of their time "branching"—that is, visiting store locations to learn the local idiosyncrasies of every community. Retailers believed that America was thoroughly homogenized—that the folks in Chicago loved the same fashions that the people in Detroit did—so it made sense to stock the same merchandise at most every branch store. In any event, the logistics of traveling to all of the sixty-six Marshall Field's, Dayton's, and Hudson's stores scattered throughout the Midwest was impractical. "Our buyers are lucky if they get to each store once a year," explained Dan Skoda, Field's president since 1992.

In short, buyers no longer had the freedom to impose their will (or their taste, for that matter) upon stores that had become fixated on the bottom-line performance above everything else.

This was the assembly-line, bottom-line apparel of the nineties that shoved fashion forever aside. In the 1960s, "before television and communications dictated a lot of the fashion, the department store used to be your first visual contact with fashion," said Allen Questrom, who served as chairman of Federated Department Stores from 1993 to 1998. "You came into the store to see what was available. In those days, the buyers spent a lot of time in the art of fashion; they knew more about fit, construction, and fabric. They could pick things that fit within the context of their store for a certain ilk of customers. They got to know the customers who shopped that store. The downtown store and later the mall had the advertising and special events that made the store *the* authority."

Such retail rituals disappeared by the 1970s, the era of the designer boom and nationally advertised fashion brands. Once designers became household names in apparel, accessories, perfumes, and bedding, their brands "created the ultimate consumer demand which you didn't have twenty years ago," said Philip Miller. "The department store used to be the vehicle that introduced merchandise concepts to the customer, but today, it's the brand. The designer is now communicating directly through national advertising and editorial and through fashion shows. The consumers see it in many instances as fast as we retailers do."

As designer brands moved onto center stage in the 1980s, department stores abandoned their practice of organizing sales floors in categories such as "better dresses" or "women's sportswear." The floors were reconfigured in brand-name boutiques under banners such as Liz Claiborne, Ellen Tracy, or Jones New York, which were among the most popular labels sold in America. As such powerful brands began to dominate department stores, buyers became less inclined to try out new and unfamiliar labels that shoppers would most likely overlook. "Most people don't have a natural sense of fashion and they are insecure," said Questrom. "The person who can afford to stay in the Ritz Carlton Hotel won't go out to experiment and try some exclusive inn they've never heard of. They need an authority, and today the authority is the brand. They have confidence in that label."

———

DAYTON HUDSON DIDN'T believe in hosting lavish black-tie benefits the way Field's had under Miller. Instead, the corporation quietly donated 5 percent of its annual pretax profits directly to charities—or about a million dollars a week, in the late 1990s. Nevertheless, Dayton Hudson knew the significance of maintaining ties to Chicago society. So Field's continued its longtime tradition of hosting a major fashion show benefit every fall. Traditionally Field's fashion shows were posh and elegant, where couture originals were shown on Chicago's top models—the teenage Cindy Crawford had once been a runway favorite. But Dayton Hudson decided that Field's shows needed to be more populist, to reach the broad audience that management now wanted to attract.

In August 1991, Field's added a new fashion show to its calendar, "Cause for Applause," which was billed as "a show of entertainment and fashion trends, rather than designer fashions presented on a runway." The program was modeled after Dayton's annual "Fash Bash" musical revue which had been a big hit with Minneapolis audiences for years.

"Cause for Applause," held at the Chicago Theater near Field's on State Street, indeed turned out to be a fashion show that made the headlines, but not the ones Dayton Hudson was expecting. Actor Mandy Patinkin, a Chicago native, was a jovial host. He got a few laughs when he passed out boxes of Frangos to the people in the front rows. But the evening droned on for nearly two hours, during which sixty models and dancers paraded the new fall styles, consisting of career clothes from Nippon, J.H. Collectibles, and Adrienne Vittadini—and hardly an evening gown in sight. Clearly, there wasn't much cause for applause from the Gold Coast crowd.

Genevieve Buck, the *Tribune*'s fashion editor, was sarcastic in her review: " 'Cause for Applause' was obviously ushering in a new fashion era at Field's," she wrote. "Gone were the upscale Calvin Kleins, Oscar de la Rentas, the Giorgio Armanis and Yves Saint Laurents of past shows that opened the fall season after Labor Day."

"Cause for Applause" encored in 1992, when carnival jugglers shared the stage with models, only to get another thumbs-down from Buck and her Gold Coast readers. Dayton Hudson gave up after that, and Field's returned to its high-toned fashion-show benefits for the fall season.

But that didn't mean a return to Field's upscale agenda of the eighties. "The way we do it today is different," explained Gerald Storch, Dayton Hudson's executive vice president of store planning, in 1997. "Our ultimate goal is to have the merchandise that most [shoppers] want, the national brands like DKNY, Dana Buchman, Perry Ellis, and Tommy Hilfiger."

BUT WHAT DID America's shoppers really want? Since the 1980s, designer brands had a spotty track record as they grappled with focusing on what to produce while department stores weren't sure of what to mark down and what to sell at full price.

Still, the chains kept multiplying. By the early 1990s, retail space across the nation had mushroomed at an astonishing pace. America overflowed with thousands of shopping centers—but fewer customers. There were more than 35,000 malls in operation by 1992, an estimated 18 square feet of retail space for every man, woman, and child in America, or nearly triple the number that existed in 1972. As America's suburban migration slowed in the late 1980s, the population of young women trawling the malls began shrinking as well. More and more, supply was exceeding demand, but unfettered, retailers continued to open more branch locations.

"The way retailers made money in the past was to open new stores every season," said Carl Steidtmann, an economist at Management Horizons, a retail consulting firm. "They are so wedded to this experience that it is difficult for them to change."

Beginning in the 1970s, retailers had a reason to expand so rapidly: a new generation of baby-boomer career women who were filling their closets with clothes to wear to work. Thus began the explosion of women's brands like Liz Claiborne, Jones New York, Chaus, and J.H. Collectibles, which dominated the women's floors in department stores. Those mighty labels were joined by dozens of specialty chains like The Limited, its sister, Express, and Casual Corner and Ann Taylor, all with their own private-label fashion lines. Discounted women's fashions were plentiful at Marshall's, Loehmann's, T.J. Maxx, and the factory outlet malls, while Sears and Penney's beefed up their fashion selections. Even Wal-Mart couldn't resist. By 1992, the Bentonville, Arkansas–based powerhouse had $82 billion in annual sales—with nearly $30 billion coming from apparel and sheets and towels.

Ironically, it would also be fashion that eventually put retailing on the skids. The buoyant women's apparel industry hit a pothole in the fall of 1987 when designers made a concerted push to bring back short skirts—at a time when women had spent the past few years building wardrobes of calf-length hemlines. The miniskirt revival that began in spring 1987 was universally endorsed on the high-fashion runways and tested on such popular prime time TV series as *Dynasty*, where actress Joan Collins could be seen plotting her schemes in sexy short dresses. One Bloomingdale's newspaper ad blared "SHORT" in three-inch type: "Never ones to flash a leg in vain, we applaud the outright appeal of a hemline above the knee." Chasing the wave, Liz Claiborne spent hundreds of thousands of dollars to shorten skirts already in production for its fall deliveries.

But the minis suffered a maxi-crash that year because millions of women just said no. National Public Radio's Nina Totenberg, for one, was outraged, and on the air, she urged women not to buy into the hype. Sisterhood was indeed powerful. For the first time in a decade, there was a drop in the sales of women's apparel. The backlash took the industry by surprise, and fashion writer Irene Daria concluded, "the female American population seemed to mature overnight."

Apparel marketers were stumped—and panic-stricken. Racks and racks of short skirts languished unsold, alongside blazers, blouses, and sweaters, as more women boycotted fashion in general. Claiborne, Limited, and U.S. Shoe, the holding company of Casual Corner, pointed to fashion as the reason their profits fell in 1987. A few years later, shorter skirts finally did catch on with most women, but apparel marketers were starting to learn a hard lesson: They couldn't dictate fashion as they used to.

Maybe if they just tried harder, or made fashions cheaper, lightning might strike again. But alas, Seventh Avenue continued to suffer with a string of designer flops in the 1990s—like the "waif" look of frilly velvet and droopy ruffled blouses, the unkempt "grunge" look, and the "fishtail" dress with its asymmetrical hemline.

The apparel industry had laid the groundwork for this rebellion by disrupting its own fashion cycles, which had always induced women to update their wardrobes. By espousing the notion of "individual style" and "investment dressing," designers had unwittingly persuaded women to stop buying so many clothes.

By 1994, the apparel industry had entered a third straight year of slumping sales, and retailers and designers alike were baffled. In 1993, women's apparel prices fell 4.4 percent from the previous year, the sharpest price decline since 1952. During the 1994 Christmas season, Liz

Claiborne revealed just how bad things had gotten: Only about 20 percent of Claiborne's fashions had moved at full price in department stores.

As for those enthusiasts who kept shopping, many women were buying far fewer clothes and paying less for them. The average retail price of a dress fell in 1994 to $35.78 from $39.30 in 1991; blazers dropped to $37 from $41.

The fallout of women's apparel had more to do with working women than fashion. As everybody shifted into wearing casual clothes most of the time, it was easy for women to become blasé about fashion. Indeed, American women were focusing more on their careers instead of their clothes. In the early 1980s, the New York advertising agency Wells, Rich and Green had surveyed hundreds of women about their fashion habits, concluding that "the more confident and independent women became, the less they liked to shop; and the more they enjoyed their work, the less they cared about clothes." Demographics were another vital component. As America's population skewed older, many women already had closets bulging with clothes they could still wear. They were also saddled with mortgages and bills for their children's education. So keeping up with the latest fashions was simply no longer a priority.

Such signals were immensely distressing to apparel marketers, who realized women's cooling attitudes toward fashion were likely to be permanent. "In women's apparel, what you're seeing in many ways is the end of an era," Carl Steidtmann, the economist, told *The Wall Street Journal* in 1994. "Businesses which grew up in the past fifteen years when the industry was growing dramatically and everything seemed to work are now in an era of no growth when nothing they are doing seems to work."

Across America, there were just too many retailers selling too many clothes at a time when many women were winnowing their wardrobes. Starting in the early 1990s, a retail shakeout began, when The Limited

Inc., which had 3,300 stores in 1990, began shuttering hundreds of its Limited, Express, and Lerner's stores. Some of the most popular apparel marketers like Merry-Go-Round, Gillian Group, and J.H. Collectibles went out of business altogether. Even the mighty Liz Claiborne was forced to shutter its seventy-five-store First Issue chain.

NOT EVERY RETAILER was confounded by fashion, however. As more women shopped for clothes that were affordable, comfortable, and casual, the retailer they now turned to was the Gap. With its combination of well-made classic clothes, the right price, and a hip, modern image, Gap had became the new fashion destination for millions of women and men. The Gap, along with its sister divisions Banana Republic and Old Navy, gained an incredible market share in the 1990s and became the world's second largest apparel brand, behind Levi's. In 1998—the year in which it opened a new store every day—Gap generated $8.3 billion in sales in its 2,237 stores, which included 953 Gap Stores, 637 Gap Kids stores, 258 Banana Republic stores, and 282 Old Navy stores in the U.S., with the remaining Gap stores in Japan, the UK, Canada, France, and Germany.

"For years, we and so many others defined fashion as 'designers,' but fashion is no longer that," said Patrick McCarthy, editor of *Women's Wear Daily*, in December 1997. "The big shift started about 18 years ago, but didn't reach fruition until the last 5 to 7 years . . . [when fashion] went from designer to moderate and everything in between. People are now defining Gap and Banana Republic as fashion, even though those stores are charging $30 for a dress."

Gap was founded in 1969 by Donald Fisher, a California real estate developer, who opened his first Gap (as in generation gap) boutique in San Francisco selling Levi's jeans and discounted records and tapes. As

Gap caught on and expanded into hundreds of stores over the next decade, Fisher bought Banana Republic in 1983, the year he made the best decision in his professional career, hiring Mickey Drexler, the former president of Ann Taylor. An MBA with the instincts of a designer and extraordinary vision, Drexler hired designers to create Gap's own extensive collections of jeans, T-shirts, and sweaters in a broad range of sizes and colors. And thus began Gap's antifashion explosion.

Gap's unpretentious, "real clothes" stance reflected the changing consumer attitudes across America starting in the late 1980s. "Fashion had ground to a halt in the 1990s, and Gap was right there to initiate the casual, dress-down trend in a big way," said David Wolfe of Doneger Group retail consultants in New York. "Gap slowed down the evolution of fashion. Every six weeks, Gap has a totally fresh assortment—not necessarily based on new designs, but on new colors. You walk into a Gap store and the consumer gets the message right away."

But just as important as Gap's easy-to-read clothes was its image. Gap began with its "Individuals of Style" campaign of black-and-white ads, putting Kim Basinger in an oversize white Gap men's shirt and pearls and Dizzy Gillespie in a Gap mock turtleneck. With its ubiquitous, seductive advertising, Gap created its own fashion moment in 1984 with a $12.50 pocket T-shirt that continues to be a wardrobe staple for millions of Americans. Next came Gap's vintage photographs of celebrities with the tagline "Humphrey Bogart wore khakis," and "Gordon Parks wore khakis." In the world according to Gap, fashion was beyond the clothes, and all about the individual who wore them.

As Gap's credibility climbed, the chain became retail's most formidable fashion authority, usurping the role department stores had owned for years. Gap didn't need designer pedigree, it didn't need snob appeal, it didn't need high prices. And, ignoring fashion's revolving door, Gap still managed to make money, even though its clothes didn't go out of style each year. Shoppers kept coming back for more Gap basics, attracted by the new colors and other flourishes Gap created to keep its styles fresh—underscored with Gap's marketing magic.

Like Marshall Field's in its heyday, Gap played big to both ends of the spectrum. Whether they were affluent or working class, folks were proud to admit that their clothes came from Gap. They were members of a modern elite: individuals secure in their own style and beyond designer hype. "That is the big shift in fashion. People now consider moderate, inexpensive clothes as chic," McCarthy said.

Department stores could only look at Gap—and take notes.

THE WOMEN'S APPAREL debacle of the early 1990s, and the triumph of Gap and its many imitators, hastened the already declining fortunes of department stores. Much more business had shifted to the discounters, who became the powerhouses of retailing. By 1996, discounters accounted for about 41 percent of general retail sales (up from 27 percent in 1987). Wal-Mart now sold more apparel than all department stores combined. And department stores' overall market share had slipped to 14 percent, down from 20 percent in 1987.

It was against this backdrop that so many entrenched local department stores were either driven out of business or compelled to merge with their one-time competitors. By 1997, more than half of all department store sales came from four conglomerates: Federated Department Stores (the owner of Bloomingdale's, Macy's, Burdines), May Department Stores, Dillard's, and Nordstrom.

Taking advantage of size, these conglomerates learned how to make more money by operating more efficiently. They centralized their buying operations—as much as 85 percent of the merchandise sold in any one location could be sold in virtually any other store in the chain.

Returning to the origins of America's first department stores in the nineteenth century—and copying the success of Gap—the amalgamated chains further democratized fashion. Federated dropped high-end merchandise from almost all its stores. "Outside of Bloomingdale's, we have an eyedropper of designer merchandise," said Terry Lundgren, president of Federated. In 1997, only 45 of Federated's 420 stores carried bridge brands—such as Ellen Tracy, Emanuel, Anne Klein, and DKNY— priced a notch below top designer labels. Across the rest of Federated, the likes of Liz Claiborne were the top of the line.

Department store retailing had become increasingly about minimizing fashion risks. But even though department stores had revamped their strategies, they would never reign supreme again. In 1997, economists at Management Horizons predicted that the department store industry "is not growing and probably won't for the foreseeable future." Management Horizons projected that sales at department stores from 1996 to 2001 would rise annually at a meager 0.5 percent, compared to growth of 2.2 percent between 1991 and 1996.

Department stores now depended on getting their fashion authority from their key suppliers, known as "matrix" brands. In menswear, for example, the big three were Polo Ralph Lauren, Tommy Hilfiger, and Nautica, which accounted for 40 percent of the men's sportswear sold in department stores in 1997. "There are maybe eight key women's apparel brands and three or four men's brands who have their systems hooked into the computers at the stores," explained Robert Buchanan, an analyst. "The matrix puts stores on automatic pilot, and relieves the buyers from having to go to so many meetings. It's just easier and more efficient for stores to operate that way."

Stores also depended on matrix brands to take on many of their former responsibilities. A typical example was Eileen Fisher, a New York designer of loose-fitting women's casual apparel priced from $40 to $250. Fisher, who founded her company in 1984, was one of the lucky ones. She felt fortunate to be on the matrix at Field's, where her collection was carried at all of its fourteen stores. She depended on getting big orders from department stores after the independent shops she used to sell to in the 1980s went out of business in the 1990s.

Fisher personified the modern fashion house of the 1990s. She designed her business to be as straightforward and conservative as her styles. Fisher didn't get distracted by throwing expensive fashion shows and hobnobbing with the press. She knew that in order to be popular with women, she first had to be an important player inside department stores.

So Fisher took care of business: designing, manufacturing, and shipping merchandise to stores. She shared the cost of building in-store shops—at a cost of several thousand dollars each—in department stores. She also forked over thousands to subsidize newspaper ads and store catalogs where her merchandise appeared.

Fisher dispatched her own team of retail coordinators to pay visits to every store branch—just like buyers did in the old days—to set up in-store displays in department stores and orient the salespeople. The designer also did her part to make certain that Eileen Fisher fashions sold before markdowns. Whenever full-price sales fell below a certain level, Fisher had to pay a rebate—in the form of a discount on future orders—to department stores. "Retailers are very serious about making their profit margins," she said.

And that's why Fisher went the extra mile to ascertain what the computer printouts couldn't tell her. What styles were missing from her collections? Did women prefer silk to rayon? Fisher fine-tuned her collections from consumer feedback she gleaned from her own chain of a dozen Eileen Fisher boutiques—and not from Field's. "At the department stores, their buyer isn't on the floor; she doesn't know," Fisher said.

As department stores directed more and more of their business to powerful matrix brands such as Eileen Fisher, they began to look alike. "The worst thing that happened to fashion in department stores was when they got carved up into all of those in-store boutiques. That's what turned stores boring," said Ellin Saltzman, a former fashion director of Saks Fifth Avenue and Macy's.

Nevertheless, boring spelled success for May Department Stores, the 240-store chain that had the best annual growth rate among department stores in the 1990s. Industry experts dubbed May's aggressive use of matrix brands the "May-onnaising" of department stores.

May's divisions included Lord & Taylor in New York, Foley's in Houston, Hecht's in Washington, D.C., and May/Robinson in Los Angeles. May's stores were clean, brightly lit, and neat, and well-stocked with the most popular mainstream brands—merchandise that was conservative, affordable, and satisfactory to May's clientele. "May has never had any pretenses," explained Aronson, the retail consultant. "It's a middle-class Sears dictated out of St. Louis."

May even managed to give the discounters a real run. Lord & Taylor, for example, frequently tempted shoppers with 20 percent off coupons on any single item already on the markdown racks. During such promotions, a dress originally priced $180 could go for as little as $54, or 70 percent off the original price.

But if Lord & Taylor could afford to give away a dress at such a steep discount, was the dress overpriced at $180 to begin with? Such steep sales made more people more skeptical. The original prices on clothes had come to resemble the "list" prices on items like stereos, prices that were steeply marked up so that they could be marked down.

As more shoppers became trained to hold out for the best deals, markdowns had indeed become a way of life. In a 1996 consumer survey of 6,300 households, 80 percent said they were motivated to buy clothes because they were advertised bargains, up from 71.7 percent in 1992. "Shoppers say, 'I can wait until the next sale or go to factory outlet malls and get it today,' " said Field's Skoda.

With so many retailers overflowing with fashion merchandise, markdowns were indeed the only way to keep the goods flowing through stores. Department store powerhouse Liz Claiborne sent fresh merchandise to stores every four to six weeks. Most department stores started marking down those goods nine weeks after the clothes hit the sales floor—if not sooner. The rationale behind this practice was that the longer merchandise was hanging on the racks, the harder it was to sell. So retailers wasted no time moving out their mistakes and moving in fresh fashions at full price.

But this revolving door also worked against fashion. When a new trend didn't sell promptly, the style disappeared before shoppers ever had a chance to catch up. A 1995 study by the retail consulting firm Management Horizons observed that the markdown syndrome had effectively blocked fashion novelties from ever reaching department stores, in an era when the chains "desperately need to be more unique." Retailers "focus on keeping the goods moving rather than experimenting with new merchandise that might differentiate them with their competitors. The unhappy result is that many department stores look shockingly similar and risk losing market share to smaller innovative specialty stores," Management Horizons concluded.

So if conventional department stores had turned into cookie-cutter operations with the same brands, what happened to the best designer fashions, the crème de la crème? Where are the 28 Shops of today? Field's continued with its 28 Shop at only two locations: State Street and Water Tower Place. But the 28 Shop of the 1990s bore little resemblance to its glorious past incarnation. At State Street, the special elevator and rotunda foyer were gone. The 28 Shop was simply another department on the eighth floor, with designer dresses from Yves Saint Laurent, Christian Lacroix, and Bill Blass grouped together on metal T-stands.

Stepping up to claim the best designer business in the late 1990s were the few high-end specialty department store chains, namely Saks Fifth Avenue, Neiman Marcus, and Barneys New York—as well as the designers themselves, such as Gucci, Escada, Jil Sander, and Giorgio Armani, who opened their own stores in cities like New York, Chicago, Houston, Los Angeles, and San Francisco.

Meanwhile, the young designers like Isaac Mizrahi, who emerged in the early 1990s, had fewer retailers left to support them. Bloomingdale's, for one, used to nurture new designers by carrying their money-losing collections for a few years until they caught on. "If we really believed in a designer, we would continue to buy them for several seasons, even if the line didn't sell well," said Kal Ruttenstein, fashion director at Bloomingdale's. He recalled that back in 1989 Bloomie's even bought a big ad in *The New York Times* to help expose Mizrahi to the public. "But today, we wouldn't do that anymore," Ruttenstein lamented. And now everybody knows that even Bloomie's sponsorship failed to save Mizrahi a decade later.

With fashion's new condensed time frame, new designer brands came and went—in a hurry. There was no point in standing behind a slow-selling newcomer when there were plenty of other new designers that stood, perhaps, a better chance at selling. "We give them about a year and if they don't make our projections, we tend to drop them," said Joan Kaner, fashion director at Neiman Marcus.

Meanwhile, the fashion authority poised to lead in the next millennium is Gap, the juggernaut which, through its various divisions, serves shoppers' needs for apparel, shoes, cosmetics, fragrances, and underwear at every price range. And at the top of its pyramid, Gap's $1 billion-a-year Banana Republic chain distinguished itself in the late 1990s as formidable competition to tonier designer brands. Its 280 shops generated retail sales of about $636 a square foot, or more than twice as much as similar mall chains.

In the fall of 1998, when Banana Republic draped itself in suede jackets, shirts, pants, and vests, the retailer pulled off an unprecedented fashion coup. Ignoring cues from Paris, Milan, or Seventh Avenue, Banana Republic decided to push suede—a material that nobody was using of late—into a major fashion statement. "We felt the opportunity in the marketplace that we could go aggressively after suede," said Gap's CEO Drexler. "Suede was a luxurious fabric and it speaks to the consumer about high quality."

And once again, the Gap organization designed the way it knew best, putting its familiar casual silhouettes, shirts, jackets, vests, and pants into buttery suede fabric imported from Italy and priced reasonably at $100 to $400. Then Banana Republic blitzed magazines and the TV airwaves with ads with stark images of the lush sportswear above the caption: "Banana Republic. Suede." The store provided free alterations on suede, which helped move almost all of the merchandise before markdowns. After Banana Republic's suede crusade, a number of the sharp-eyed merchants on Seventh Avenue began whispering the unthinkable; they were ready to copy Banana Republic, to come out with their own suede fashions for fall 1999. Banana Republic had effectively turned suede into what's known in retailing parlance as a "category killer," by creating such a demand that suede merchandise alone drew thousands of shoppers into the store.

The end of fashion has led straight to Gap, which has mastered a modern way of marketing clothes that is working according to the principle that Marshall Field's had drummed into his people long ago: "give the lady what she wants." To borrow a 1998 cover line from *Fortune* magazine: "Gap Gets It." Which means the shoppers get it, too.

IN 1995, MARSHALL Field's marked its fifth year under Dayton Hudson—but there was little to celebrate. Field's had become more populist with its "13-Hour" sales, but the novelty of a more affordable Field's wore off because every other store in Chicago was promoting lower prices as aggressively as Field's was. "We were promotionally driven into the mid-1990s but it didn't feel good and we didn't do it as well as our competition," admitted Field's Skoda. "We kept hearing from our guests [what Field's always called their customers] that this isn't what they want. This isn't why they shop here. 'I want better merchandise, great service and exciting new things. I want to be proud to have it in a Marshall Field's box.' "

Finally, management stepped back in search of a new solution that would revive its upscale image—at the expense of turning off all those bargain hunters. Phase two began when Field's gutted many of its storewide promotions—causing sales to plummet; Dayton Hudson reported that operating profit at all of its department stores plunged 41 percent in 1995 from 1994.

As Dayton Hudson management finally saw the wisdom of catering more to Field's sophisticated, hometown market, it transferred twenty-five buyers back to Chicago. "Chicago is the fashion capital of the Midwest and having more buyers here allows us to sense the pulse of a fashion city and Michigan Avenue," said Skoda.

Field's had a lot of making up to do on the fashion and image front. Field's used to rank along with Nordstrom and Crate and Barrel as a top-quality place to shop, according to Series Industry Research Systems, a market research firm that based its findings on telephone interviews with consumers. But in the 1990s, consumers had given Field's lower marks. "We're not looking at Kmart, but they have certainly dropped from the elite," Chris Ohlinger of Series Industry told the *Chicago Tribune* in September 1997. Even so, shoppers ranked Field's ahead of Bloomingdale's in terms of quality and service.

Dayton Hudson could afford to be patient while it revamped Field's, Dayton's, and Hudson's, because its core business, Target Stores, was growing faster than ever and shoring up the corporation's balance sheet. By 1997, Target's 736 locations accounted for $17 billion, or 70 percent, of Dayton Hudson's revenue and 80 percent of its operating profits, while the department stores registered 12 percent of revenue and 8 percent of profits.

Target had carved out a niche as an upscale discounter by offering apparel and household merchandise—and it became one of the most sophisticated and efficient retail operators in America. Target used the same tactics as supermarkets: It knew exactly how much space on each shelf went to a particular brand of deodorant.

Just like Gap's Old Navy, Target had given $10 knit shirts and $19.99 jeans a fashion image. Target's apparel and housewares were a notch above budget, but its merchandise didn't look cheesy. It became fashionable for well-to-do shoppers to visit the store they nicknamed "Tarjay," with a French pronunciation.

In 1997, Target rolled out an arch, high-fashion ad campaign, "Fashion and Housewares," that wooed shoppers with humor. One of the first ads shows a bald man in a $7.99 knit shirt with an $18.99 desk fan slung across his back. Target became the first discounter that successfully positioned itself as hip.

Field's, Dayton's, and Hudson's benefited by being a part of Target's family, not only because of its profits, but also its model efficiency. Accordingly, the department store division trimmed its expenses by $50 million in 1997, sharpened its list of vendors, and hired more salespeople. Moreover, the division maximized its productivity. "In the old days it would take us maybe three or four days to unload a fifty-three-foot trailer that was full of merchandise," said Hank Lorant, Field's regional director of stores, in 1998. "Now we can get all that merchandise unloaded and onto the sales floor in three or four hours."

Field's was also busy designing a new image for itself, as a department store that offered value and customer service, tarted up with a dash of glamour. The cheeky advertising strategy that worked wonders on Target did the same for Field's. In 1997, Field's came out with a new advertising tagline: "Where else? Marshall Field's." The ads were shot throughout the expansive, historic State Street store in order to underscore the breadth of merchandise that shoppers could find only at Field's. In one of the TV commercials in the Walnut Room restaurant, three modern Holly Golightlys—in black sheath dresses and big black hats—were seated at a table. The announcer recited breathlessly, "Yves Saint Laurent, Ungaro, Escada, Missoni—and *Vivienne*," referring to the smiling waitress who suddenly appeared to serve them.

The message from this commercial—that Field's employees aimed to serve its shoppers—reflected the store's new emphasis on training its sales associates to perform specific duties. Some staffers were assigned to "push teams," whose jobs were to rearrange merchandise on markdown displays, while others concentrated on selling to customers full time. Field's also motivated salespeople by paying commissions for the first time, to individuals in such key areas as fashion apparel and shoes, which attracted a better caliber of salespeople.

While Field's was still wedded to its matrix list of national brands, the store was also beginning to benefit from having more of its buyers in Chicago. "They are now on hand to attend the local social events, to see where the trends are, and they convey this to our partners in Minneapolis," Skoda said.

While such tinkering began to take effect, Field's still had a long way to go. In 1997, Donna Karan agreed to be the featured designer at Field's annual fall fashion benefit. But after executives from Donna Karan International made a visit to Field's, the designer changed her mind and pulled out of the event. Karan begged off, citing conflicts in her hectic schedule, but that wasn't the real reason why she wasn't coming to Chicago.

"We couldn't believe how Field's had gone down," said one Donna Karan official who recalled his walk through Field's. "I mean, they put *one* Saint Laurent dress on a hanger and call that their designer department. There are practically no designer goods at the store. It would have been bad for our image for Donna to do that event."

But if the Donna Karan people had returned to Chicago a year later, they might have felt better about Field's, where improvements were starting to kick in. One Field's shopper, Kathy Robinson, told the *Chicago Tribune* in July 1998 that she had recently bought furniture, shoes, and clothes at Field's on State Street. "They're slowly but surely roping me in. If I'm going to a department store, it's Field's," Robinson said.

Field's new polish penetrated more than just the surface. Dayton Hudson reported that its department store division had risen impressively all through 1997, when pretax profit grew 59 percent to $240 million from the year before. And Field's was on track in 1998 to post another stellar year. In August 1998, an executive at Field's hometown rival,

Carson Pirie Scott, paid a rare compliment to Field's in the *Chicago Tribune.* "They recognized they weren't going in the direction they should have been. They did something about it and it seems to be paying off," said Ed Carroll, Carson's executive vice president of marketing.

Basking in its recent good fortune, Field's threw its September 11, 1998, fashion benefit with a newfound confidence. It was a night of déjà vu as designer Carolina Herrera was the featured designer at the black-tie benefit at the Museum of Contemporary Art, which was only a few blocks away from Water Tower Place, where Herrera had attended Field's most memorable bash a decade ago.

"An Evening of Fashion and Art" was the theme of the party, which began with cocktails under a tent behind the museum. After a fashion show featuring Herrera, Sonia Rykiel, Ungaro, and Calvin Klein designs, the Venezuelan-born Herrera, regal in her white satin shirt and a full gray taffeta skirt, took her runway bow, caressing a bouquet of white calla lilies.

An Andy Warhol portrait of Herrera hung on the wall in the corridor at the museum where a gourmet dinner of lamb chops and grilled shrimp salad was served. The evening was elegant and low-key, with guests going home around 11 P.M. carrying gift bags with two miniature Herrera perfume samples.

While some Chicagoans still believed that Field's fared better without Dayton Hudson, the truth was that Field's would have never would have survived on its own. Under the stewardship of Dayton Hudson, Field's initially stumbled badly, but also remade itself for the future by adopting many of Target's best practices.

Working the room at the party was the blond and bubbly Sugar Rautbord, a fixture on Chicago's Gold Coast scene for more than twenty years, who was dressed in a steel-gray Herrera gown from Field's. She was having a swell time, smiling and posing for photographers. She didn't seem to mind at all that the party wasn't so lavish.

"Thank God, the eighties are over!" she declared. "Everything is now pared down; people don't want to be overdone nowadays. This is the smart way to do philanthropy in the nineties." Then Rautbord let it be known that she loved to shop at Field's again: "Field's is on its way back. The store is making a renaissance."

GORED IN A BULL MARKET: WHEN

DONNA KARAN WENT TO WALL STREET

*No, I'm not your typical CEO—far from it. But to take a company
from zero to $700 million says something about how we operate. Do we
do it by the straight and narrow? Of course not. We cut on the bias.
I'm a creative thinker with a vision.*

—DONNA KARAN, May 1997

*I don't watch the stock price. The stock price is like hemlines.
It goes up and it goes down.*

—DONNA KARAN, October 1996

*F*or Donna Karan, the last week of
October 1996 was about as harried as it gets. The first lady of American
fashion was once again caught up in the frenzy of producing two major
fashion shows—and more. She opened the week with the introduction of
D, an experimental collection of avant-garde sportswear, and closed it
with a fashion show of her Donna Karan New York couture collection.
In between the traffic on the runways, Karan had to be *on*, especially on

Wednesday evening when she met with a group of Wall Street money managers—a group that was decidedly not in her fashion tribe.

The Week That Was began on Sunday, October 27, under the fashion-show tents set up in Bryant Park behind the New York Public Library, the venue where Bill Blass, Todd Oldham, and Nicole Miller and forty other designers were unveiling their spring 1997 women's collections. That afternoon, D debuted under a special tent designed to meet Karan's exacting specifications.

The big tent was now a study in beige, its ceiling and walls draped with hundreds of yards of filmy gauze fabric. The rows of folding chairs were gone, replaced with long benches with individual seat cushions covered in creamy muslin. The atmosphere was intimate and ethereal, a setting in keeping with Donna Karan's recent embrace of spiritualism and New Age philosophy. Behind the gauzy layers were models, hairdressers, makeup artists, and technicians whose efforts would culminate in a twenty-minute presentation that would cost nearly half a million dollars.

Seated under the beige top were about 650 fashion editors, photographers, and retailers. In the front row—and oblivious to flashing cameras pointed at her—was actress Demi Moore, still sporting her *GI Jane* buzz cut. (Earlier that year, she and her husband, Bruce Willis, had modeled in Karan's print ads.) The press release placed in each seat described D in a flurry of alliteration: "directional, definitive, distinctive, downtown and daring." Models paraded down the runway in see-through asymmetrical tops worn in layers with tight tube skirts.

D was also derivative, in the minds of a number of fashion sharpshooters in the audience, who whispered to each other as they spotted the references to minimalist designers Helmut Lang and Jil Sander. Retail buyers, who had had their fill of such looks during the Paris and Milan shows just weeks earlier, were perplexed, figuring that

D, which was pricier than Karan's sporty DKNY line, would be difficult to sell to women. In any event, the press reviews of the show were generally upbeat, if guarded. "Women will decide whether they enjoy playing with Karan's lean, body-clinging pieces to create an effortless effect," opined Mimi Avins in the *Los Angeles Times*.

Meanwhile, back in the heart of New York's garment district at 550 Seventh Avenue, Donna Karan's corporate headquarters, staffers scrambled to prepare her showroom for the rest of the week. The long, black-walled space on the fourteenth floor would be doing double duty, as the venue for Friday's fashion show as well as the Wednesday night dinner Karan was hosting for fifty Wall Street institutional investors.

Of all the hectic weeks for Donna Karan to play hostess! It wasn't her idea. But then, there was no way she could turn down Morgan Stanley, the investment bank that had led her namesake fashion house to Wall Street in a $258 million initial public offering four months earlier. Josie Esquivel, Morgan Stanley's apparel industry analyst, talked her into it, insisting that it would be a good idea for Karan, the chairman and CEO, to get acquainted with some of the key people who would hold considerable sway over her stock.

On Wednesday evening, Karan came dressed in all-black, as usual, her hair in a floppy cheerleader ponytail with long bangs. She was with Stephen Ruzow, her trusted chief operating officer. They led the group on a tour throughout the building and through more offices around the corner at 240 East Thirty-ninth Street, to give them a feel for what was behind the $510-million-a-year Donna Karan franchise: women's and men's apparel, sunglasses, handbags, athletic shoes, backpacks, perfumes, and cosmetics. Afterward, everybody sat down at tables on the showroom runway, which was now dim and cozy, with dozens of flickering scented candles from the Donna Karan Home Collection. While they dined on chicken and salad, two models strolled around in the styles from the spring couture line that would be shown on Friday.

What grade did the Wall Street suits give Karan for the evening? Somewhere between Satisfactory and Incomplete.

"It was all very opulent, very impressive," recalled one portfolio manager who was there. "But I can tell you that I didn't leave there feeling any more optimistic about the outlook for the stock."

He and the other money managers had reason to be skeptical about Donna Karan International. Back in June, when the company made its bow on the New York Stock Exchange, investors were psyched, lining up for the 10.8 million shares, representing 50 percent of the company, that were for sale in the initial public offering, or IPO. As investors deemed Donna Karan the most fashionable deal of the season, the stock commanded a respectable opening price of $24 a share.

But the excitement surrounding Donna Karan, listed under the symbol DK, didn't last long. On June 28, the first day of trading, DK bounced up to $30, then settled to close at a respectable $28, as many investors flipped their holdings, collected their one-day profits, and bailed out. Just thirty days later, DK slumped below its offering price to $21—and then the race to the bottom began, as the shares skidded like a run in a pair of sheer DKNY pantyhose.

By October, DK had tumbled to $15.50, in response to the company's lower-than-expected third-quarter earnings. A few months later, more bad news surfaced: a $1.7 million net loss in the fourth quarter. The company red-flagged some troubling signs: Its businesses were "too broadly focused" and internal expenses had ballooned way over budget. CEO Karan vowed to slash costs, and she ordered "management to take measures to insure that this trend doesn't continue." By the end of 1996, barely six months after the opening day, DK shares had tanked to the $9 range.

As speculation swirled that DK was headed for a meltdown, stock-brokers started wisecracking about the glossy fashion issue that was now as deceptive as a well-placed shoulder pad. Among traders, DK just happened to have another meaning, as in "don't know." A stock is "DK'd" when a broker can't complete a trade because he doesn't recognize the transaction, arguing that he didn't make it and doesn't know who did. And DK shares were certainly an enigma.

The House of Karan was now in the thick of it, taking a hazing on Wall Street. There was no escaping the reality that it was no longer business as usual. The very fact that Karan had been forced to entertain those Wall Streeters right in the middle of the hectic fashion-show week was a wake-up call if ever there was one.

Many people acquainted with Karan weren't at all surprised, suspecting that the pressures of being a chief executive with real fiscal responsibilities hadn't sunk in yet for the forty-seven-year-old designer. And they were right. Karan was clueless about the rules of Wall Street. Public companies are under pressure to keep everything up: revenue, earnings, and the stock price. There's nowhere to hide, because securities regulations require public companies to issue quarterly income statements as well as to disclose promptly any material developments that could affect future earnings, such as the sales of assets, lawsuits, and executive changes. And whenever bad news comes out, the reaction is swift: The stock price takes a tumble, followed by a flurry of negative news articles.

Accustomed to setting her own agenda and projecting upbeat, larger-than-life images of herself and her fashion house, Karan wasn't ready for prime time on Wall Street, which was like living in a fishbowl. She wasn't used to people questioning her abilities. Every so often, fashion editors would nix her runway collections, but they never grilled her about business matters.

So why did Karan go to the trouble to take her fashion house public and put herself under such a hammer? She was up against a wall. Takihyo Inc., the financial backer who had launched her company in 1985 and owned 50 percent of it, was ready to cash out. Takihyo partners Tomio Taki and Frank Mori had become embittered with Karan, after having locked horns with her on the company's business strategies during the 1990s.

When a divorce between the parties became imminent, going public was the obvious option. "Unfortunately, we never really discussed the concept of why we were going public and what that meant. It was not just getting the money," Taki recalled. "Now, we had different objectives than she did. . . . The investment banker explained everything to her in advance. But I just don't think it registered in her mind."

After the offering, Mori and Taki took their share of the proceeds—$58 million in cash and about 25 percent of the outstanding shares in the public company—and bowed out, leaving Karan to fend for herself for the first time in the company's eleven-year history.

Karan had always held the title of chief executive officer, but hers was largely a ceremonial role without real fiduciary responsibilities. Back in 1993, when Karan first floated the idea of going public, Wall Street analysts immediately raised concerns about her ability to run the company without Taki and Mori. But she didn't heed that warning. Karan refused to give up her CEO title then and she refused again in 1996. She loved the title and she felt confident that Ruzow would continue to do the heavy lifting on financial matters, as he had done in the past.

For years, Karan relished her role as the company's creative visionary, an artsy image that had played well for her, and she fully expected her expanded role with the big boys on Wall Street would play even better. Anna Wintour, editor of *Vogue*, thought her readers might like to see Karan up close and personal, as a CEO on the verge of taking her company public. Karan had kept a diary during the sixty road-show presentations she and Ruzow made before institutional investors in America and Europe, in the effort to drum up interest in DK shares. "Going Public," by Donna Karan, ran in the September 1996 issue of *Vogue*.

Poking fun at herself as a fashion creature trapped inside a world full of suits, Karan recounted how, on the long plane rides between stops, she got up to speed, memorizing accounting lingo like "EBIT" (earnings before income and taxes). She was incredulous at how nosy those professional money managers could be: "What going public really means is that everybody gets into your business quite literally."

Her entry for Day Six in Portland, Oregon: "These guys are really most interested in margins—what makes money? Growth and how to support it. It's not about luxury and cashmere and fabric and color. It's the bottom line."

While the designer CEO came across as amusing, if a bit flaky, in *Vogue*, the shareholders who read the article weren't laughing, because their DK holdings were tanking. Taki was among the exasperated. "She made it sound like a game," he said of the article. "Everybody already thinks that she doesn't know anything about [being a CEO]. The investors are thinking, 'She is the CEO and I am depending on *her* to manage the company with my money?' It is ridiculous!" Taki and Mori, as selling shareholders in the original offering, were obliged to hold on to that big block of shares they owned for at least a year before they could start cashing in. Their wait would be painful. By mid-September, their DK holdings had lost more than $40 million in value since the June offering.

In July 1997, after a full year of hard knocks in the stock market, Karan aired her frustrations in a speech before an audience of fashion industry executives: "I have been a CEO for ten years, yet nothing in my experience prepared me for the challenge of going public. Like having a baby, it doesn't matter how much advice you get, how much reading you do—until you go through it yourself, you have no idea what's coming."

By then, it had become clear that Karan's days as chief executive officer were numbered. But the jury was still out on how long the celebrated fashion house would stay in style on Wall Street.

DURING THE 1990S, the "monastic" look, "grunge," and fishtail hemlines were among the fleeting runway fads that barely lasted a season before they disappeared into fashion oblivion. But what did catch on, the trend that every fashion house wanted to knock off, was going public. The climate was perfect for new stock issues, with interest rates low and a roaring, unstoppable bull market. A record number of retail and fashion issues went public starting in 1992, with forty such companies coming to market between October 1995 and November 1997.

Besides Donna Karan, the newcomers to the New York Stock Exchange and the Nasdaq over-the-counter market included Gucci, Tommy Hilfiger, St. John Knits, Jones Apparel Group, Kenneth Cole Productions, Polo Ralph Lauren, Mossimo, Marisa Christina, Starter, He-Ro Group, North Face, Nautica, and Guess.

A number of these new issues seemed highly unlikely to produce the long-term growth and profits that public companies were supposed to sustain. For one, there was Mossimo, a West Coast maker of casual menswear best known for its $28 volleyball shorts with a funny script logo. Another questionable contender was He-Ro Group, which specialized in cocktail dresses marketed under the designer label Oleg Cassini—not a familiar name to most women. Cassini's big moment occurred more than thirty years before when he dressed First Lady Jacqueline Kennedy. Compared to those companies, Donna Karan International looked downright solid. Nevertheless, Donna Karan was vulnerable to instability given that 70 percent of its business came from expensive and trendy clothes for women and men.

Traditionally, the companies behind some of the top-performing apparel stocks projected an aura of invincibility. For example, VF Corp. (1998 sales of $5.5 billion) marketed commodity staples—Lee and Wrangler jeans and Vanity Fair bras—items that millions of people would always need to replace, regardless of what was in style. Likewise, Warnaco Group Inc. (1998 sales of $2 billion) contained a good balance of sturdy fashion licensed brands: Victoria's Secret lingerie, Chaps by Ralph Lauren, and Calvin Klein underwear. And the longtime stronghold in department stores Liz Claiborne Inc. (1998 sales of $2.5 billion) had been the apparel maker favored by legions of career women since the early 1980s. Such consistently solid performers made a lot of sense as public companies.

Nevertheless, Wall Street rolled out the welcome mat to a number of iconoclastic businesses during the go-go stock market of the 1990s. "The market has broadened," observed Linda Killian of Renaissance Capital Corp., a firm that specializes in evaluating new stock issues. "When you look back in the sixties, seventies and eighties, the typical IPOs were bio-tech and high-tech companies. But companies that were never viewed as being suitable for the public market were suddenly attractive in the 1990s. The list includes pet supermarkets, Internet stocks, gaming, and fashion—they all are the new industries in the IPO market."

Despite the ephemeral and unpredictable nature of fashion, more apparel companies were viewed as attractive investments in the nineties because designer names and fashion brands had become powerful hooks in the marketplace. "Part of the valuation that goes into a company is brand equity," Killian explained. "The fashion companies now have the ability to license across a number of products not only at the high end but at the lower price points."

Never before had apparel companies had such reach. For example, Guess Inc. (founded in 1981) was one of the hundreds of apparel makers that cashed in on the designer jeans boom. Guess marketed the sexy "three-zip Marilyn jean," which it advertised on the fetching German model Claudia Schiffer. As demand for designer jeans ebbed and flowed over the years, Guess could have easily slipped off the fashion radar. But instead, Guess spent millions on advertising to position itself as a power brand and a full-fledged fashion house, which attracted many licensees. In 1995, the year before it went public, Guess had sales of $440 million, $48 million of which came from royalties it collected from twenty-six licensees that made Guess infants' and children's wear, eyewear, footwear, active sportswear, and sheets and towels.

As fashion moved into the forefront of pop culture, Wall Street became seduced by the celebrity of designers. Donna Karan's best design effort ever may have been her road shows for investors. Her campaign began with a stock prospectus sporting an unusual black cover that resembled her fashion-show invitations. Investors who attended the presentations took home a DKNY baseball cap, sunglasses, a T-shirt, and cosmetics.

Karan played to standing-room crowds on most stops on the circuit. Instead of lecturing her audiences, she dazzled them with a touch of glamour: a little fashion show. Apologizing for not looking like a supermodel, Karan made quick changes behind a folding screen near the podium. She switched jackets—from black to white to lime green—to demonstrate the versatility of her signature "seven easy pieces" formula, suitable for day-to-night, office-to-black-tie dressing. A video montage followed, featuring Karan alongside her pal Barbra Streisand. There was

President Bill Clinton in one of Karan's draped wool crepe suits and First Lady Hillary Rodham Clinton hosting her first White House state dinner in 1992 in Karan's famous "cold shoulder" gown in black.

"Investors were starstruck to watch her up there," recalled Esquivel of Morgan Stanley. "It was the whole celebrity aspect of her. Everybody felt this was a deal they *had* to be in."

The glamour factor "certainly helps sell the stock initially," said Killian. "But ultimately, a fashion stock reverts to form over time." In other words, "what investors are looking for are not accolades for their fashions or from their peer group, but more consistent growth—sound financial growth and management."

As always in the erratic world of fashion, past performance was never any guarantee of future results, which was why fashion issues would always be high-risk investments.

"Fashion companies can be good, family-owned businesses, but most of them aren't cut out to be public companies," asserted Arnold Cohen, the principal of Mahoney Cohen, a leading accounting firm on Seventh Avenue. Cohen knew this first-hand from his years as chief financial officer of Puritan Fashions, a popular New York dress manufacturer in the sixties and seventies. When Puritan began trading on the New York Stock Exchange in 1965, its annual sales exceeded $100 million and its top-selling dress label was Forever Young by Gloria Swanson, a licensed brand named for the ageless star of *Sunset Boulevard*. But in the late sixties, when the fashion winds blew in the opposite direction—pantsuits—Puritan was caught flat-footed, and it scrambled to shift into slacks. Cohen remembered: "Puritan couldn't survive in this environment."

Thanks to the tenacity of Carl Rosen, Puritan's visionary chairman, the dressmaker managed to hang on and even enjoyed a renaissance in the late 1970s, when Rosen took the leap to become the jeans licensee for Calvin Klein. But like so many apparel companies, Puritan had no executive management to speak of. So when Rosen died in 1983, Calvin Klein Inc. rushed to acquire Puritan in order to protect what had been Klein's core designer jeans business.

Cohen related a story about one of his clients, a privately owned maker of women's coats, that illustrated a recurring theme in the rag trade. This coatmaker had enjoyed healthy sales gains for years until two consecutive warm winters hammered sales, leaving the maker stuck with too much unsold inventory. So the owner elected to cut back sharply on the number of coats he produced in 1997, a decision that caused his annual sales to plummet to $74 million from $100 million. The owner had no one to answer to but himself. It would be *his* call when—if ever— to pump up the volume again. "Now that doesn't smack of a public company, does it?" Cohen asked. "Once you are public, no way can you go backwards, even if the bottom line is better at $74 million than it was at $100 million. There is always that pressure for public companies to grow."

Still, going public offered many advantages to owners, such as when aging founders were ready to cash out of their businesses. And when more fashion houses were looking for growth outside the U.S., which was another trend in the 1990s, being a public company, with an enhanced ability to raise capital, made it far easier to expand internationally.

In the early 1990s, a handful of showcase fashion IPOs started the stampede to Wall Street. All of Seventh Avenue looked on with envy and awe as Jones Apparel Group, maker of Jones New York women's apparel, went public in 1991 at $14 a share. Jones's fortunes rose with its stock price—and its founder, Sidney Kimmel, became much richer. By selling blocks of shares he owned at the right time, Kimmel personally pocketed more than $300 million between 1991 and 1997. And shareholders made out quite handsomely, too. A $1,000 investment in Jones at the May 1991 offering was valued at $5,607 by March 1997.

Then along came Tommy in 1992. Menswear maker Tommy Hilfiger Corp. issued a $15-a-share IPO on the New York Stock Exchange. Hilfiger's fashions at retail became hotter than a pistol in the ensuing years, as the popular brand gained market share to become one of the top three menswear brands in department stores, along with Polo Ralph Lauren and Nautica. An initial $1,000 investment from the Hilfiger offering at $7.50 a share (adjusted for a stock split) was worth $6,866 by March 1997.

Those fashion issues were among the few best-case scenarios—and the examples everybody on Seventh Avenue repeated as the justification to go public. But some of the most touted fashion issues also turned out to be dogs, whose stocks collapsed within a year of their coming to the market. A $1,000 investment in Guess Inc. at the time of its August 1996 IPO had shrunk in value to $611 by March 1997. Likewise, $1,000 spent on Mossimo's shares in February 1996 were worth $548 twelve months later. And only nine months after Donna Karan's June 1996 IPO, a $1,000 investment in DK had a value of $458.

Donna Karan's sorry performance broke the spell and cast a dark shadow around the entire sector. "The Donna Karan IPO did a lot to hurt the perception of the apparel business among today's investors," Margaret Mager, apparel analyst at Goldman Sachs, told *WWD* in 1998. Subsequently, there were far fewer new issues after Donna Karan, as Wall Street began losing its taste for fashion.

Clearly, Donna Karan's travails were unique to its operations, but Wall Street wasn't necessarily buying that argument. To quell the skeptics, at least one apparel maker adopted a new spin for its IPO. When Columbia Sportswear, a Portland, Oregon, maker of parkas and jackets geared to snowboarding, skiing, and fishing (1997 sales of $350 million), went to the market in early 1998, it took pains to distance itself from the likes of Donna Karan and Mossimo. In road-show presentations to institutional investors, Columbia skirted the F-word, preferring to describe clothes as "outdoor" apparel instead of fashion.

"High fashion and Wall Street are like oil and vinegar. They don't mix," declared Alan Millstein, a New York fashion industry consultant. "The best public companies out there, like Liz Claiborne, Jones Apparel, and St. John Knits, are safer than the others because they don't depend on selling runway clothes." But for Donna Karan, the runway was the center of her fashion universe, where the yellow-brick road to going public all began.

IN 1985, KARAN opened the doors of her fashion house to such fanfare that in record time, she shot to the top as America's best-known designer, beloved by executive women. And she became the last women's designer to cross the threshold into the major leagues. There have been no shortage of promising, media-savvy talents coming on the scene since then—such as Isaac Mizrahi, Marc Jacobs, Michael Kors, Todd Oldham, and Cynthia Rowley—but none of them flew very high, nowhere near the $100-million-a-year mark in sales. And many crashed, notably the celebrated Mizrahi, who shuttered his business in 1998 after ten unprofitable years. "Donna is an innovator; the only world-class designer to ever come out of Seventh Avenue since Anne Klein," said Millstein.

After Karan, it was as if some invisible hand had pulled up the drawbridge. The fact that Karan had managed to break through the ranks when so many others couldn't owed a great deal to her extraordinary talents as a designer and marketer. But Karan also lucked out, with a number of pluses that greatly facilitated her ascent.

Timing, for one. Karan got in on the ground floor during the designer wave of the 1980s, when she was able to fill a need for a new generation of affluent women, many of whom were advertising executives and investment bankers over thirty. These women could afford to wear the luxurious designer creations by Bill Blass or Oscar de la Renta, who were the favorites of Nancy Reagan and the ladies-who-lunch set. But high-powered baby boomers wanted a designer of their own generation and there weren't many to choose from—Giorgio Armani had barely begun his push into women's wear. So women gravitated to Karan, who gave them clothes that were glamorous, sophisticated, and very modern. What's more, Karan's target customers could easily identify with a designer who was an ambitious career woman, married with a daughter.

Furthermore, Karan had been blessed by having secured what young designers didn't get anymore: deep-pocketed private investors who were also experienced managers in apparel manufacturing. When Ralph Lauren and Calvin Klein went into business in the late 1960s, they didn't need a wealthy benefactor—each was able to scrape together the $10,000 or so that it took to open a fashion company. But that was long before the marketplace became inundated with fashion designers and the price of entry rose dramatically. Launching a prestigous designer business in New York in the 1990s required real capital, at least a million dollars. And because establishing a new fashion house took years, and success was such a crapshoot, few independent investors were willing to take a flier on an untested designer who was more likely to fail than to succeed.

Financiers such as Taki and Mori were rare and the last of their kind. They poured more than $10 million of capital into Donna Karan for more than a decade, and their business acumen was critical in turning Karan's dream into a thriving enterprise.

It has often been said that fashion designers are born, not made. And true to legend, Donna Ivy Faske had fashion in her bloodline. She grew up in the sixties in suburban Woodmere, Long Island, where her mother,

Helen Richie Faske, known as "Queenie," was a showroom model and sales representative for manufacturers in New York's garment district. Her father, who died when she was three, was a tailor, while her step-father, Harold Flaxman, toiled in the rough and tumble of the rag trade's dress business.

Young Donna, by her own admission, was a terrible student, one who cut classes and lied about her age to land her first job, selling clothes at a neighborhood boutique at age fourteen. "I was always a working person," she once recalled. "I knew fashion was a part of me whether I'd be a retailer or an illustrator or what. I knew I was artistic. Whether I was artistic enough was a real question in my mind."

With her shaky high school record, Donna had to use her mother's connections with Seventh Avenue designer Chester Weinberg in order to get admitted into New York's Parsons School of Design, one of the top fashion schools. Finally in her element, Donna flourished at Parsons alongside classmates Louis Dell'Olio, Bill Robinson, and Willi Smith, who would go on to become famous designers. Donna stood out by winning student awards for her designs, and she caught the eye of designer Anne Klein, the doyenne of American sportswear at the time. Klein took a shine to the spirited young talent, who dropped out of Parsons to become one of her assistants.

But Donna was unfocused on the job and proved to be a handful for the demanding Klein, who fired her after a few months. Over the next eighteen months, Donna finally got herself together, as she moved on to another sportswear house, then settled down and got married to Mark Karan, a Long Island boutique owner. In 1974, she went back to Anne Klein, who gave her a second chance.

Knocking on Anne Klein's door the year before was Tomio Taki, a wealthy Tokyo businessman who had come to Manhattan to buy a fashion company. Taki had no experience on Seventh Avenue, but he was deeply rooted in apparel making, having spent his early career in his family's business, Takihyo Group, a two-hundred-year-old apparel, textile, and consumer products company based in Nagoya, Japan.

In 1960, Taki's father put him through a test. Young Taki had to develop an apparel factory in Okinawa, an island where labor costs were high. Taki first had to determine which garments the Okinawan workers could make efficiently and would also generate healthy profit margins. He settled on producing cotton raincoats, which the factory eventually exported to the U.S. by the thousands.

Landing in New York, Taki once again had to figure things out. He went about doing some practical market research. With the help of several business contacts, he sent dozens of ordinary women on a shopping mission: to secretly cut out the hang tags from clothes by their favorite upscale designers. From the thickest stacks of tags—Bill Blass, Halston, and Anne Klein—Taki began making overtures. He ultimately bought a 50 percent stake in Anne Klein & Co. from investors Gunther Oppenheim and Sandy Smith, leaving designer Anne Klein and her husband, Chip, who ran her sales showroom, owning the other half of the business.

Gunther Oppenheim was a legendary garment district impresario, who liked to make his money fast, without a lot of hassles, to "get the order, make it, ship it," remembered Dexter Levy, the former chief financial officer of Anne Klein. As America's most acclaimed designer sportswear brand, Anne Klein was a perennial top seller at department stores—so Oppenheim had no complaints about sales.

But what made him furious were the spiraling expenses Klein incurred in the design studio, where she spent lavishly on fabrics and samples to create her famous collections. Levy remembered: "Anne was legendary for flying all over the world, looking for the best fabrics, at any and all costs." He estimated that she spent as much as $1 million a year just in sample fabrics, at a time when the company's sales were about

$10 million. As the studio's bills swelled with her creative whims, Oppenheim flew off the handle. "Gunther was always battling with Anne, telling her 'You've gotta sell this! I ain't Chase Manhattan Bank!' " Levy recalled, adding that Oppenheim was obsessed about costs because "half of the money in the company was his, and he was tightfisted."

When Taki showed up, Oppenheim was in his seventies, had recently remarried, and was good and ready to cash out of Anne Klein. Levy said: "Gunther wasn't interested in fighting the fights with Anne and Chip anymore. Tom [Taki] made them [Oppenheim and Smith] a fair offer and they left the business."

Less than a year after Taki entered the picture, in October 1974, Klein suddenly died of cancer. Taki promptly promoted her top assistant, Donna Karan, who was twenty-six and about to give birth to her first child at the time, and he hired her Parson's buddy Louis Dell'Olio to help her. (Taki eventually acquired the rest of Anne Klein from widower Chip Klein.)

In the beginning, according to Levy, Taki was more of a passive investor in Anne Klein, spending most of his time in Tokyo in his family's business. But in 1975, he hired Frank Mori, a seasoned garment industry veteran and Harvard MBA, to run Anne Klein. The fashion house continued to thrive under Karan and Dell'Olio, and Karan quickly gained confidence, Levy noted. "Donna grew in the job. When the Saks buyers came in, she sold the line herself in the showroom. She began to think she was Anne Klein reincarnate, that *she* represented the organization."

And Karan, just like her late mentor, was a big spender. "She had picked up all of Anne's bad habits," said Levy, who remembered one time in the mid-1970s: "I went to what I thought was a dry run for the fashion show and I came back the next day and Donna had worked all night, completely changing the second half of the show." Karan and Mori often argued bitterly about her penchant to waste money. "They had some life and death struggles, but generally she would cave in to Frank," Levy said.

Taki and Mori, partners in Takihyo USA, however, got along quite well in business. "There are no power plays here," Mori once said about their relationship. Taki's low-key cerebral style was a sharp contrast to Seventh Avenue's tightly controlled family businesses. When managers visited Taki's office in New York, they had little reason to be intimidated. Instead of a traditional desk in his office, there was a round mahogany table with four armchairs. Taki invited visitors to "sit wherever you want."

Over the next decade, Karan and Dell'Olio proved that the Anne Klein trademark could have a long afterlife. The formidable design duo won three Coty Awards, fashion's equivalent to the Oscars at the time. They also designed Anne Klein II, which was one of the first bridge collections, priced a notch below designer brands and sold in department stores. Anne Klein had more than twenty licensees for jewelry, scarves, belts, and such, and its annual sales grew to more than $400 million at its peak in the late 1980s.

By 1983, Karan felt she had outgrown Anne Klein. She wanted to stretch, to express herself with her own high-fashion collection. As she became harder to manage, Mori made it easy for her to leave: He fired her. Karan had an employment contract with an annual salary of $1 million, which meant that Mori and Taki were obliged to pay her for the remaining years of the contract.

"Donna pushed this thing to the brink—and they realized the liability," said Levy. "So they made an arrangement with her to use her severance pay to back her in business. They felt that they could cap their liability and control how much they would have to put in the business. They didn't worry because Donna was a great designer, a proven commodity."

In 1985, Taki and Mori spun off Karan into her own house, leaving Dell'Olio to continue at Anne Klein. Karan now had everything going for her. She had divorced Mark Karan and married an old flame, Stephan Weiss, a sculptor and a divorcee with two children. And she had her very own fashion house where she wasn't simply an employee, but an equal partner.

The fact that Karan always owned 50 percent of her company seemed highly unusual because moneymen typically weren't so generous. Financial backers always retained the majority stake so that they could retain the power to control. But when Karan negotiated with Taki and Mori, she insisted on owning half of her namesake company. Taki, who was known to be generous in his business dealings, came around to agree that she needed a substantial stake in the venture. Taki recalled: "I wanted her to be confident and by owning half of the company she would have that confidence. I gave it to her to encourage her to build her own equity base." But down the road, he would regret his largess.

Karan also got something else that Taki agreed was important for the company's image: the title of chief executive officer. Although they never put it in writing, Taki claimed, "it was always understood that she made the marketing and fashion decisions, and we made the financial decisions. This is the way it was supposed to be. And it wasn't a problem at the beginning. At the start, it was the three of us. Usually if we said no to anything, she wouldn't say anything more."

But this harmony would change after Karan's husband, Weiss, became more involved with the company. During the first few seasons, when the fashion house was mired in production and delivery problems, Weiss stepped in to help. "I needed a fire helmet because I was putting out fires all day," he told *Working Woman* in 1993. Weiss also admitted that he wasn't comfortable during the times his position put him in an "adversarial role with Donna, which I didn't like." Eventually, Weiss bowed out of the day-to-day management and shifted his energies to directing the company's new ventures and licensing.

Taki characterized Weiss as a diligent, hard worker, one who was learning on the job about the fashion business. Weiss once approached Taki to seek his own stake for himself in Donna Karan. Taki responded to him: "Go talk to Donna," who eventually split her 50 percent interest in her house with him. Soon, Weiss was attending the partners' quarterly planning meetings, where all the company's key decisions were made.

With Weiss joining in the mix, the meetings became more confrontational, since Karan now had an ally. Taki remembered, "Unfortunately, the combination of Donna and Steve became too much of a problem. Sometimes, it was Donna and Steve against me and Frank, or Steve and Frank against Donna. I had to calm them down."

The high-strung Karan was famous for throwing fits when she couldn't get her way with Taki and Mori. According to Taki: "She would sit down on the couch, scream, yell, and cry to influence us. She'd walk out of the meeting. So what were we going to do? I might have to say, 'Okay, Donna.' " In other words, "Donna always gets what she wants."

And to some observers, Karan had been getting what she wanted for a very long time. When Karan finally arrived on Seventh Avenue, all the fashion editors and top retail executives, like Dawn Mello, president of Bergdorf Goodman, were rooting for her. Her fashions hit the ground selling—first at wholesale, then in stores. The fact that Takihyo owned Anne Klein provided real leverage with department store buyers; every major retailer who carried Anne Klein was inclined to give Karan's fashions good play on the sales floor.

It wasn't as if retailers needed much convincing, because Karan designed clothes that were special and very salable. Her fashion concept was built around the idea of a man's wardrobe—interchangeable tops and bottoms, rather than outfits. Women loved Karan's staples: a body suit—a fitted blouse that snapped in the crotch so that it never came untucked—a slim dress, a wrap skirt, pants, and a jacket. Everything came in sophisticated solids like navy, black, burgundy, or cream in luxurious silk, cashmere, and fine wool. The collection, priced from $150 for a bodysuit to $2,000 for a skirt and jacket, had an urban edge with a touch of sexiness. In addition, Karan got plenty of mileage from her earliest celebrity customers such as Candice Bergen, Diane Sawyer, and Barbara Walters, who were fashion role models to millions of women.

But the best role model for Donna Karan New York was Karan herself. She had the ultimate credibility because she looked like her customers: big-boned and hippy, a healthy size 12. Her designs were slimming and flattering: Her gathered wrap skirts hid tummies while her wedge-shaped dress made women look taller. And women swore by Donna Karan's opaque pantyhose, made by Hanes. The designer stockings were a breakthrough, fortified with Lycra, which made women's legs look firmer and longer—and every hosiery maker rushed to copy them.

Indeed, she had the golden touch. Never bothering to do any market research, Karan confessed, "I design from my guts. Before every season, I open up my closet and see what's missing. Then I design what I want to wear." From her guts came another winner—the casual, urbane DKNY sportswear collection that became a $100 million business in its first year, 1989, and ultimately the backbone of her company. Karan herself dreamed up the catchy name; she said that DKNY had a nice ring to it, like NYPD.

But coupled with Karan's canny fashion sense were her quirky work habits, which threw a wrench into the system. Donna Karan's signature collection always came in late, arriving weeks after other designer collections were already on the sales floor. Late deliveries were a chronic problem that plagued the company from the start and continued to wreak havoc a decade later. It seemed illogical that Karan couldn't meet a deadline.

"In my opinion, Donna is the most brilliant designer in the market," said Stephen Ruzow, "but the collection is her personal signature and it changes as Donna changes." While other designers prepared their spring collections in time for buyers to order in February for June delivery, Karan's collection was never ready until after her April fashion show, which made it impossible to turn orders around quickly. "Retailers complain about this consistently, but Donna is on her own time frame," Ruzow explained. To work around her habits, the company created another label called Donna Karan Signature, designed by a team of her closest assistants, which arrived at the stores ahead of her top collection, to ensure that the store shelves weren't empty. Fortunately, her bread-and-butter DKNY collections, which was designed by a separate staff, made it to the stores on time.

Late deliveries were more than a mere inconvenience to stores. In the 1990s, designers stepped up their pace in delivering fresh merchandise to stores every few weeks. Stores marked down slow sellers to make room for the next round of deliveries. So Karan, running on her own clock, was ruining the flow of merchandise—and causing her company to miss out on sales. Timing played a big role in how Escada, a German fashion house, built a mighty $700-million-a-year business in the 1980s. Escada didn't do fashion shows and instead designed its production timetable so that Escada fashions always beat other designer brands to the sales floor.

Nevertheless, retailers put up with Karan's late deliveries for years because during most seasons, her clothes managed to sell briskly whenever they arrived, which was a testament to her tremendous pull with women. Karan built a cult following of well-to-do women who dressed head-to-toe in whatever Karan served up each season. Karan herself was the consummate saleswoman when she made in-store appearances like the one she did one February morning in 1993 at Bergdorf's. Karan was a whirling dervish, darting from one dressing room to another, telling perfect strangers exactly what to try on and what to buy—just like girlfriends do when they shop at the mall. Bergdorf's clients were wide-eyed, hanging on her every word, and many left with shopping bags full of Donna Karans. During those heady years when Karan played personal shopper, Bergdorf's could sell as much as $800,000 worth of merchandise over the span of a few days.

Karan achieved this loyalty by designing her fashion image to be as important as her clothes. Image marketing was the mark of fashion houses in the 1990s, and Karan, along with Calvin Klein and Ralph Lauren, was among the best. Karan was already thinking about fashioning her image back in 1984, before her house even opened, when she hired advertising whiz Peter Arnell. He helped her create a persona that permeated everything, starting with her sleek Donna Karan New York black and gold logo. Karan's advertising was evocative without having to show clothes— such as a black-and-white shot of the Brooklyn Bridge on a foggy day. In the early years, Karan always took her runway bow to the recording of her chosen anthem, "A New York State of Mind," belted out by her buddy Barbra Streisand.

Karan's ads also featured an idealized image of herself: brunette model Rosemary McGrotha, who once was shown in a speeding limousine, balancing a Filofax and a baby. Another memorable ad, "In woman we trust," featured McGrotha being sworn in as president, with a lacy black bustier peeking out from the top of her blouse. Karan fortified her feminist, go-getter message through a dialogue with her fans in her *Woman to Woman* newsletter. A typical excerpt:

"To me, the future is all about personal style, not designer dictates. My role is to offer women the freedom and tools to pull it together in a completely modern, sexy way—with simplified pieces that are timeless, luxurious, and flexible enough to go day into evening. This is not about a season; it's about everything I stand for. . . . That's why I think of these clothes as a celebration of personal style. From one woman to another."

With her squinty smile, a sweater tied around her waist, snuggling next to her handsome hunk of an artist husband, Karan seemed to be having it all. She came across as one smart cookie with a head for numbers. In a September 1989 cover story for *Manhattan Inc.*, writer Jennet Conant noted that Karan was "intimately acquainted with the bottom line."

But four years later, during another interview, she revealed more honestly to *Working Woman*, "What's business to me isn't about facts and figures but the image of the company that all begins with product. When I see a balance sheet the small print drives me crazy. For me, it all has to be visual."

So while Karan wrapped herself around the "product," Mori and Taki and Ruzow and others took care of the nitty-gritty fine print. As Ron Frasch, a former Neiman Marcus executive, explained to *Working Woman:* Ruzow "insures that a company with a creative head and diverse divisions is pulled together—and that Donna gets the credit."

Once a week, Karan broke away from her creative agenda when she and Ruzow got into the habit of meeting in her Manhattan apartment to review business matters from a long to-do list that tumbled out of her overstuffed leather tote. Often, Ruzow had to rein her in to keep her from taking on too many new projects. "She would do everything tomorrow because she is so prolific. My job is to keep the business in focus," Ruzow said.

As a private company, the fashion house was cleverly designed just like a Donna Karan pantsuit: to capitalize on Karan's strengths and compensate for her flaws. But harking back to the years of Anne Klein, Taki and Mori would always object to the outrageous expenses coming from the design studio, which was the deep, black hole at every fashion house.

In the trial-and-error process of creating high-fashion collections, designers spent hundreds of thousands of dollars to make sample garments for every collection. Karan's studio was her baby—her special sanctuary where she created her runway collections, where her ego and her artistic reputation were on the line. Accordingly, Karan pulled out the stops, just like her mentor Anne Klein had done. "We creative types like to spend," an unflinching Karan said in October 1996.

Every year, Karan and her design team traveled to Paris to *Premier Vision*, the leading fabric trade show, which drew the top producers from around the world. Such business trips, and side trips to London and Milan, yielded a bounty: scores of seven-meter fabric samples and lots of research material, clothes bought from auctions and flea markets and from the trendiest independent boutiques, like Egg, Karan's favorite haunt in London.

Returning to her New York studio, alongside pattern makers, sewers, fitting models, and other design assistants, Karan got down to the nuts and bolts of designing a collection. Some designers such as Dell'Olio worked from their own sketches, from which they envisioned an entire collection. This was the efficient way to design, minimizing the number of sample garments that needed to be made.

But Karan, who didn't sketch well, tinkered painstakingly with sample garments that were made many times over. And because Karan manufactured her samples in Italy as well as New York, and made many, many changes along the way, costs mounted quickly.

"Donna is the most brilliant artist, but she has a hard time deciding," said one of her former studio assistants. "Right up until the day before the show, she is still making changes on the collection." (According to this assistant, Karan would be so taxed during this process that she began taking vitamin B_{12} injections to fortify her for the countdown crunch right before her fashion shows, and she encouraged her assistants to do the same.) The design team got used to the company's bean counters, who carped about the problem of "oversampling" and the need to cut back. "But nothing ever happened, because nobody ever says no to Donna," this former staffer said. "She'll have a hundred fabrics pinned up against the wall and she wants to see how all of them look made up."

So why didn't anyone stop her before she killed the budget again and again? Taki and Mori swallowed hard when Karan overspent, but they stopped short of turning off the spigot. "In creating financial success, you have to support creative people and what they want to do. That is an obligation," Taki said.

So then it was left to Ruzow to juggle, to work around Karan's unorthodox ways. "Whenever the costs got over budget, we shipped more goods to stores to help fix the bottom line," said Ruzow.

But Karan's overspending and constant bickering wore down Taki and Mori. The drama finally came to a head in 1992, when Karan was ready to introduce her first perfume.

Since the 1980s, designer perfumes had become like a license to print money. A popular designer perfume could generate fat profits year after year—and the beauty of it all was that it had to be designed only once. Given the mystique surrounding Donna Karan, her first fragrance was certain to be a sure thing. But in order to take off, the perfume needed a high-octane launch: tens of millions of dollars in advertising and marketing. That's how Calvin Klein created his succession of blockbuster fragrances like Obsession, Eternity, and CK One. He left the marketing to the experts, which in his case happened to be his fragrance licensee, Unilever, which, as is typical in licensing deals, was responsible for all development costs and advertising. Calvin Klein rolled up his sleeves during the development phase, but after that he could sit back and collect a big royalty check every year, amounting to millions of dollars that were virtually free and clear of expenses.

But not Donna. After she made the rounds to experts Estée Lauder, Revlon, and Cosmair, she wasn't satisfied. She wanted a higher-than-usual royalty fee and, not surprisingly, total control. She and Weiss talked it over and agreed that they could do it better themselves, so the perfume should be done in-house.

That's when Taki and Mori hit the roof. They were apparel makers who knew their limitations—even if Karan didn't. "We had so many people who wanted to give us money to do her fragrance. We didn't need to do it ourselves," Taki said.

But again, Donna had it *her* way. Weiss, the sculptor, designed the black and gold bottle for the Donna Karan New York fragrance, which was meant to resemble the torso of a female nude seen from the back. The high-concept scent was a blend of cashmere, suede, Casablanca lilies, "and the back of my husband's neck," in Karan's words. The smell was faint, perhaps too subtle. "The scent was meant for me and my husband and not for someone across the room or the next woman in the elevator," Karan told *Vogue*.

"I know this is not the way fragrances get developed. But we wanted to make something so special and precious, it needed plenty of tender loving care. We have started something from nothing and if I'm going to make a mistake, it had better be a small one! Because it could damage the heartbeat of our huge apparel company."

Those were famous last words. The Donna Karan New York fragrance became a cautionary tale on how *not* to do it. In the first six months, the perfume registered losses of $5.9 million, on sales of $4.1 million. That seemed implausible. No designer as high-profile as Karan had ever *lost* money on a perfume!

But this was amateur hour—a case study of a fragrance launched on the cheap. There was no advertising blitz—not even scent strips inserted into magazines. Furthermore, Donna Karan fans were forced to hunt for the perfume, which was initially available only at Bloomingdale's or through a toll-free mail-order line. The telemarketers taking the orders couldn't even pronounce the designer's name correctly, greeting callers with a chipper "Hello, Donna KO-ran." And Weiss's sculpture-of-a-spray-bottle was prone to leakage, leaving a trail of unsatisfied customers.

The fragrance debacle was a watershed, the coup de grâce for Taki and Mori, who were tired of tussling with Karan. The backers got ready to back out.

SO IT WAS time to head to Wall Street. With the help of investment bankers at Bear Stearns, the company began to make the necessary preparations for an initial public offering. The preliminary prospectus, filed in August 1993, revealed that Taki and Mori would be exiting the company, leaving Karan and Weiss to become the company's co-chief executive officers. The company's annual sales at the time were $258.5 million, with a net income of $29 million—and 90 percent of the sales came from DKNY and other women's wear. All of the newer divisions—children's wear, menswear, and fragrance—were unprofitable to date.

Understandably, the institutional investors who read that first outline were reluctant to jump on board. Despite its popularity, the House of Karan had a long road ahead to prove that it could succeed moving other merchandise besides women's clothes. And leading the charge in the future would be two creative, nonbusiness people, Karan and Weiss.

Just as Wall Streeters began to take a closer look, to search for the substance behind the Donna Karan style, many would-be investors got cold feet. Some unsettling news had hit the fan involving Leslie Fay Companies.

In 1993, the venerable Seventh Avenue dressmaker was embroiled in a messy accounting scandal. During a year-end audit that January, Leslie Fay's corporate controller admitted that he and others in the back offices had been overstating the company's sales and income by making false entries into the company's books. When Leslie Fay dropped this bombshell in February, its shares took a nosedive on the New York Stock Exchange. By April, the beleaguered company was forced to reorganize under Chapter 11 bankruptcy.

During an internal investigation of Leslie Fay in the following months, so much bad news trickled out that the company's reputation was forever ruined. As it turned out, the books had been cooked at Leslie Fay for years. Leslie Fay wound up having to restate its earnings for the past three years, effectively wiping out $81 million of previously reported net income that never existed. The price of Leslie Fay shares fell to under a dollar a share, which forced the company off the New York Stock Exchange. The controller who blew the whistle and the company's chief financial officer were eventually indicted by a federal grand jury, while John Pomerantz, Leslie Fay's CEO, who claimed absolutely no knowledge of the scheme, managed to escape charges—but not embarrassment—and was eventually cleared of any wrongdoing after the investigation. The mystery of Leslie Fay continues as the two indictments have yet to result in any punitive damages or jail terms, seven years after the fact.

As the Leslie Fay soap opera played out during 1993, all of Seventh Avenue was aghast and sullied by association. Leslie Fay personified the ugly stereotype of the old-time garmento who played it fast and loose— a depiction that legitimate apparel makers had been trying to shake for years. With the overhang of the Leslie Fay scandal, 1993 was hardly the climate for Donna Karan to go public.

What's more, Donna Karan had its own problems to contend with, since the sales of its women's collections began to slump that year. There was no way the fashion house would meet its internal earnings projections. Any stock offering embarked upon against that backdrop—if indeed it managed to squeak through—would depress the overall value of the company. So Karan, Weiss, and Mori held a press conference in New York to call the whole thing off, for the time being.

After that very public false start, the Donna Karan organization retreated back to business, somewhat as usual. Weiss was now in the executive suite, with Karan as the company's co-chief executive. As Weiss went about issuing orders around the office, he crossed many people at the company, especially Frank Mori. Most people in the industry thought that Weiss, the artist-turned-CEO, was in way over his head.

"He wasn't credible," said Millstein, the consultant. "He was inexperienced. . . . He had the job because his wife wanted him to come to work every day in a suit and tie, not in [an artist's] smock."

Karan told *New York* in May 1996 that the relentless bashing of Weiss "burns my butt. I cannot believe after all these years we are still discussing that about my husband who has done an extraordinary job. . . . If anybody thinks I did it [alone], we did it."

SOMEWHERE ALONG THE way, Karan got religion. During the early 1990s, she had embarked on a new personal journey of self-introspection and she began to explore her spirituality through Eastern philosophy and the teachings of New Age guru Deepak Chopra. Eventually, Karan's newfound beliefs found their way into her business. Her fashion-show music also became more ethereal, like the time the models walked down the catwalk to a recording of Chopra reading his poetry. And the clothes looked otherworldly, too. Karan had all but abandoned her signature sexy sleek and began experimenting with dowdy-looking long skirts and baggy tops. A lot of retailers and customers missed the sexy Donna look, but Karan didn't seem to care. She had to keep evolving.

Given her rocky relations with Mori and Taki, Karan had to hold her company together in order to make another pass at Wall Street. She must have been heartened after watching Gucci make a splash with its IPO in 1995. The Italian fashion house had been riding high with Tom Ford, the hottest designer of the moment, and a red-hot stock. Investcorp, the Bahrain-based investment bank that bought Gucci in 1987 for $245 million, made $1.6 billion on selling Gucci shares, in two deals: an October 1995 IPO and a secondary offering five months later.

By the spring of 1996, the house of Karan was all dressed up and ready to go to the stock market again. The company's balance sheet was now cleaned up, and the fashion house looked a lot more promising: annual sales were $510 million, or about double the 1993 sales. There were no more losses in menswear—the men's division was actually profitable and growing—and children's wear had been discontinued. Only the beauty business—the fragrance, lotions, and skin-care line—still wasn't making money.

In the 1996 offering, Karan was now listed as the chairman and the sole CEO of the company, while Weiss held the title of vice chairman, continuing to oversee the company's beauty business and legal and licensing departments. The prospectus gave a cryptic definition of his new role: "While Mr. Weiss's office will not necessarily be a full-time position, he will spend substantial amounts of time as vice chairman." No one understood what that meant.

Surprisingly, one aspect of the offering, a royalty payment to Karan and Weiss, managed to pass muster with prospective investors. The royalty payment was in connection with the company's most valuable asset, its trademarks, which after the offer would belong to Karan and Weiss through Gabrielle Studio, a company named after Karan's daughter. For the use of the "Donna Karan," "DKNY," and "DK" trademarks, the public company agreed to pay an annual royalty, based on a percentage of sales, starting at 1.75 percent for the first $250 million plus 2.5 percent of the next $500 million in sales, and so forth. It seemed unusual—and downright greedy—that Karan and Weiss would take ownership of the trademarks, which were the most valuable asset the company had other than Karan herself. At other publicly owned designer companies such as Tommy Hilfiger, Liz Claiborne, and Polo Ralph Lauren, the trademarks belonged to the company, not the designers.

Here's how it worked. In the offering, Karan and Weiss collected the same as Taki and Mori—$58 million, and about a 25 percent stake in the public company. In addition, the creative couple was entitled to a $5 million royalty from Gabrielle Studio. After the IPO, the company would continue to pay millions in royalties to Gabrielle Studio every year.

Morgan Stanley, the lead underwriter in the deal, advised against this arrangement, as did Taki and Mori. But Karan and Weiss flatly refused to relinquish the royalty stream, claiming that it was Karan, after all, who was the company's visionary and who deserved to own the trademarks that she alone had made valuable. Taki was pissed. He countered that if anybody deserved to share in the ownership of the trademarks, it should have been him and Mori, who put the fashion house in business and had put up with Donna all those years.

But the royalty payment didn't seem to faze all those wide-eyed investors, who couldn't wait to get their hands on DK shares. Later, when the company's fortunes began to evaporate, most institutional shareholders felt as if they had been duped.

One bright spot that DK shareholders had been looking forward to was the company's plan to grow through lucrative licensing deals. Everything was right on track in early 1996, after Donna Karan had signed an agreement with jeans maker Designer Holdings Inc. to make DKNY jeans. Designer Holdings made an initial $6 million payment to the public company, and agreed to pay $54 million more over the next four years, plus 7 percent royalties on sales every year.

Designer Holdings, itself a recent new listing on the New York Stock Exchange, had done a fine job with Calvin Klein's jeanswear. In just two years Designer Holdings had more than tripled sales of Calvin Klein jeans to more than $400 million in 1996. Arnold Simon, Designer Holdings' chairman, vowed to do the same for DKNY jeans, whose sales were about $50 million in 1995. Simon had visions of a $300 million DKNY jeans business after only about three years.

But the DKNY jeans deal came unzipped only months after it was signed. In March 1997, Donna Karan and Designer Holdings agreed to dissolve the partnership, citing "unexpected difficulties." The day the news broke, DK shares dropped again to $11.25—or less than half the offering price.

After the fact, Simon spilled the back story: the frustrating back-and-forth exchanges he endured in dealing with Karan and a number of the company's executives, all of whom, it seemed, wanted to put their two cents in about the terms of his contract. The sticking point was fundamental: Karan wanted to limit Designer Holdings to making denim jeans and nothing else; Simon insisted on making a jeanswear collection, as he had for Calvin Klein.

"The contract stated I will have a jeanswear license comparable to other jeanswear licensees in the industry," asserted Simon. "Of course I know what that means. I can't just make five-pocket jeans, but a whole collection of tops and bottoms. But they were only going to let me do jeans and two T-shirts. I mean, how do you go into this business with *two T-shirts*?"

But Ruzow sustained that the deal with Designer Holdings was "very explicit" because Donna Karan had never intended for its licensee to produce a jeanswear collection that could cannibalize its own DKNY sportswear collections made in-house. "Arnie signed the license knowing that. He just went ahead, knowing that he would eventually get what he wanted," Ruzow said.

In canceling the contract, Donna Karan agreed to give back the $6 million payment to Designer Holdings and $4 million more in development costs. But having already counted on the $6 million windfall, Donna Karan had already splurged on a new advertising campaign starring Demi Moore and Bruce Willis. The stars were paid in clothes, and $2.3 million went to buy ad space, mainly in Europe, where the company was getting ready to open boutiques in Stockholm, Moscow, Amsterdam, Berlin, and Barcelona. Management figured it could afford to spend more on advertising because, according to Ruzow, "We were on track to make our ad budget for the year and the pictures were fabulous. It was a once-in-a-lifetime shot, we felt that it was a good time to increase our exposure."

But at year-end, those ad expenses stood out like a sore thumb on the company's income statement in a year that Donna Karan didn't meet its earnings targets. DK shareholders reacted bitterly to the broken deal with Designer Holdings. They promptly filed a class-action lawsuit against the company in federal court, charging Karan and her top officers with mismanagement. (The suit was dismissed in 1998.)

Because Takihyo still owned Anne Klein, a competitor with Donna

Karan, Mori and Taki were legally barred from being involved with internal Donna Karan matters. But Mori was too frustrated to stand by and watch Takihyo's stake of 5.4 million DK shares slip any further in value. Mori appealed to the board of directors to waive the restriction and let him back in so that he could restructure the company he had built. But the Donna Karan board members said no. Still, the directors were motivated to act, and thus began a search for a new CEO to replace Karan.

Karan got a phone call from an eager thirty-nine-year-old candidate, John Idol, who was president of Polo Ralph Lauren's licensing divisions. The polished executive, who resembled a young Harrison Ford, was determined to win Karan and the board over, which he did. When the company announced his appointment as CEO in May 1997, Karan told reporters how impressed she was with him, remarking that he was also "cute." Karan held on to her titles as chairman and chief designer.

To be sure, Idol's arrival didn't sit well with Ruzow, who for so many years had been the de facto CEO without having the title or real authority over Karan. In the public offering, Ruzow had received a $5 million onetime payment for his efforts over the years. But there was no way that Ruzow was going to report to Idol, so he resigned from the company. He became CEO of Kate Spade, a designer handbag company, then left there after three months and became president of Calvin Klein underwear at Warnaco Group Inc., Klein's licensee.

Idol quickly began polishing the company for Wall Street, signing up Liz Claiborne to make DKNY jeans and Estée Lauder to take over the troubled beauty division in 1997. The beauty division had chalked up an estimated $100 million in losses since 1992, with its lineup of skin treatment products and fragrances named Chaos, Water Mist, Ice, Sunlight, and Rain.

Idol went about cost cutting, slashing some $40 million in annual expenses, which included layoffs of 285 employees, about 15 percent of the total workforce. Employees saw many of their perks, like clothing allowances and cellular phones, disappear. There would be no more free clothes given away to movie stars, including Barbra Streisand. And Idol was determined to come up with a new system to get the collection delivered to the stores earlier. The aggressive restructuring write-offs took the company deep into red ink in 1997—a net loss of $81.4 million on sales of $639 million. Nevertheless, Karan and Weiss enjoyed a splendid payday, collecting $17.6 million in Gabrielle Studio royalties in addition to their combined salaries of $3 million.

Having cleaned house, Idol promised good times and profits in 1998, but excessive spending wasn't the only problem at the House of Karan. Fashion was, too. Donna Karan's $37-million-a-year menswear division was doing just fine until 1997, the year Donna suddenly had a thing for men in tight suits.

Karan was playing with fire when she decided to change her menswear silhouettes. Her men's suits were expensive—$800 and up—and a big part of their appeal had always been the loose, draped silhouette that flattered men over forty, her target market. But Karan had gotten carried away with the trends coming out of Milan from Prada and Gucci, where the jackets were tight, with high armholes, worn with skinny pants. And so tight became the order of the season—on virtually all of Donna Karan's menswear.

The results were disastrous at stores like Barneys New York and Saks Fifth Avenue. It was said that some retailers didn't even bother with markdowns, they just sent the collection back to Donna Karan. During the closeouts, delighted Donna Karan fans had a field day finding bargains at Men's Wearhouse—that is, the ones who could fit into tight suits.

The fallout was even more stunning as the brand lost credibility with men who moved on to other brands like Zegna and Armani. "Consistency in menswear is critical," said Ruzow. "It's hard to win the customer back once you've disappointed them."

The tight suits didn't appear on John Idol's watch, so he had no qualms about criticizing them as a "one-time fashion moment" that would never happen again. "We will continue to break new ground in fashion, but in the future we will try to evolve and not radically move completely off into something new."

The rain poured on the women's collections as well. Idol pulled the plug on the experimental D line that had never caught on. In the past, the company had goosed up sales by shipping DKNY sportswear indiscriminately to many accounts, disregarding the fact that $400 blazers would never move in certain store locations. Idol finally cut off one hundred store locations and slashed prices of DKNY by about a third, noting that it was "ridiculous that DKNY's khaki pants were $130 when Banana Republic was selling them at $68." What's more, Donna Karan's fifty-odd outlet stores were so poorly merchandised that they weren't making money. There would be no more of that. "This is The New Donna Karan," Idol promised to investors at the Goldman Sachs Global Retailing Conference in September 1998.

Idol had much to prove—and an incentive to prevail. His $898,000 annual salary guaranteed him lucrative stock options based on the company's future stock price. "I think this will be one of the great turnaround stories on Wall Street," he promised. But with the stock trading in the $5 to $7 range at the end of 1998, he still had a lot of turning around to do.

In the meantime there was no way that Karan would be denied. She dug into her own pocket to make up for the shortfall in her design studio budget. In 1998, Karan was said to be still spending heavily, continuing to buy as much expensive fabric as she wanted. "I'll pay for it myself," she was said to have told one of her assistants. Later, in corporate filings, the company disclosed that at the end of 1997, Karan made a personal loan to the company of $7 million. The loan was characterized as a "cash cushion" for the company. "We may have to borrow from her again. We don't intend to, but we could," Joseph Parsons, the chief financial officer, explained in a statement.

But the next time Karan pulled out her checkbook, she weighed in with a gift instead of a loaner. She had found a great location on the corner of Sixtieth Street and Madison Avenue across from Calvin Klein, where she set out to build her first flagship store, to open in 1999. Her magnanimous commitment, to spend "many millions" of her own money to fund the store, played like another DK joke around Wall Street.

Meanwhile, Idol continued to sweat to make his earnings targets. In 1998, the company eked out a profit of $128,000, or one cent a share. Spinning out this thread of good news, an assured Idol pronounced, "We've turned the corner," on March 24, 1999, the day of the 1998 earnings release.

Still Wall Street wasn't impressed; the stock remained stuck in the mud at $7.25.

The year 1998 was supposed to be pivotal for Donna Karan, whose underwriter, Morgan Stanley (which became Morgan Stanley Dean Witter in 1997), had visions of DK shares bubbling up in the mid-thirties range in 1998. One of the investment bankers involved in the deal remarked in hindsight in May 1998: "Had I known then what I knew later, I would have never recommended that we do the stock offering."

———

WHILE DONNA KARAN'S travails stayed in the headlines, other fashion stocks were also having trouble staying afloat, including Guess, Marisa Christina, and Mossimo. "The post IPO of certain companies has been sloppy," said Elizabeth Evillard, managing director of PaineWebber specializing in fashion stocks. "For the first one, two, or three quarters, if the company does not make the estimates that were projected by the analysts, the market is unforgiving."

While Donna Karan International performed its comedy of errors, fashion's theater of the absurd starred Mossimo Inc., the maker of volleyball shorts, in Irvine, California. Mossimo, which took Wall Street on a wild ride, was the parable of the overhyped designer who landed into an overheated stock market.

The stock charted like a parabola. In February 1996 Mossimo went public at $18 a share, and soared steadily within months to a remarkable $51 a share, buoyed by Mossimo's grand plans to expand. But as Mossimo failed to deliver and started to screw up, the stock crashed to under $10 a year later. By October 1998, Mossimo's share price had plummeted to $2.50.

The tale of Mossimo had a storybook beginning, fueled by extraordinary luck. In 1987, Mossimo Gianulli dropped out of the University of Southern California to begin a modest apparel business in a garage with a $100,000 loan from his father, a landscape architect. Always more of a salesman than a designer, Gianulli hit the jackpot on a fluke. He put his name, "Mossimo"—scribbled in a bold, black flourish—on the T-shirts and shorts he produced. It didn't take long for the Mossimo signature to become the coolest of logos at surf shops along the West Coast. Gianulli began to think big. He hired designers to help him expand into woven shirts and casual sportswear.

It wasn't fashion innovation that caused Mossimo to pull in $44 million in sales by 1994. It was Gianulli's ability to market himself as a latter-day version of rat-packer Dean Martin, who was his idol. With his swarthy good looks, pompadour hairstyle, and sideburns, Gianulli was hired in 1994 to play a hunk in Janet Jackson's "You Want This?" music video. Moss, as his buddies called him, was a smooth, martini-drinking swinger on Hollywood's celebrity circuit, who became a cult figure among Generation X-ers on the West Coast. Starstruck young women and beach boys lined up to meet him whenever he appeared in stores.

When Mossimo went public, Gianulli entered the record books. At thirty-two, he became the youngest CEO of a New York Stock Exchange company; all of his senior executives were in their early thirties and none had ever run a public company. Mossimo's shares doubled to $37 after just three months on the stock market, giving the plucky Gianulli, who owned 70 percent of the shares, a net worth of more than $500 million, which got him listed in *Forbes* as one of the 400 richest people in America in 1996.

The cocky young fashion mogul set his sights on becoming the next Calvin Klein. Mossimo pulled out of Pacific Sunwear shops and *Surfer* magazine, and sallied into the world of Bloomingdale's, *GQ*, and *Vogue*. His luck was holding out through 1996, when Mossimo's sales climbed 30 percent to $108 million, with $10.7 million in net income, reflecting Mossimo's push into casual men's sportswear and a new women's line.

But overexpansion and inexperience did Mossimo in. By early 1997, the company was sinking under the weight of design problems, cost over-runs, late deliveries, and slumping retail sales. The Mossimo logo now seemed like a short beer in a very tall glass. By fall, shareholders headed into court to sue Mossimo, alleging that the company's officers made false and misleading statements about Mossimo's financial condition. The class-action suit charged that as Mossimo expanded, it had lost control of its operations and finances. Mossimo denied the allegations and vowed to fight the charges in court.

In March 1998, Gianulli relinquished his CEO title to become the company's "visionary." Replacing him as CEO and president was John Brinko, fifty-five, a turnaround specialist whose last rescue effort was at the troubled Barneys New York chain after it fell into Chapter 11 bankruptcy in 1996.

But Mossimo's stock only started to show signs of new life in January 1999 after the company hired a new CEO, Edwin Lewis, the former Tommy Hilfiger Corp. chief executive who retired in 1994. Ready for a new challenge, Lewis poached a few of his trusted Hilfiger executives to help him build Mossimo into the next Hilfiger. The news of Lewis's arrival lifted Mossimo's shares to the $7 to $9 range in early 1999.

IRVINE ALSO HAPPENED to be the home of one of the strongest fashion companies on the New York Stock Exchange, St. John Knits. With 1996 sales of $200 million, St. John Knits was unique—a maker of $1,200 women's knit suits that was grounded in conservative practices for more than thirty years.

For starters, St. John had amassed a loyal following of executive businesswomen who loved its Chanel-inspired suits, which had become fashion classics. At Saks Fifth Avenue, St. John's sales rose to $75 million to become Saks' most profitable vendor.

Founded in 1962 by the husband and wife team of Robert and Marie Gray, St. John invented a silk and rayon knit yarn called Santana, which it patented. Santana gave St. John's garments an edge; the clothes retained their shape and remained wrinkle-free—appealing properties that made St. John a favorite of traveling executives. St. John had few quality problems it couldn't control; the company spun and dyed Santana yarn, and produced all of its garments, buttons, and jewelry inside a sprawling industrial park in Irvine.

St. John advertised in *Vogue, Harper's Bazaar*, and the rest, but stayed clear of the hype on Seventh Avenue. "I never believed in fashion shows," said Robert Gray, St. John's CEO, in November 1997. "Whenever you get good press from those shows it always comes from some outrageous fashions—and we don't make outrageous fashions. We aren't part of that scene. If you try to create 'fashion,' that's a pretty tough job to make something different that is still wearable. We make something that is stable, with three different skirt lengths, that looks good on women. We try to satisfy the biggest customer base we can."

For a long time, the Grays, who were joined in business by their designer daughter, Kelly, didn't consider their company as a candidate for Wall Street. "It was never in my plans to go public," Gray said. "All of our growth came internally. We kept putting money back in our own company. It felt good to be running my own ship."

In 1989, the Grays sold 80 percent of their interest in St. John to Escada, the German fashion house, for about $56 million. The Grays continued running St. John, using the funds to open seventeen boutiques in Europe and Asia. But when Escada ran into its own financial troubles, it spun off St. John onto the New York Stock Exchange for $117 million in March 1993, which landed the Grays on Wall Street.

During St. John's pre-IPO road shows, Gray didn't try to fascinate potential investors with the glamour of the fashion business the way Donna had. Gray said he played it straight when he told them: "I'm a product man. What I try to do is sell product. We have had the same team for thirty-five years. We know what we are doing. We aren't trying to sell fashion or reinvent the wheel. We are trying to invest in clothes that women enjoy wearing."

St. John's impressive five-year earnings growth rates—averaging 31 percent a year on sales gains of 24 percent—made institutional investors salivate for higher and higher earnings. Gray knew he could push more merchandise out the door, but he was thinking long term. He had watched too many luxury brands lose their cachet because their merchandise was sold in too many stores. "We're not going to flood the market with goods," he said.

But even the rock-solid St. John demonstrated that old Seventh Avenue adage: You're only as good as your last season in stores.The knitwear maker got snagged in the spring of 1998 when it came out with more complicated, trendier designs. It was a wise fashion move to draw younger women into St. John's fold, but too many of the new styles had too-short skirts, which its traditional customers didn't like. And disappointing its fans even more, St. John's spring line suffered from uneven quality: dyes that didn't match, crooked pockets, and loose buttons. Redfaced, the company recalled the irregular goods from irate retailers. As expected, Wall Street was unforgiving. When St. John disclosed that for the first time in five years it wouldn't meet its earnings targets, the stock tumbled 11.5 percent to $39 on the very same day.

The market turmoil in the fall of 1998, and other internal problems at St. John's struggling Amen Wardy home furnishings division, depressed its earnings for the rest of the year. There was also an embarrassing class-action suit from shareholders, charging that management had misled investors. St. John vigorously denied the charges alleged in the lawsuit. When Gray came to New York to speak to Wall Street money managers in October 1998, he was visibly grumpy. "You know we have been getting a lot of bad press lately."

As St. John struggled to unravel its recent mistakes, there was reason to be optimistic about its future. After its long, stellar run, St. John had hit an iceberg when it got sidetracked by fashion and production problems. But the company was still profitable and imminently fixable. Women who loved the brand would be patient, at least for a while, because St. John offered a look that was unique in fashion. Nevertheless, Wall Street would make St. John pay for its errors, and the stock wouldn't recover until the company proved itself again.

But Gray didn't wait for St. John's stock to rebound. In December 1998, Gray and his family launched a $500 million buyout offer for all the outstanding St. John shares they didn't already own, in a move to become a private business again—distancing itself far from the prying eyes of Wall Street.

CLEARLY, WALL STREET is a level playing field that throws all types of companies onto the same track and expects them all to perform up to par every quarter. In the mid-1990s, Wall Street had been drawn to fashion issues, like moths to a flame, but such stocks were an enigma—glamorous, yet highly volatile—as well as investments where they could get burned. Conversely, fashion companies such as Donna Karan viewed Wall Street as a cash machine, without taking into account that institutional investors were essentially gamblers who didn't understand fashion cycles and who shot from the hip. Whenever weaker apparel stocks underperformed, everybody paid, and fashion stocks across the board took a hit.

But that's the way the Street plays fashion—tough and quick. The fashion businesses that made the leap to Wall Street had raised the bar for themselves, putting their brands under financial pressure beyond the day-to-day challenge they already had in designing and second-guessing consumer tastes. Publicly traded fashion companies had to meet a financial standard, which by definition is at odds with what is traditionally defined as fashion: that is, a trendy and unpredictable product. When a company goes public, it's the end of fashion. It means the end of too-tight pants and fashion for fashion's sake. It means commodity merchandise—polo shirts, jeans, sweaters, and blazers—that sell year in and year out. Such consistency kept the earnings up and the stock price rising at Liz Claiborne, Warnaco, VF Corp., and others.

In the mid-1990s, when Liz Claiborne's sales peaked at $2.2 billion, and its stock floundered at less than $30 a share, the apparel maker didn't find an answer from fashion. Instead Claiborne took its case directly to the people. Claiborne spent $1 million to conduct an exhaustive market research study of more than six hundred consumers, mostly in focus groups. The study, conducted in 1995 and 1996 by Arc Research in New York, employed psychologists who visited women at home, looked into their closets, and spent the day shopping with them. The intelligence Claiborne gleaned about women's preferences in fabrics, styles, fit, accessories, and colors were used by Claiborne's design teams. The strategy worked, as Claiborne's sales and profits started rising again in 1996.

But Donna Karan couldn't let go of fashion. The predicament at Donna Karan was deep-seated. John Idol's grand restructuring eliminated most of the waste, but his plans were merely scaffolding. He couldn't fix the core problem, which was Donna Karan herself. She was through and through a victim of the old school of fashion, and her spoiled habits had been tolerated, even nurtured, by Takihyo for years.

As Donna went about her personal fashion discovery, she had broken her promise: "from one woman to another." Where were the magnificent seven—the easy-to-wear wardrobe pieces that her fans depended on? They got drowned out, replaced by "twisted parachute" skirts, padded dresses, and D tube tops. Idol vowed that "The New Donna Karan" would give women what they wanted. But just as Dayton Hudson learned when it tried to make over Marshall Field's, the consumer will let you know when you get it right. The House of Karan had miles to go—at least a couple of years—before it could turn itself around, while New Age Donna had yet to find herself in the religion of Wall Street.

OUTSIDE OF THE BOX: ZORAN

You don't have to be scientist to do fashion.
You have to **sell,** *and that's that.*

ZORAN, February 1998

$\mathcal{T}$he two hundred fashion enthusiasts who showed up for the noon session of a fashion symposium at New York University on November 6, 1998, were primed to meet Oscar de la Renta, the dashing, Dominican-born couture designer who caters to American socialites and First Lady Hillary Rodham Clinton. But de la Renta—jockeying between couture assignments for Balmain in Paris and for his own Seventh Avenue house—was forced to cancel at the last minute. Instead, the audience would get a heady dose of high-fashion stimulation from Zoran Ladicorbic, a New York designer who they probably didn't know sold clothes that were more expensive than de la Renta's. In the world of fashion, he was known simply as Zoran. The Z in his logotype was a bold slash, the mark of a swashbuckler. And if ever there was a designer who had cut through the established order, it was Zoran.

Zoran was the vision of a modern Einstein that day, with his bushy gray hair and thick beard, in a baggy black pullover and loose black pants. Instead of making a speech, Zoran answered questions, expounding on his minimalist take on fashion, which had served him splendidly for more than twenty years. As he held forth in his scratchy Slavic accent, dropping his articles and prepositions, a blond model canvassed the room dressed in several combinations of his luxurious styles: a sarong skirt, a quilted jacket, pants, and a floor-length shift gown, all in cashmere, silk lamé, taffeta, or wool. About thirty minutes later, Zoran turned to the left of the stage and asked the model, "Are you ready?" She walked toward him, toting a Zero Halliburton stainless steel briefcase, the same type that hip L.A. lawyers carry.

The Halliburton contained every garment she had just modeled, all neatly folded inside. A collective gasp swept the room, as many women in the audience stood up to get a closer look. Zoran had cooked up this little gimmick to illustrate what he called "jet-pack fashion." A Zoran wardrobe—from day to evening wear—was not only chic, but portable enough to fit into a small bag, ready to be tossed in the overhead compartment on a plane.

No fuss. But surely some muss, ventured one woman in the audience. Stuffed into that tiny case "the clothes will get wrinkled," she contested. Zoran countered that his fine fabrics weren't prone to wrinkles, and besides, "Woman arrives in hotel, hangs clothes in shower, and wrinkles fall out." His presentation finished, Zoran snapped the briefcase shut and walked off, toting his compact collection like the top secret that it was.

Zoran was an enigma, a fashion creature stranger than fiction. Colorful, difficult, and often outrageous, Zoran was a Yugoslavian immigrant in New York, a hairy bohemian whom some nicknamed Rasputin, after the mystical, nineteenth-century Russian spiritual adviser. Zoran was indeed otherwordly, among the breed of eccentric designers, those who made fashion the edgy and exciting industry it had become. Fashion had always been a sanctuary for strange birds like Zoran, but all too many of these exotics were destined for extinction. All show and little substance, they usually burst on the scene for a moment of glory, only to burn out, making room for the next wave of young talents.

Not so with Zoran. He was weird, yet purposeful. His unconventional ways hadn't prevented him from building one of the most successful high-fashion businesses in America. Since 1976, when Zoran launched his first collection, he had managed to grow his business steadily in what was indisputably the most difficult sector to turn a dollar: expensive women's clothes. Zoran had succeeded on his own terms—not Seventh Avenue's. And his unique success sprang from two sources: an intimate understanding of his customer and a business approach that worked perfectly for a company his size.

IN CONTRAST TO Emanuel Ungaro's ornate couture frocks, festooned with bells and whistles that screamed "expensive," Zoran's fashions were spartan, lacking what was known as "hanger appeal." Without sharp tailoring, shoulder pads, or linings, the clothes looked downright humble as they drooped and slouched on hangers. It wasn't obvious, for example, that Zoran's pull-on pants with an elastic waistband were made from the finest $60-a-yard Tasmanian wool and retailed for ten times that amount. Or that a long folded square was really a lush $1,000 silk sarong, the bottom half of an elegant black-tie ensemble. But it just so happened that Zoran's untailored look was right on target, hitting the spot where a growing number of well-to-do women had landed in recent years.

What's more, Zoran's economic accomplishments were as unexpected as his designs. Right from the start, Zoran's clothes stood out because they always *sold*. By the late 1990s, when Zoran's contemporaries such as Calvin Klein were pushing millions of jeans and underwear— and hardly any high fashion—Zoran was still focusing on a single collection, whose pared-down simplicity was in the height of fashion in the 1990s. Saks Fifth Avenue became Zoran's best wholesale account; his collection was sold at twenty of Saks' fifty-five branch stores by 1998. At Saks alone, Zoran's business amounted to an estimated $30 million, at retail—which meant Zoran outsold the couture collections of every other high-end designer. More startling were the profit margins that Zoran pulled in; his fashions always retailed at full price—and never went on sale. Ever. Zoran's solid success without markdowns was an anomaly in fashion. (At Saks Fifth Avenue, no more than 50 percent of designer merchandise sold regularly sold at full price.)

Zoran ran an exemplary fashion house that offered a successful business model for designers large and small. He proved that a niche player could survive in a cutthroat marketplace, where affluent women were buying fewer designer clothes and were more likely to trade down than up when they did. Zoran's little business was an exquisite combination of all the designer businesses profiled in this book, one that incorporated many of their strengths and avoided most of their mistakes and pitfalls.

Granted, Zoran had neither the fame nor the fortune of de la Renta, Blass, or Ralph Lauren. Nonetheless, Zoran was very much a multimillionaire, having succeeded at playing the same game as the top industry players. In the spirit of Armani, Zoran offered simple styles that delivered the tangibles and the intangibles: high quality, as well as the cachet that his well-to-do clients expected. Zoran kept repeating the same styles, making him an extreme version of fashion's great recyclers like Armani and Gap. Like Karan in her early years, Zoran devised a formula that revolved around the functionality of a few good staples that were the basis for a wardrobe. The venerable St. John Knits didn't court the fashion press or hold fashion shows—and neither did Zoran. It took Zoran all of nineteen years to run his first paid advertising in magazines, and even then, he advertised in the most economical, low-key way possible, by sharing a space with Saks Fifth Avenue.

Unlike his peers, Zoran was adamant about keeping his business small, distributing his merchandise to a select group of the best retailers. Zoran knew his own limitations—and the limitations of luxury goods, which derived much of their allure from being scarce, forcing people to search for them. This strategy was a mind game grounded in reality. There would always be a finite market for expensive clothes.

Zoran's narrow focus allowed him to operate at maximum efficiency with minimal hassle. If he ever had any inclination to "think pink" or to fiddle with his signature style, he had thus far resisted, saving his company millions in research and design expenses, and sparing himself the nerve-racking creative stress that hounded designers like Donna Karan.

What goes around in fashion had come around to Zoran, whose business was reminiscent of couture's legendary renegade, Cristobal Balenciaga. Fashion editors had often used the expression "the ease of Balenciaga" to convey the wearability and comfort of his styles. And the same could be said of Zoran.

BORN IN 1947, Zoran grew up in a well-to-do family in Kikinda, near Belgrade, where his father was a landowner and a banker. He studied architecture at the University of Belgrade before leaving Yugoslavia in 1971 after his sister, who had earlier emigrated to Long Island, sent him a plane ticket to America.

In New York, Zoran shifted into fashion's fast lane. He checked coats at the Candy Store disco; he sold clothes at designer Pierre Balmain's Madison Avenue boutique, and worked as a collaborator with designer Scott Barrie. In those days, Zoran was a dandy who loved to wear expensive suits and rakish fedoras—a happy-go-lucky party boy who hung out until he figured out his next move.

Halston's sleek simplicity was all the rage in 1976 when Zoran dreamed up his own formula of basic pieces, which he first turned out in $8-a-yard silk crepe de chine. Zoran recalled spending $100 to buy the fabric and then hiring a Manhattan handkerchief maker to sew the garments for $3 apiece. He was lucky to land his first retail order with Marion Greenberg, an enthusiastic buyer at Henri Bendel, who bought his first run of about forty garments. Bendel's sold them quickly and immediately ordered more. Zoran claimed he sold about $40,000 at wholesale in his first year.

While Greenberg proved to be an invaluable sponsor to Zoran in his early years, the two later parted bitterly in 1983 after Greenberg sued Zoran, charging that she was an equal partner in his business by oral agreement, and that Zoran couldn't have made it without her input and professional connections. A New York state court judge eventually dismissed the suit in 1995.

While the extent of Greenberg's contribution was debatable, there was no denying that Zoran benefited from his early round of fawning coverage by the fashion press. For a few years, Zoran was even a favorite of *WWD*'s editor, John Fairchild, "who was initially quite impressed by him," recalled Ben Brantley, who was *WWD*'s fashion editor at the time. "Zoran's clothes were so damn photogenic. He was always very canny about hiring models who would make the clothes look good—like Esme and Josie Borain. Zoran got a lot of page-one pictures. And so many women in the office really got into wearing Zoran."

But *WWD*'s reporters were always searching for novelty in fashion, and Zoran wasn't delivering, which meant that he was no longer newsworthy. Fairchild cooled on Zoran and began deriding Zoran's plain clothes as "furniture covers," Brantley remembered. Fairchild, who loved

Paris couture, didn't consider Zoran a true craftsman. "It bored him ultimately," said Brantley, who recalled a *WWD* photo layout of a model dressed as a nun next to Zoran with the headline "Chairman of the Bored." Eventually Zoran disappeared from the pages of *WWD*. Without a PR machine of his own, Zoran stopped getting covered in the press.

But Zoran didn't lose much sleep. By that time, he was off and running with a thriving little business, so he hardly fretted that *Vogue* and *Harper's Bazaar* didn't come calling. He *had* the customers. And how those clients came into the Zoran fold is a story unto itself.

Zoran always chose to fly below the fashion radar. Ever the contrarian, Zoran refused to join the Council of Fashion Designers of America, the prestigious New York fashion industry trade group, which had repeatedly invited him to join. Zoran hated the fawning ways of the fashion establishment, the big parties, the hype, and the "hullabaloo," as he called it. Like Garbo, he wanted to be left alone. This pretense worked splendidly to his advantage. Keeping a distance from Seventh Avenue fueled the mystique he had cultivated as New York's most difficult fashion artiste. Most people were self-conscious around him, having heard all the tales about his quirky temperament—they didn't want to risk being insulted, or worse, rejected. Whenever his name came up, many fashion insiders dismissed him as a drunk and a crazy man.

"Zoran is a man of great mood swings," said Brantley. "I have seen him be very kind and generous to people, and I've seen him be very cruel. He doesn't mean to be cruel, but to be outrageous, he must be confrontational."

ZORAN WAS A night owl who cut up after hours when springloaded with his beloved Stolichnaya vodka. Late one night in November 1994, in his lower Manhattan loft showroom, Zoran was holding his usual salon around a large table with about a dozen friends and clients, most of whom happened to be in his clothes that night. The talk turned to hair. Suzanne Orenstein, a Minneapolis buyer, casually asked Zoran whether she should continue to let her shoulder-grazing locks grow. Zoran hated long hair on women, so she knew what he was about to say.

"NO!" Zoran boomed. "You need to cut it—now." He sprang from his chair, leaving a trail of Marlboro smoke, and disappeared behind a long white wall. Zoran came back with two huge pairs of fabric scissors. He grabbed the tablecloth from a nearby table and draped it around Orenstein. Working by candlelight, Zoran started whacking away. He wasn't *that* drunk; he slowed down when he got to the nape of her neck. "Zoran is always cutting somebody's hair. He did mine once," one woman said.

A fast ten minutes later, he was done. Orenstein grabbed a hand mirror to inspect her ear-length bob. A little lopsided, but her hair looked better. She laughed and gave Zoran a big hug as everyone clapped. Why did she let him do it? Orenstein insisted that it never crossed her mind to question Zoran. "He wanted to do it," she said. "I know he is strong-willed and I have confidence in him."

On another evening, Zoran was primed for a little mischief, hours after having a steak dinner at Peter Luger's in Brooklyn. He was celebrating the birthday of one of his few buddies in the press, Cathy Horyn, a fashion writer for *Vanity Fair*. Their last stop, around 2 A.M., was at a bar in lower Manhattan. Although Horyn said she was ready to call it a night, Zoran wasn't. Just one more round of Stolis for the road, he insisted as he lit up another Marlboro.

The bar's jaded regulars weren't sure what to make of Zoran. Who was this homeless-looking fellow? Why couldn't he sit still? Why wouldn't he shut up? Zoran zeroed in on two city sanitation workers who were now seated at the bar after having parked their garbage truck outside.

"I want you to take her to hotel in garbage truck," he demanded in his raspy, thick accent.

The garbage guys barely looked up. Zoran persisted. "I want Cathy to ride in garbage truck." He dug into his pocket and pulled out a crisp $100 bill. "For birthday."

Moments later, Horyn was perched high above the street, waving good night to Zoran while seated next to a driver whom she remembered "was quite cute, a really good-looking man." As the white truck rolled through the silent streets toward the Wyndham Hotel, Horyn was tickled but wistful. "I just wish somebody had seen me *get out of that truck*."

Passion and humor certainly summed up Zoran when he was at play, when he could sometimes be quite calculating. Actress Lauren Hutton recalled the evening she was at his studio in the early 1980s, not long before she was due to appear on stage as a presenter at the Academy Awards. "I told him I was planning to wear this puffy red Halston dress," Hutton said. Zoran walked over to a long rack of clothes and pulled out something of his. "Take a look at this," he demanded.

"It was a pair of long boxer shorts in this incredible gold material and a sweatshirt top that matched. He said, 'I think this looks better,' " she remembered. "And I wore it."

Amid a sea of big hair and ballgowns, Hutton was starkly simple— and smashing on stage. Photos of her Oscar fashion coup cropped up in a number of publications. "When I got home, people kept calling me up; I kept getting all these messages about my outfit," she remembered. Zoran got a number of calls, too, from friends who spotted his clothes on TV. Long before Armani had conquered the Oscars, Zoran was feeling quite smug.

Yet for all his bluster and his aloof facade, Zoran kept abreast of all the to-ings and fro-ings inside the fashion loop. He burned the phone lines daily, gossiping with his circle of well-connected clients, buyers, and a few fashion editors. Zoran's friends were often surprised at how plugged in he was. Often, it was Zoran who told them first about the drop in the price of Donna Karan's stock or who showed up out at Armani's latest store opening.

Zoran was crazy—like a fox—when it came to running his business. In the world of expensive clothes, Zoran had mastered the art of marketing luxury fashion, the art of getting the most bang for the buck. He accomplished this without any offshoots from his one and only collection. There were no Zoran perfumes, jeans, or handbags, none of the sundry extras that designers like Blass relied on to compensate for the money they didn't make from their top-drawer couture designs.

Zoran's success exemplified the end of fashion. He proved that high fashion lived on, but under a new definition that was actually quite old-fashioned—a throwback to the era of Balenciaga, when couture houses were small and exquisite. By staying focused on his own special niche—and by not being too greedy—Zoran made sure that his company grew steadily and profitably for more than a decade. Then came the 1990s, the best of times for Zoran, when his business exploded. Suddenly, more and more affluent women had a yen for Zoran's low-voltage, casual style.

Zoran got rich on the most primary of concepts. His fashion formula was essentially a top-of-the-line Gap: T-shirts, tops, tunics, pants and skirts, boxy shifts, and loose jackets. These were clothes that you just threw on, without any embellishments or fastenings. No zippers. No buttons. Everything came in only one size, and always in the best fabrics. The woman who loved the look of a $50 slouchy cotton sweater from Gap could finally get perhaps the best version of that classic from Zoran, in the richest cotton for about $600, or in four-ply cashmere for $1,200.

This was a luxury that was anonymous, a tad frumpy and appealing to Wasp sensibilities—and checkbooks, as it was quite common for women to spend $30,000 or so a year on a Zoran wardrobe. "With their implicit disdain for frippery they are also, perhaps, the ultimate snob clothes," wrote Ben Brantley in a 1992 profile of Zoran in *Vanity Fair*.

And among the sexiest too. Curiously, Zoran's loose, covered-up styles were a turn-on to some men. Brantley, for one, was amazed when he once observed how a group of men reacted to one woman in Zoran. "There was this sexual charge that came out of her; men were just falling over her. I think that part of the appeal is that these are clothes that you can slide out of very quickly."

ZORAN WOULD LIKE everyone to believe that he had his successful strategy all figured out from the start. But he wasn't *that* savvy. He was just stubborn. He loved simple, plain clothes and saw no reason to change them every season. This turned out to be a brilliant business tactic. Zoran's classics built a steady consumer following, effectively turning his label into a potent trademark.

Fashion's Rasputin was also a guru who instilled fear, respect, and unwavering loyalty in his most faithful private clients, about a hundred women known as the Zoranians. They were his truest believers, the ones who trooped downtown to visit him at his white-walled loft showroom—first on Sullivan Street and then on Chambers Street—where Zoran made them over. It was there that he told them what they *needed* to wear—his clothes, of course—which they tried on right in front of him, *before* he permitted them to look in the mirror. "I am your two eyes and *I* tell you what looks good," he said.

Zoran was brutally frank in his assessments of women. He never failed to point out when someone was too fat or when clothes were too tight: "You like to look like slut," Zoran barked to one journalist in noting her penchant for short, fitted dresses. Short, carefree hairstyles completed the Zoran look, which was why he was so scissor-happy to create a nifty bob. He told the Zoranians to ditch their fussy trimmings, their scarves, their belts, to "give jewelry and diamonds to housekeeper."

Zoran's "don'ts" went right down to the feet, where stiletto heels and slingbacks were verboten. "Woman should be like man," he said. Of course he suggested the only footwear that complemented his look: his own high-tongued $400 suede loafer. There was nothing more chic than a woman who didn't have to think about what she was going to wear, he said. "I don't talk them into dressing simple and plain. You either get it or you don't, and if you don't, I don't sell to you."

It sounds like a cult, doesn't it? But Zoranians said their gruff leader hadn't washed their brains; he simply cleaned up their fashion sensibilities and shored up their own sense of personal style. "Zoran has an incredible eye, this great sense of proportion; he can look right at a person and tell you what is right for you," said Ann Free, a former Washington lobbyist who bought her first Zorans in 1985. "These are fabulous, understated clothes. Once you open your eyes and get acquainted with his approach, you get the feel of being simple and unadorned and that gives you a real confidence. As women get older, they get a lot smarter. You find a style that works for you. And once you get there, it's effortless."

Like Balenciaga, Zoran figured out long ago who the true customers of expensive clothes were: wealthy women over thirty-five, those who led active professional and social lives and who weren't fashion victims. Accordingly, Zoran's styles flattered mature women: Nothing was tight or clingy. His skirts and pants had elastic waists and his dresses, jackets, and loose coats draped gracefully when a woman walked.

Like Armani, Zoran had his share of famous clients, such as Gloria Vanderbilt, Candice Bergen, Diane von Furstenberg, Lauren Bacall,

Isabella Rossellini, Queen Noor, Elizabeth Taylor, and the late Jacqueline Onassis, who bought her Zorans at Henri Bendel but never met the man.

But celebrities weren't Zoran's favorite customers. The stars required high maintenance—too much trouble for him to be bothered with. Zoran liked to sit on his throne waiting for women seek him out, instead of chasing them. He wouldn't suck up, and with few exceptions, he wasn't giving away clothes, which the stars expected. "If they want to wear my clothes," he snapped, "let them go to Saks, like Elizabeth Taylor does."

Zoran was much more impressed with the self-made millionairesses next door, the executive women who were elegant, understated dressers such as Roberta Arena, a former executive vice president of Citicorp. A fervent Zoranian since the mid-1980s, Arena looked the part with her short brunette bob and slender figure. Arena owned hundreds of pieces of his clothes, with her favorite styles in every fabric he'd ever offered— alongside a few sweaters from Gap. A jet-pack Zoranian, Arena logged in hundreds of thousands of miles of business travel; she regularly boarded the Concorde clutching a small carry-on bag packed with enough Zorans to take her through two weeks' worth of board meetings, dinners, and cocktails. Naturally, she and Zoran got chummy along the way, hanging out together in Naples, Florida, where they both had vacation homes.

Another longtime enthusiast was Nancy Friday, the best-selling author, who fondly referred to her favorite Zoran outfits in her books. On the back of the dust jacket of her 1996 book, *The Power of Beauty*, Friday was pictured in a black boatneck sweater and pull-on pants, both by Zoran. "I feel that I look as good as I can in Zoran," Friday said. At five ten and a half with cropped blond hair, Friday said she wore Zoran not to blend in but to stand out. "Zoran's clothes are plain in the same way that a Picasso line drawing is plain, absolutely elegant and perfect. I have Zorans that are twenty years old and I can wear them and wear them."

Friday and her husband, Norman Pearlstine, Time Inc.'s editor-in-chief, passed many a cocktail hour at Zoran's downtown studio, where Friday took her time scouring Zoran's wall-length rack of clothes.

Of course, Zoran's kooky persona added some juice to his curious mystique. Zoran had treated many women to one of his spontaneous shearings. But the vast majority of Zoran's clients would never get a haircut or share a Stoli with him. One Bendel's client had been spending between $30,000 to $40,000 a year on her Zorans for a decade before she finally got around to meeting the designer in 1996.

Fashion trends have always been a sign of the times. And Zoran's surging popularity in the late 1990s came as more wealthy women had put aside the eighties frou-frou to recast themselves as serious people. "They are separating what they consume from who they are. These women don't need to be reaffirmed with expensive jewelry," said Steve Barnett, a New York management consultant whose clients include international marketers of luxury goods.

Thus, Zoran's highly nuanced "dog-whistle fashion" summoned that woman who could discriminate from afar that his $2,200 six-ply cashmere cardigan was as precious as any fur. "The smaller the group that recognizes it, the more luxurious it is," said Barnett.

Zoran's snob appeal and cachet endured because he saw the virtues of staying small for the long haul. He never forgot what happened to Halston when the celebrated minimalist got greedy in the 1970s and rolled out a cheap Halston III collection for JCPenney. The tony Bergdorf Goodman promptly dumped Halston's couture line—and suddenly the golden Halston trademark had turned to rust. That message wasn't lost on Zoran, who was keenly aware of the limitations of his simple formula— try to stretch it too far and disaster would follow.

Indeed, Zoran had already watched such a collapse. In 1987, an ambitious young Dallas designer, Sandra Garratt, introduced Multiples, a collection of cheap polyester-cotton knit sportswear that was the hottest label during the eighties trend known as "modular" dressing.

Multiples' connect-the-dots concept was easy and affordable: For $200 a woman could buy several of its twenty-four components, including pants, shirts, skirts, jumpsuits—and put together a stylish, versatile wardrobe. Each piece came in only one size, packed in a plastic bag with a how-to chart that tempted women to experiment mixing and matching the pieces, which was easy enough to do.

Multiples, as it turned out, was also a Zoran rip-off, or so he claimed. Zoran believed that Garratt was no creative genius, just a former employee of his who quit working for him after only a few months. Garratt maintained all along that she had already dreamed up modular clothes a couple of years before Zoran went into business. Back in 1974, Garratt won a student award as the "most promising star" at the Los Angeles Fashion Institute of Design and Merchandising, for her senior project: a collection of one-size knit sportswear pieces made to be worn in layers. Garratt said that Zoran had hired her based on her work for her student portfolio.

During the late 1980s, Zoran watched on the sidelines as Garratt basked in the spotlight. Garratt's first year with Multiples yielded her a fat $2 million royalty check on sales that hit $100 million at retail. But Zoran guessed—and probably hoped—that Multiples would be a flash in the pan that would stumble on its own success. It was a reasonable bet. Fashion gimmicks tend to have a short shelf life, and Multiples was no exception. Indeed, Multiples' flimsy knits hardly had much life left in them after several machine washings—a problem that caused many early enthusiasts not to buy more.

Furthermore, the idea was so simple to execute that in no time there were multiples of Multiples—such knockoffs as Elements, Switches, and Linkup. Ironically, Multiples' biggest rival was Units, a brand that Garratt herself created. Garratt had launched Units in 1986 with the help of venture capital partners. But after a few months, Garratt fell out and split with her financiers, who retained the rights to Units. The financiers sold the trademark to JCPenney, which pressed on with a chain of two hundred Units boutiques.

Months later, Jerrell Inc., a Dallas apparel maker, offered Garratt a licensing deal to come up with another version of Units. And thus Multiples was born. But after one terrific year of sales, Garratt sued Jerrell, claiming that Jerell's own line of knockoffs was cannibalizing her Multiples business. A court settlement left the beleaguered Garratt with $130,000, and by October 1989 she was out of business. (Units lasted until 1994 before folding.)

Zoran delighted in recounting the rise and fall of Multiples, if only to underscore that *he* knew the marketplace. More to the point, he was still around to get the last laugh. "I knew I could make big money if I did cheap clothes, but I wanted this to last long time," he explained. And the sure way to command couture prices year after year was to do what Zoran did: remain exclusive, maintain the highest quality, and—fundamentally—design the styles that women want.

Quality was easier to maintain when a fashion house was like Zoran's and filling orders by the dozens and not the thousands of dozens. Zoran's seamstresses cut each garment individually, finishing the edges by machine with perfectly straight topstitching. His signature label was then barely tacked on, making it easy to remove, if it didn't fall off on its own. This was done on purpose because, as Zoran liked to say: "Labels scratch." His aversion to labels later became a sore spot when the Federal Trade Commission took issue that missing from Zoran's clothes were fabric-care labels that are required by law. Without admitting or denying guilt, Zoran paid $14,000 in 1998 to settle with the FTC. He then began attaching a "dry clean only" label to his garments.

Ever the purist when it came to natural materials, Zoran refused to use the new high-tech synthetic blends that designers like Armani now favored. "My clients expect the best fabrics. Only 100 percent," he said.

As Zoranians paid dearly for his heavy "double georgette" silks, they expected not to see themselves coming and going. Wisely, he had the good sense not to produce too much. Women couldn't just breeze into the mall to Nordstrom or Lord & Taylor, for example, and pick up a few Zorans. The only chain that stocked Zoran in America was Saks. (He finally added Neiman Marcus in the fall of 1999.)

Worldwide, Zoran did business with only about sixty retail locations, usually no more than one specialty store in each city. For the entire state of New York, Zoran sold only in Manhattan, and only at two locations: Saks Fifth Avenue and, more recently, Bergdorf Goodman, which he added to replace Henri Bendel in 1998. Both Saks and Bergdorf's bustled with business; it was more typical than unusual for either store to move $40,000 worth of Zorans in a single day.

This kind of clout gave Zoran the upper hand over his retail clients. He shipped merchandise to stores not necessarily when they requisitioned an order, but when *he* thought it would sell. All too often, retailers required designers to ship seasonal fashions too early—spring fashions in December, for example, when shoppers were still buying winter clothes. Zoran knew this was ridiculous—and he refused to go along. He continued to ship linen clothes to stores in the middle of July, when the summer goods in the rest of the store were marked down to 50 percent off. And since his retailers weren't going to mark down the linens at the end of the season, it didn't matter when they sold—which was usually sooner rather than later.

———

AS FAR BACK as 1983, when Zoran thrived on small orders from more retailers, he flew into a rage, abruptly canceling accounts that he accused of selling knockoffs of his designs, stores such as Bergdorf's and Saks Fifth Avenue, and I. Magnin in San Francisco.

Linda Dresner, who operates boutiques on Park Avenue and in Birmingham, Michigan, said she cut off Zoran by her own design in the early 1990s. After having "great success with Zoran for about eight years," Dresner decided to drop the line—ironically, for the same reason some women swear by Zoran. "Our sales slacked off with him because he stuck with too much of the same things and our customers needed more change. It was just too repetitious." She also bridled at Zoran's rude treatment of women. "He could be insulting to people. He would tell them to lose weight. I guess some people like to be insulted, but I found it was too much."

Imperious as Zoran was, he continued to satisfy Chicago's Ultimo, whose twenty-year-relationship with Zoran grew into a $2 million annual business in the late 1990s. Since Zoran personally followed the sales of all his retail accounts—the stores faxed him reports daily—he could fill Ultimo's needs as ably as Joan Weinstein, Ultimo's owner. Zoran "understands his product better than anybody," Weinstein said.

Over the years, Weinstein evolved into a Zoranian herself, as she wore Zoran "95 percent of the time." The blond Weinstein, who resembled actress Jeanne Moreau, usually dressed in all-black or charcoal Zorans that she wore *her* way, layering a silk top asymmetrically across her shoulder, tied at the waist. She also piled on stacks of cinnabar bangles at each wrist—a flourish Zoran chose to ignore. "Zoran covers all the bases," said Weinstein. "You can wear it sexy, you can make it look young. It looks different on everybody."

For a long time, Zoran also protected Ultimo's local monopoly; Zoran wouldn't sell to any other store in Chicago. Zoran finally relented in 1998, adding Saks in Chicago. Weinstein wasn't happy about that—but she couldn't complain because her Zoran business still remained steady.

ZORAN'S ONE-SIZE concept wasn't as simplistic as an extra-large T-shirt that fit everybody. Only Zoran's sarongs fit all; the other styles flattered different body types: the "skinny pant" fit sizes 4 through 6; the "regular pant" fit up to a size 10, and the "pajama pant" fit sizes 10 up to 14. The same went for his "square top," which came in four or five different silhouettes.

Eliminating sizes was just one way Zoran made business simple and kept costs down. Most fashion houses spent millions to create samples to prepare every collection; Zoran spent zero. His seamstresses kept using those same patterns—some so old they were held together with yellowing tape. Whenever he was in a creative mood, he thought about new shapes and fabrics, nervously twisting his beard. Once he decided to shorten a sleeve by a few inches. He walked over and told the seamstresses to make the change.

Zoran held up a 1976 version of his tunic top next to the 1995 model. The difference? "I close up side slits." After years of opening and closing slits and shifting around fabrics, Zoran said his collections provided infinite variety—more than 25,000 combinations—enough to keep his fans intrigued and collecting the latest variations on his theme.

But designing still had its challenges and frustrations, namely scouting out mills that could deliver the precious fabrics that Zoran required to make his simple shapes pop. Nowadays, it was harder to locate the $100-a-yard fabrics he favored in the past—not even the top Paris couturiers ordered such materials in quantity anymore. Thus, many of the best mills in Italy and Switzerland that Zoran relied on for years had closed down—or stopped making the materials he needed.

Instead of pure fashion, Zoran was selling fabulous fabrics. And his clients knew it. Some of his fans admitted that they tried to cut corners by taking their old Zorans to their local dressmakers to copy. "But they don't come out the same because you can't get those fabrics," said Ann Free.

AFTER A TWELVE-YEAR absence, Zoran agreed to return to Saks Fifth Avenue in 1993, and Saks soon became his biggest account. Saks chairman, Philip Miller, assigned June Horne, a senior buyer, to work with Zoran. Miller made it clear that he expected Horne to bond with the difficult designer because Saks had big plans for him. Horne recalled that she was anxious: "I had heard all the stories about him."

In 1995, Horne made her first visit to Zoran's Chambers Street headquarters, inside a huge twelfth-floor loft that functioned as design studio and factory. A long white wall bisected the room. The factory side was crammed with bolts of fabric, a long plywood cutting table, and rows of sewing machines for ten seamstresses. On the other side was a vast open space, virtually empty except for an endless rack of finished garments arranged by color, mostly black.

Horne arrived at sunset, when Zoran "was sitting with his back to the wall, so there was this silhouette of him and his beard. I thought, oh my, he is sitting there like God. He reminded me of Jerry Garcia," she remembered.

She came equipped with a Polaroid camera and an order pad, ready to get down to business. But at five o'clock, Zoran was just sitting down to a late lunch of salmon and pasta, sent over by Balducci's. Out came the Stoli and champagne. Horne hung around for three hours during which they discussed everything except his clothes, though they were "over on that wall staring me in the face the whole time." Their repartee was lively. "I remember we got into a slightly heated argument about politics."

Weeks later, after three or four of these get-togethers, Horne finally got around to writing Saks's order. She fully expected to do the paperwork with assistants, but it was Zoran who sat down beside her and told her what to buy. "I've never met any designer who is so involved with the line on a day-to-day basis. He stays on top of every detail," she marveled.

Zoran was adamant and pushy, of course. He insisted on sending alpaca to Saks through April, even though Horne told him not to. The twenty $2,000 alpaca jackets he sent to the store "all sold immediately," she confirmed. Zoran agreed, just for the hell of it, to meet Saks shoppers in Palm Beach in December 1997 where he parceled out bits of fashion advice to shoppers, something he generally avoided. "The most time you have with customer is five minutes, and there is nothing I can do for you," he said.

Zoran refused to disclose profits, but given his low overhead and frugal habits, he was clearly cleaning up. His operations were as stripped down as his fashions. All garments were made in-house, by thirty or so employees in New York and Milan, except for sweaters, which were knitted by outside contractors near Milan. The employees who didn't sew performed many odd jobs. Jude Goldin, a former waiter at Mr. Chow's, managed Zoran's New York office, answered the phone, did paperwork, packed boxes of clothes, and styled store windows at Saks and Bergdorf's. Still playing the waiter, Goldin also served Stoli and champagne whenever the Zoranians dropped by.

Zoran found many ways to save money. In 1997, he left his Chambers Street loft and moved his factory into the garage of his nearby townhouse residence. So, while seamstresses toiled in the ground-floor garage at his townhouse, Zoran turned the second floor into his showroom and hangout for the Zoranians, leaving the third level for his private living quarters. The seamstresses liked their new garage factory, which was air-conditioned, while the Chambers Street studio wasn't. ("I'm European," he said about his indifference to air-conditioning.)

Frugality, indeed, was the byword at the house of Zoran, where there were few indulgences. The fashion master cut his own hair and wore the same outfit every day—a white T-shirt (bought at Wal-Mart), black or khaki pants (made in his studio), and Cole-Haan black moccasins without socks. He spotted a nifty $19 black nylon windbreaker at Old Navy and bought a dozen for himself. Zoran either walked or cabbed around Manhattan, and when he traveled to Milan or Florida, he always flew coach.

In keeping with his love of architecture, Zoran had bought and sold several homes over the years. Besides his TriBeCa townhouse, he owned an 1831 plantation home in Charleston, South Carolina, and a beachfront spread in Naples, Florida.

While Zoran managed just fine without secretaries and design assistants, he couldn't mind his business without an excellent chief executive. In another sign of his head for business, Zoran didn't find his CEO on Seventh Avenue, but on Wall Street: Gary Galleberg, a lawyer and former mergers and acquisitions associate at the prestigious Wall Street law firm Cravath, Swaine & Moore. Handsome, urbane, and terse, Galleberg, who was born in 1957, was the kind of guy who would be successful at running any type of business. He was also modest, discreet, and a calculated risk taker—a casual fellow who came to work in a polo shirt and Zoran chinos, accompanied by his dog, a Rhodesian Ridge-back named Red.

Galleberg and Zoran met by chance, when they struck up a conversation over drinks at a downtown bar in 1985. After they became friends, Zoran asked Galleberg in 1988 to work for him. "I was intrigued by the challenge of running a small business," recalled Galleberg. "I didn't know anything about fashion, but that didn't matter to me. The company was already in good shape when I came. It was a solid company with a good brand and I thought it would be fun to be involved in that."

So Galleberg became Zoran's first official CEO. He computerized the company's books and became an active investor in the stock market, for himself and for Zoran's own portfolio. By the late 1990s, Galleberg was pulling down the equivalent of a senior law partner's salary, without the killer hours and the stuffy protocol.

Zoran provided the creative brains and Galleberg the business brawn. Galleberg came along at the perfect time, just as sales spiked in the late 1980s and paperwork began to take up too much of Zoran's time. Galleberg liked that the business was no-nonsense and hummed with profits. "The hardest part about the business is controlling growth," Galleberg said. Zoran's business with Saks alone more than doubled between 1995 and 1997. "We are doing a lot more work with virtually the same number of people," Galleberg said. "Except for the seamstresses, we haven't added any more senior assistants, so we're trying to operate more efficiently. And that takes a great deal more coordination."

Galleberg was relieved that he didn't have to bother with coordinating fashion shows, which Zoran hated. "I always thought fashion shows were a waste of time, because buyers write orders in showroom, not runway," Zoran observed.

About once or twice a year, Zoran got the urge to host a modest fashion soiree, a dinner party for about one hundred guests in his showroom, where he presented a few outfits on a couple of models. In March 1995, Zoran staged such a dinner in Milan at the start of Milan's fashion week, when designers like Giorgio Armani and Gianni Versace were doing their big runway shows. Zoran's dinner for 150 at Biffi Scala was a prized invitation to a select group of wealthy Italian clients—an A-list of what he called "the contessas and marquessas"—and a few members of the fashion press and European boutique owners, including Milan's Marisa and Pupi Solari, among his biggest accounts.

Zoran hardly needed to enlist the three models he hired for the night. His guests were a walking Zoran fashion show. The Italian women, regal in carriage, faithfully turned out in their Zorans, demonstrating the endless ways his designs could be worn—spare, the way he loved them, or gussied up with antique earrings and pearl necklaces, the way most Italians preferred.

Helping Zoran host the dinner was Mirella Pettini Haggiag, herself a striking Italian socialite who wore her Zorans with panache. Haggiag was another one of Zoran's lucky finds. A former model who worked for Valentino, Haggiag was a fixture on the Italian social whirl. With her movie producer husband, Roberto Haggiag, she owns homes in Rome, Milan, Venice, and New York.

Before dinner, Zoran rolled in a long rack of clothes and set up a makeshift changing room for the models: a folding screen in front of the restaurant's bar. While guests were finishing their tiramisù and espresso, Zoran pulled a few items from the rack, handing them to his assistant, who dressed the models. Zoran, in a baggy black sweater, escorted each model through the dining room. "The cut is marvelous," purred Gae Aulenti, the noted Italian architect, when a model twirled by her in a stiff white silk gazar shift. At the end of dinner, the guests headed over to the clothes rack and began sifting through the clothes. Zoran shooed them away, inviting them to come over to his Milan showroom, which many did for the next few weeks.

The tab for Zoran's veal and risotto dinner party came to about $10,000—far less than the $500,000 designers usually spend on a runway show. Later that week, Armani and his licensees spent nearly $1 million on a black-tie fashion-show dinner party and disco.

When Zoran traveled to Milan in the springtime, he usually stayed over for his birthday, March 7, when he liked to do a little celebrating. After his triumphant dinner party, Zoran decided to return to Biffi Scala with a party of six for his birthday. But instead of reserving a cozy banquette in the corner, where he most likely would be recognized, he called with a special request. "Is kitchen available?" he asked the maître d'. "Kitchen is chic-est place in restaurant," he explained.

Kitchen dining became popular in Italy during the late 1970s, when acts of terrorism attributed to the Red Brigade were prevalent. Back then, many rich people and politicians didn't like to dine in restaurants, fearing they'd be gunned down, *Godfather*-style, over a plate of pasta. So several fine Italian eateries allowed their most special clients to dine incognito in the kitchen. Restaurant kitchens thus became the height of inverse chic in Italy, where danger could be not only exclusive but glamorous.

Zoran loved this sort of thing. Biffi Scala's kitchen was in the basement, a cozy place where the scurrying chefs were in full view. A waiter prepared a table with small stools for Zoran. After that fancy party earlier in the week, Zoran sipped his Stoli, relieved not to have to play the gracious host.

But not quite. Halfway through the pasta course, a video crew from a local TV station and a Milanese socialite bolted down the steps in search of Zoran. He came in on cue, complimenting the woman who was dressed in navy taffeta and velvet Zoran. "You look great," he said.

Suddenly, blinding strobe lights came on, as the camera rolled. "Here we are downstairs in the kitchen of Biffi Scala with the famous Zoran," the reporter began, in heavily accented English, shoving a microphone in Zoran's face. "Tell us about what you do," he asked. Zoran, who was smoking, didn't flinch: "I do fashion." Then the reporter posed the same question to Galleberg. "I work for him," he deadpanned.

IN THE SUMMER of 1997, Zoran was feeling a bit restless—but serious, for a change. He was getting ready to reintroduce his signature suede loafers, which he had stopped making a few years ago. And he thought about creating his first handbag.

But what Zoran was really thinking about was expanding—perhaps even buying an existing fashion house. And he couldn't think of any finer name than one of America's premier couture houses, Bill Blass.

At seventy-five, the debonair Blass was Seventh Avenue's most prominent designer-statesman, a philanthropist who once bestowed a $10 million gift on the New York Public Library. Blass's couture collections sold mostly in trunk shows—and hadn't been profitable in years. But Blass had a cash cow: a valuable network of forty licensees that made his sheets, perfumes, jeans, and menswear. Zoran said that Galleberg could further exploit those licensees while he would update Blass's couture line. "Bill and I have same customer," Zoran said, referring to some of his socialite clients.

Zoran had bumped into Blass in 1996 on a freezing night after a CFDA fashion awards ceremony at Lincoln Center. Zoran was shivering in a nylon windbreaker, standing outside beside Ron Gallela—Jacqueline Onassis's famous stalker—and other paparazzi, who were waiting for Mick Jagger and other celebrities to leave the party. Zoran almost got hauled off by the police because he had attracted a group of homeless people who watched him give out twenty-dollar bills to other street people. One police officer tried to stop Zoran and they got into an argument.

Blass suddenly emerged, carrying the silver CFDA trophy he had received for his lifetime achievement in fashion. Zoran walked over to say hello. Stunned, Blass muttered something and scurried off to his limousine. Lauren Hutton, also leaving the event, recognized Zoran and wondered what he was doing outside when all the fashion people were inside. Zoran never attended such affairs, but that evening he just happened to be in the neighborhood and decided to wander over to Lincoln Center for the hell of it. Zoran cracked up as he remembered the look on people's faces who recognized him: "They all thought I was drunk!"

A few months later, Zoran called Blass and invited him for lunch at Da Silvano, an Italian restaurant popular with the fashion crowd, in the West Village. Both Blass and Zoran liked to smoke and drink, and they were having a fine time when Zoran finally leaned in and told Blass that he wanted to buy his fashion house. Incredulous, Blass thought Zoran was only kidding—and besides, where would Zoran get the millions to buy his business? Zoran insisted that he could afford to buy Blass out, but only at the right price. He wanted Blass—cheap. Zoran told Blass that he would send Galleberg to go over the numbers and perhaps they could strike a deal whenever Blass was ready to sell.

Blass's reaction to Zoran's proposition was more intrigue than real interest. Blass was hardly ready to retire, having enjoyed excellent sales from his 1997 spring couture line. So nothing came of Zoran's initial pursuit. Undeterred, he vowed to pursue Blass again, confiding to his buddies that eventually "Bill will sell to me."

It seemed incredible that Zoran, the stellar model for the future of fashion, and not its past, would be genuinely interested in Blass and his old-school way of business. How serious was Zoran about Blass? Clearly, he seemed to relish the impossibility of it all—that David *could* actually buy Goliath. Zoran would have gotten a kick out of flipping the finger at all those fashionistas. He could just hear the gasps reverberate across Seventh Avenue.

But after Zoran's initial overture to Blass in 1997, and Galleberg's subsequent meeting with Blass in 1998, no business combination resulted from the talks. So Zoran settled back down to concentrate on his own company, which continued to advance quite smartly. In the fall of 1999, Zoran added a major new client, Neiman Marcus, which he said placed an initial wholesale order for about $8 million for the first year. Neiman's would keep Zoran occupied and stimulated for a while. But fashion's Rasputin, who liked to brag that he hadn't designed anything new in fifteen years, was still searching for something more to do.

e p i l o g u e

ON MARCH 29, 1999, the longest-running bull market on record crossed a monumental threshold when the Dow Jones Industrial Average broke the 10,000 barrier, encapsulating America's stunning economic rebirth, energized by the boom in information technology that now compelled every sector in business to learn to operate faster, cheaper, and more efficiently. "Companies that stumble in the computer room are all too likely to be devastated in the marketplace," opined *The Wall Street Journal*.

A case in point: Levi Strauss & Co., the world's largest clothing maker, whose sales peaked to $7 billion in 1996, only to unzip two years later to $6 billion. It seemed unfathomable that Levi's, the inventor of jeans, American fashion's calling card for nearly 150 years, had lost its groove with young people who for decades swore by low-slung Levi's 501's as the coolest jeans on the planet. But by the 1990s, jeans-wearing teenagers had moved on, preferring the hipper image of jeans marketed by the Gap, Polo, and Tommy Hilfiger—as well as bargain versions from Sears and Penney's—all of which chipped away from Levi's market share in recent years.

Just like the French couture houses fell out of touch, Levi's had become too inbred, too complacent, and too slow to react to changing fashion trends and savvier competition. At the end of fashion, even the formidable Levi's could no longer take its dominance for granted in a world where shoppers were fickle, fast-moving targets when it came to clothes. In 1997, the San Francisco–based giant hunkered down, embarking on an unprecedented $1 billion worldwide restructuring, closing half of its U.S. apparel factories and laying off thousands of workers.

Peter Jacobi, Levi's president and chief operating officer who resigned in 1999, told an audience of textile industry executives: "The alarms were going off, but frankly, we hit the snooze button a few too many times. We were left behind, stuck in a rut of internal focus, the same old business model and the same old products . . . In the last several years, we the manufacturers and marketers have seen our authority falter. Our consumers know what they want and, whether we want to believe it or not, we no longer have much choice in the matter. . . . unfortunately what's the most common among [consumers] is their lack of commonality."

Levi's recruited a new president and CEO from outside its ranks: Philip Marineau, the former president of Pepsico's North America division. After five months on the job on February 21, 2000, Marineau admitted that the monumental task of turning around Levi's would take at least another couple of years. Meanwhile, Levi's 1999 sales slipped further, to $5.1 billion, effectively pushing it off its vaunted perch. The world's biggest apparel maker was now Levi's arch-rival, VF Corp., maker of Lee and Wrangler jeans, with sales of $5.6 billion.

THROUGHOUT THE 1990s, sport shirts and khakis had displaced suits to become the de rigueur office uniform, even at the most traditional Wall Street firms like Goldman Sachs and JP Morgan, which finally succumbed to the "all casual all the time" edict in 2000 in order to better fit in with a new generation of young Internet entrepreneurs who were rewriting America's business culture. The pervasive casual trend had succeeded in stunning Saks Fifth Avenue, which conceded that it was having a harder time selling its stockpile of dressy designer creations. In late 1999, Saks said it would retool its merchandise mix to bring in more of the "elegant casual" clothes that its upscale clientele were now demanding.

PARIS AND MILAN dominated fashion news in 1999 and 2000, but the big headlines weren't coming from the runways. High fashion was now engulfed in the trend of corporate takeovers as a wave of consolidation—led by the voracious LVMH—became the order of the day.

After a long protracted battle, LVMH succeeded in amassing a 34 percent stake in Gucci and appeared to be closing in for the kill in early 1999. But Gucci would be rescued by a formidable French ally: François Pinault, the billionaire who controlled Pinault-Printemps-Redoute, the biggest nonfood retail group in Europe—and who happened to be Arnault's arch-rival. In its role as Gucci's white knight, Pinault snapped up a 40 percent stake in newly issued Gucci shares for $3 billion after having shelled out another $1 billion to buy Sanofi's beauty products division, which included the famed House of Yves Saint Laurent. Pinault flipped Sanofi over to Gucci, in a play to create a multi-brand luxury brand group, run by Gucci's CEO Dominico De Sole and designer Tom Ford.

Ironically, the end of fashion had circled back to Paris, where the walls that had been hastily erected at the start of the decade to protect French fashion from the encroaching Italians and Americans had fallen down. Only five years ago Saint Laurent had shamed Ralph Lauren for knocking off his couture gowns. Now the Saint Laurent trademark had become the ward of two Americans—De Sole and Ford—at the helm of a new Italian fashion group.

The battle for Gucci was "emblematic of the New Europe that is taking shape with the launch of the common currency and the globalization of the industry: two Frenchmen squaring off for control of a Dutch-based Italian company, run by a U.S.-educated lawyer and an American designer advised by London-based American investment bankers," wrote Thomas Kamm in *The Wall Street Journal*.

Meanwhile, the losing side of the "war of the handbags" refused to retreat. Still Gucci's second largest shareholder and a raging bull not about to be upstaged by Gucci or Prada, LVMH had set about its own luxury-goods agenda in acquiring the designer businesses of Jil Sander and Helmut Lang, and pressed on to fortify its $8 billion luxury-goods empire, focusing on accessories—especially pricey purses—which had displaced perfumes as the must-have designer totems of the moment.

Executive women who had traded their business suits for khakis and cashmere were now inclined instead to splurge on fancy accessories like expensive handbags from Gucci, Fendi, and Prada. By 1999, handbags had upstaged dressy clothes as fashion's new stars—and profit makers—prompting a new round of deal making in the upper reaches of high fashion, and a reassessment of how the world dresses up.

Round two of the "war of the handbags" centered around Fendi, the Rome based fashion house that had been stone cold in the 1990s until it rebounded with a runaway hit—the "baguette" handbag—a saucy number that tucked under the arm like a loaf of French bread, accented with a boisterous double-F rhinestone buckle. In another telling sign of fashion's new globalization, LVMH paired with an Italian partner, Prada, to take control of the House of Fendi, for $900 million—a stupendous price that drew clucks among fashion insiders while underscoring fashion's current predicament.

"This media circus of the runway shows is all about selling products other than clothes," remarked David Wolfe of Doneger Group, retail consultants. "Designers aren't doing their job," he said. Stylish shoppers continue to be interested in fashion and are "so flush financially and anxious to buy something, but the runway clothes are unwearable. So they go out and buy an $800 Gucci bag."

But, as often happens when the fashion world moves en masse to chase the next Big Trend, already there were signs of a dressing down.

Designer Jil Sander quit her eponymous house after only five months under Prada, while menswear designer Hedi Slimane resigned his post at Saint Laurent. Both designers balked at taking orders from outsiders—a worrisome portent to all those newly formed fashion conglomerates that believed the designer companies they bought would simply do what they were told. The cost-saving synergies and economies of scale that worked so splendidly across a multitude of brands at General Motors or Procter & Gamble had yet to be tested in the mercurial hot houses of high fashion, where independent designers with big egos and freewheeling practices were firmly entrenched.

Awaiting his turn to run with the wolves was none other than Giorgio Armani, who announced in 2000 that he was ready to partner with perhaps Gucci or LVMH, as a new chapter of conglomerate-style high fashion was being written.

ACROSS THE ATLANTIC on Seventh Avenue, design houses were also steeped in acquisition fever—and litigation—as the rag trade's most revered designers tried to recast themselves in the new economy.

In October 1999, Calvin Klein put his venerable jeans and underwear empire on the auction block. He had his heart set on leaving his CK trademark in good hands, with an upscale European buyer like LVMH or Gucci. But after eight months, the House of Klein found no takers. The Europeans took a look, but balked at Calvin's $1 billion asking price. CK also entertained overtures from Tommy Hilfiger Corp. and Warnaco Group (the maker of CK jeans and underwear), but those talks also went nowhere.

But if Italy's Fendi could spark a bidding war and sell at $900 million, why couldn't America's Calvin Klein fetch at least a billion? The stark reality was that the CK trademark, famous for its sexy advertising and award-winning runway collections worn by supermodels like Kate Moss, was starting to fray. The bulk of Calvin's empire was jeans, underwear and perfumes, which were as ubiquitous in the bins at Costco and Walmart's Sam's Clubs as they were at Bloomingdale's.

And it was Warnaco that drove home the extent of CK's discount distribution. In January 2000, Warnaco suddenly announced its newest retail partner for CK underwear was none other than the very mass J.C. Penney. Department stores certainly didn't want to share their Calvin briefs with Penney's—and Dillard's was turned off enough to halt future orders of CK underwear. The Penney's revelation couldn't have come at a worse time, as it undermined Klein's efforts to peddle his fashion house as a luxury brand.

Decorating doyenne Martha Stewart had built an impressive $1 billion business via Kmart, which sold her sheets, towels and wall paint on the cheap, as the height of inverse chic. But Calvin Klein wasn't about to be linked with the bargain basement. Scrambling to retrieve his upscale image, Klein launched a bitter attack against Warnaco in a 64-page lawsuit, charging that his biggest licensee breached its contract and ruined his CK label by selling to cheapo channels—without Klein's approval. "This is like someone coming with a torch, a fire torch to your house and threatening to burn the whole thing up," the 57-year-old Klein fumed to *The Wall Street Journal*.

In its countersuit, Warnaco vehemently denied those allegations and vowed to prove that the house of Klein had known all along just what Warnaco was doing. But the forces on Seventh Avenue weren't buying his argument. They knew that there was no way that Warnaco could have built CK jeans and underwear into a $1 billion business—and paid Calvin Klein a $60 million annual royalty—without courting the likes of Costco.

But just days after his company sued Warnaco, an imperious Klein spent an hour on CNN's "Larry King Live" talk show, defending his actions, claiming that he had to litigate in order to protect his good name. He was hell-bent on severing his ties with Warnaco—a move that would leave his fashion house without a manufacturer for its money-making jeans and underwear. But he was willing to take the risk. Moreover, reclaiming his rights would make Calvin Klein Inc. far more salable in the future.

In the months to come, the Klein-Warnaco battle was destined to strip away the façade, to tell the whole truth: that the end of fashion had indeed arrived at its mass market reality.

THE YEAR 2000 turned out to be a stunning reversal for Tommy Hilfiger Corp. The slickest label in the 1990s was now a fashion victim, hurt by oversaturation and competition from hipper labels like Kenneth Cole and Fubu. As Wall Street investors realized that their favorite fashion racehorse was no longer a sure bet, Hilfiger shares collapsed on the New York Stock Exchange, sliding from $41 a share in August 1999 to around $7 in spring 2000—or just pennies above the perennially battered Donna Karan shares.

The $2 billion-a-year Hilfiger remained profitable but still had plenty to prove. The company retreated to bunker mentality in a corporate housecleaning that included shuttering its famed retail landmarks in Beverly Hills and London, which had been opened for less than two years. But Wall Street wasn't impressed. The Hilfiger empire sorely needed some new tricks, namely, new brands to promote alongside Tommy's 15-year-old franchise.

Ralph Lauren, too, had started to confront the limitations of his 32-year-old trademark. In 1999, Polo Ralph Lauren acquired Club Monaco, a fledgling, cutting-edge Canadian fashion chain known for its $100 knockoffs of Prada and Marc Jacobs. While Polo worked at folding Monaco into its operations, Polo whipped up a bit of high-tech froth by teaming with broadcaster NBC to create a website to sell Polo fashions on the Internet. This New, New Thing venture pushed all Ralph Lauren's buttons: Hollywood, publishing, fashion and retailing all rolled into one. Only time would tell if Ralph could turn his latest dream into a cash machine.

RALPH CERTAINLY WOULDN'T get any early encouragement from Wall Street. Never before had fashion been so out of style. Polo, Hilfiger and the rest of fashion and retail stocks were all in markdown mode in the new millennium, as profit-hungry investors cashed out of fashion and bought in to the hype and unlimited potential of high-tech and Internet ventures. And then there was Donna Karan International, still struggling to get its stock price up to $10 a share. CEO John Idol had promised that Donna Karan had indeed "turned the corner" after the company eked out a profit of $128,000—amounting to one cent a share in 1998, but the beleaguered fashion house had yet to drum up new momentum.

Donna Karan's first DKNY flagship store on Madison Avenue— replete with home furnishings and a juice bar—opened in the fall of 1999 to a blast of local fanfare that was quickly drowned out on a busy retail stretch teeming with every fancy international label in fashion. It looked like the fate of the famed Donna Karan was largely in the hands of its new licensee Liz Claiborne Inc., which had been busy marketing the DKNY jeans business and a new mid-priced DKNY women's line for department stores in 2001. Refusing to give up on the trademark that he helped to make famous, Takihyo partner Frank Mori finally joined Donna Karan's board of directors in 2000.

During her runway presentation in February 2000, the mercurial designer again weighed in with New Age music—and exposed her tin ear for public relations. As always, Donna had invited dozens of freelance photographers to cover her show, but this time they refused to be sardined into the impossibly tight space at the end of her showroom. The angry photographers marched out en masse, while a dozen more fashion-show guests, trapped in the building's elevator for more than an hour, also missed the show. Backstage with the models, a flustered Karan was overheard to shout: "Fuck the photographers!"

In its review, *Women's Wear Daily* admonished the designer for continuing to host presentations in her cramped showroom. "Whether the perceptions are fair or unfair, Donna has an image that is out of control," wrote *WWD*.

ACROSS THE MALLS, department stores held their ground amid the onslaught of the Targets and Wal-Marts while savvy specialty chains like Banana Republic and Abercrombie & Fitch continued to flex their fashion authority. In 1999, Marshall Field's kept up its campaign to be the hometown favorite again, but without sticking another thorn in Chicago's side. In March 1999, Chicagoans were outraged when they learned that Field's famous Frango chocolate mints, produced at its State Street store for more than seventy years, were leaving town. Dayton Hudson decided to close Field's candy kitchens in favor of making Frangos in Pittsburgh, where a local candy maker would be better able to fill the burgeoning demand for Frangos, which generated $17 million annually at its Marshall Field, Dayton, Hudson, and Target stores.

Harking back to the years when Dayton Hudson first took over Field's—and caused a ruckus when it tried to banish Field's signature green shopping bag—the flight of the Frangos came off as a snub to civic pride. The Frango fracas dominated front-page headlines in the *Chicago Tribune* as Chicago Mayor Richard M. Daley held a press conference where he blasted Dayton Hudson's brazen decision to discontinue a Chicago institution. "This is the candy capital of the United States," he declared. "You cannot find a candy company here to make Frango mints? Why do you have to go someplace else?"

After the candy controversy blew over, Field's continued to polish its fashion image, while the almighty Target steamrolled along, pushing its cheeky and value-minded fashion tradition, with bestselling designer merchandise like $15 teakettles by Michael Graves. The discounter was now a bona fide fashion authority, prompting Dayton Hudson Corp. to change its name to Target Corp. in 2000. At the end of fashion, an era in which many shoppers considered the cheap chic of Target far cooler than the carriage-trade appeal of Marshall Field's, the fashion industry was forced to adapt new standards and practices in keeping the new order. Still puzzling, however, were the luxury-goods fashion conglomerates such as LVMH which spent a fortune on couture fashion shows and celebrity mascots like Gwyneth Paltrow to burnish the market for $1,200 City Dior handbags.

Such luxury trinkets were bound to hit a wall even with affluent shoppers at a time when intrinsic value often trumps designer logos, nobody's dressing up, and everybody loves a bargain. And that even goes for socialite Blaine Trump, who was the fashion plate at Christian Lacroix's New York gala in 1987. In an article headlined CHEAPSKATE CHIC, Trump boasted to *The Wall Street Journal* in June 1999 that she buys her denim shorts for "something ridiculous like $9.99 at Kmart."

At the end of fashion it takes a whole lot of clever marketing to weave ordinary clothes into silken dreams.

The End of Fashion is based on 140 interviews, which I conducted between July 1996 and April 1999 in New York, Chicago, Los Angeles, Paris, and Milan, with all of the principal subjects of each chapter and people close to them. I attended all of the parties, fashion shows, and other events that took place during this period that I describe in detail. I have also used considerable secondary material from books, newspapers, magazines, and financial documents issued by publicly traded companies, in addition to my own articles from the ten years I have served as the fashion writer for *The Wall Street Journal*. In the few instances where I have used anonymous quotes in the text, I attempted to verify the account by checking with at least one other source.

A.I. = author's interview

INTRODUCTION

3 "We sold Isaac . . .": Kal Ruttenstein, A.I., 11/26/97.

4 "It looks *divine* . . .": Isaac Mizrahi, A.I., 7/2/97.

4 "All my life . . .": Michael Gross, "Slave of Fashion," *New York*, 10/1/1990.

5 "I just got . . .": Isaac Mizrahi, A.I.

6 "Look, it is all . . .": Ibid.

6 "I will always have . . .": "Isaac Mizrahi Shutting Down," *WWD*, 10/2/98.

9 "Today my style . . .": Teri Agins, "Way of All Flash: The Decline of Couture Is Seen in the Closing of a New York Salon," *The Wall Street Journal*, 4/28/92.

10 "There used to be . . .": Teri Agins, "Breaking Out of the Gray Flannel Suit," *The Wall Street Journal*, 3/23/92.

11 "Have We Become . . .": Jerry Adler, "Have We Become a Nation of Slobs?" *Newsweek*, 2/20/95.

12 "I got more . . .": Teri Agins, "Out of Fashion: Many Women Lose Interest in Clothes to Retailers' Dismay," *The Wall Street Journal*, 2/28/95.

12 "was only a bit . . .": "How to Buy a Sweater," *Consumer Reports*, December 1994.

12 "In another trial . . .": "Wash and Worry," *Consumer Reports*, May 1997.

14 "The fact is . . .": Martha Nelson, A.I., 8/4/97.

CHAPTER 1

17 "We will know . . .": Karl Lagerfeld, A.I., 4/24/98.

18 "The fact is . . .": Holly Brubach, "In Fashion: The Rites of Spring," *The New Yorker*, 6/6/88.

19 "You know, you . . .": "Lacroix Takes New York," *WWD*, 10/30/87.

19 "she felt forced, . . .": Dennis Thim, "The New Lacroix," *WWD*, 7/19/91.

20 "I believe I have . . .": Lacroix fashion show program, July 1997.

20 "When I wrote . . .": Bernadine Morris, A.I., 6/26/97.

21 "It's the same . . .": Teri Agins, "Not So Haute: French Fashion Loses Its Primacy as Women Leave Couture Behind," *The Wall Street Journal*, 8/29/95.

22 "Nowhere else in . . .": Marilyn Bender, *The Beautiful People*, New York: Coward McCann, 1966, p. 205.

22 "Worth, who invented . . .": Caroline Rennolds Milbank, *Couture*, New York: Stewart, Tabori & Chang, 1985, p. 26.

22 "The fashion system . . .": Pascal Morand, A.I., 7/9/97.

23 "They were all snobs . . .": Gerry Dryansky, A.I., 1/23/97.

24 "Christian Dior darted . . .": Bettina Ballard, *In My Fashion*, New York: David McKay, 1960, p. 60.

24 "Right after the shows . . .": Agins, "Not So Haute."

24 "better to wait . . .": Ballard, *In My Fashion*, op. cit.

25 "Most every French home . . .": Veronique Vienne, *French Style*, Columbus, Ohio: Express, 1993, p. 81.

26 "The women who . . .": James Brady, A.I., 1/9/97.

27 "The real issue . . .": John Fairchild, *Chic Savages*, New York: Pocket Books, 1989.

27 "What was amusing . . .": Karl Lagerfeld, A.I.

28 "From then on . . .": Bender, *Beautiful People*, p. 228.

28 "Dior rejected an initial offer . . .": Alice Rawsthorn, *Yves Saint Laurent*, New York: Nan A. Talese, 1996, p. 20.

29 "From 1983 to 1989 . . .": Marie Fournier, A.I., 4/23/98.

29 "all that horrible . . .": Marc Bohan, A.I., 1/24/97.

29 "suffered from 'inconsistency' . . ." and following: Colombe Nicholas, A.I., 5/2/97.

31 "My name is more . . .": Richard Morais, *Pierre Cardin*, London: Bantam, 1991, p. 150.

31 "Cardin is a very . . .": Henri Berghauer, A.I., 7/28/97.

31 "when he was forced . . .": Morais, op. cit., p. 164.

32 "His fortune was . . .": Ibid., p. 234.

32 "I don't understand . . .": Pierre Cardin, A.I., 1/22/97.

32 "Pierre was considered . . .": Henri Berghauer, A.I.

33 "A name is like . . .": Joan Kron, "Fashion Empire: Haute Couture Means High Finance at the House of Yves Saint Laurent," *The Wall Street Journal*, 9/10/84.

34 "The perfume business . . .": Patrick McCarthy, A.I., 12/10/97.

34 "was valued at . . .": Bryan Burrough, "The Selling of Saint Laurent," *Vanity Fair*, 4/93.

34 "In the next . . .": Philip Revzin and Teri Agins, "All About Yves: Saint Laurent Remains Idol of French Fashion but He Isn't Immortal," *The Wall Street Journal*, 4/6/89.

35 "If he dies . . .": Burrough, "Selling of Saint Laurent."

35 "developed a marketing . . .": Armando Branchini, A.I., 3/8/97.

35 "In one sense . . .": Fairchild, op. cit., p. 29.

36 "In 1984, Arab . . .": Kron, "Fashion Empire."

36 "It was Pierre . . .": Morais, op. cit., p. 119.

38 "In 1996, bridge . . .": Katherine Weisman, "Secondary Collections Can't Seem to Make a French Connection," *WWD*, 10/15/97.

38 "French designer brands . . .": Ibid.

38 "Mugler and Montana . . ." and following: Armand Hadida, A.I., 1/21/97.

39 "I just couldn't . . .": Elizabeth Snead, A.I., 4/99.

39 "We're really not . . ." and following: Joan Kaner, A.I., 5/23/97.

40 "When you look . . .": Agins, "Not So Haute."

41 "It is better . . .": Didier Grumbach, A.I., 7/4/97.

41 "Fashion in France . . .": Pascal Morand, A.I.

43 "Mouclier claimed that . . ." and following: Jacques Mouclier, A.I., 7/11/97.

43 "I know something . . .": Godfrey Deeney, "Ralph Cries Foul in Yves Saint Laurent Copycat Suit," *WWD*, 4/28/94.

44 "line for line . . ." and following: Godfrey Deeney, "Lauren Fined by Paris Court and So Is Bergé," *WWD*, 5/19/94.

44 "The French respondents . . .": Susan Rice, A.I., 7/95.

46 "Karl is a . . .": Bernadine Morris, A.I.

46 "All this media . . .": Karl Lagerfeld, A.I.

46 "no longer impressed . . .": Agins, "Not So Haute."

47 "Behind his angelic . . .": Nadege Forestier and Nazanine Ravai, *The Taste of Luxury*, London: Bloomsbury Publishing, 1992, p. 41.

47 "There was always . . .": Colombe Nicholas, A.I.

47 "My relationship to . . .": Forestier and Ravai, *Taste of Luxury*, p. 106.

48 "It is a massive . . .": Patrick McCarthy, A.I.

49 "looks 'like vomit' . . .": Laurence Benaim, "La Revolution de Soie," *Paris Match*, 1/19/97.

49 "People aren't going to . . .": James Fallon, "Alexander de Paris," *W*.

49 "crude and vulgar . . .": Karl Lagerfeld, A.I.

49 "For Bernard Arnault . . .": David Wolfe, A.I., 4/16/97.

50 "What is the press . . .": Colombe Nicholas, A.I.

50 "guaranteed to pill . . ." and following: Zoe Heller, "Jacob's Ladder," *The New Yorker*, 9/22/97.

51 "It isn't a question . . ." and following: Bernard Arnault, A.I., 3/19/99.

CHAPTER 2

54 "My colleagues always . . .": Charlotte Aillaud, "Emanuel Ungaro," *Architectural Digest*, 9/88,

55 "Ferragamo was prepared . . .": Ferrucio Ferragamo, A.I., 8/96.

55 "I want this . . .": Emanuel Ungaro, A.I., 7/96.

56 "Emanuel had such . . .": Grace Mirabella, A.I., 4/5/97.

56 "Nearly all of . . .": Carlo Valerio, A.I., 1/21/97.

57 "These are huge . . .": Katherine Weisman, "Ungaro's New Marriage," *WWD*, 7/8/96.

58 "had stashed them . . .": Pier Filipo Pieri, A.I., 1/21/97.

59 "During that time . . .": Ferrucio Ferragamo, A.I., 8/96.

59 "It was easy . . .": Ibid.

60 "had a perfect . . .": Aillaud, op. cit.

61 "What I can . . .": Gruppo GFT, *Emanuel Ungaro*, Milan: Electa, Milan Elemond Editori Associati, 1992, p. 38.

61 "When Balenciaga changed . . .": Beverly Rice, A.I., 6/11/97.

62 "Knapp hocked her . . .": Emanuel Ungaro, A.I., 1/29/97.

62 "One name on . . .": *WWD*, 7/65.

63 "GFT said . . .": Emanuel Ungaro, A.I., 7/12/97.

63 "But the couturier . . .": René Ungaro, A.I., 4/24/98.

63 "He makes what . . .": Catherine de Limur, from an unpublished 1984 interview with Joan Kron.

63 "Research just shows . . .": Emanuel Ungaro, A.I., 4/24/98.

64 "I sew the sleeves . . .": Emanuel Ungaro, A.I., 1/29/97.

64 "Everything evolves from . . .": Pamela Golbin, A.I., 1/29/97.

64 "full of suffering . . .": Emanuel Ungaro, A.I., 1/21/97.

65 "I try to teach . . .": Emanuel Ungaro, A.I., 1/21/97.

66 "After twenty-three years . . .": Jennet Conant, "The Heat Is On," *Newsweek*, 4/4/88.

66 "Emanuel puts a woman . . .": Lynn Wyatt, 4/17/97.

66 "turning off lights . . .": "Rich, Rich, Rich," *WWD*, 1/1/86.

67 "never spent more . . .": Carlo Valerio, A.I., 1/21/97.

67 "We have a . . .": Maura De Visscher, A.I., 6/97.

67 "I knew the . . .": Kyra Sedgwick, A.I., 7/97.

68 "hearts were shattered . . .": Ben Brantley, "Ungaro Undone," *Vanity Fair*, 3/90.

68 "I like to play . . .": Laura Ungaro, A.I., 7/11/97.

69 "heavy, clumsy and brutal . . .": Salvatore Ferragamo, *Salvatore Ferragamo, Shoe-maker of Dreams*, Florence: Centro di Della Edifimi srl, 1985 (originally published in 1957), p. 42.

69 "Salvatore became famous . . ." and following history: Stefania Ricci, *Salvatore Ferragamo, The Art of the Shoe*, New York: Rizzoli International Publications, 1992, pp. 60–86.

71 "For *them*, it was . . ." and following: Steven Slowick, A.I., 7/9/97.

72 "The Bain review . . .": Carlo Valerio, A.I., 9/97.

72 "We know he gets . . .": Ferrucio Ferragamo, A.I.

73 "thought it might . . ." and following: Peter Arnell, A.I., 6/2/97.

73 "Valerio worried that . . .": Carlo Valerio, 1/8/98.

73 "zero for the . . .": Ferragamo, A.I. With regard to Ferragamo's aversion to licensing, see Harvard Business School case study N 9-391-159 on Salvatore Ferragamo SpA, in which Fulvia Ferragamo is quoted: "If the label says Ferragamo, then there is a Ferragamo behind it from design to sale."

74 "There was little . . ." and following: Carlo Valerio, A.I.

74 "The division had . . .": Carlo Valerio, A.I., and confidential source.

75 "difficult opportunity . . .": Thierry Andretta, A.I., 4/23/98.

75 "I like the history . . .": Ibid.

76 "Laura Ungaro hit the . . .": Thierry Andretta, A.I., 9/10/98.

76 "Ferrucio is more . . ." and following: Laura Ungaro, A.I., 4/24/98.

77 "The Ferragamos are . . ." and following: Emanuel Ungaro, A.I., 4/24/98.

78 "We can't force . . ." and following: Ferrucio Ferragamo, A.I., 4/11/99.

CHAPTER 3

80 "I don't respect . . .": Ralph Lauren, A.I., 4/9/97.

81 "Lauren couldn't get . . .": Confidential sources.

81 "You know, most . . .": Frank Rich, "Stars and Stripes for Polo," *The New York Times*, 7/18/98.

81 "We've been assured . . .": Patricia Leigh Brown, "Hillary Clinton Inaugurates Presentation Campaign," *The New York Times*, 7/14/98.

81 *The Washington Times* cartoon ran on 7/19/98.

81 "A shopper at . . .": Rich, "Stars and Stripes."

82 "Congress was considering, . . ."and following quote from Rich: Ibid.

84 "It's not the jeans . . .": Terry Lundgren, A.I., 12/23/97.

85 "Ralph Lauren, who . . .": Ralph Lauren, A.I., 4/9/97.

86 "Young Ralph set . . .": Jeffrey A. Trachtenberg, *Ralph Lauren: The Man Behind the Mystique,* Boston: Little, Brown, 1998, p. 26.

86 "as Brooksy as . . .": Cathy Horyn, "Ralph Lauren, Suiting Himself; Sometimes, Criticism Can Wear a Little Thin," *The Washington Post,* 5/24/92.

86 "Frank Lifshitz was . . .": Jeffrey A. Trachtenberg, p. 20.

86 "millionaire . . .": Ibid., p. 26.

87 "Nobody was interested . . ." and following: Ibid., p. 29.

87 "The age of elegance . . .": Ibid., p. 60.

87 "buoyed by a . . .": Ibid.

88 "I elevated the . . .": Ralph Lauren, A.I.

88 "I would be . . .": Lang Philips, "Confessions of a Young Wasp," *New York,* 9/2/91.

88 "The only difference . . .": Jonathan Yardley, "King Lauren Conferring Nobility," *The Washington Post,* 12/15/86.

89 "I don't put . . .": Ralph Lauren, A.I.

89 "LVMH's Bernard Arnault . . .": Bernard Arnault, A.I., 3/19/99.

89 "Polo's licensees generated . . ." (for fiscal year ending 3/31/86): Trachtenberg, p. 263.

90 "In 1894, the . . .": Trachtenberg, p. 9. Author's note: "The Madison Avenue store generated sales of $33.8 million in fiscal 1993. Given the significant original investment in construction, as well as the ongoing expenses associated with maintaining it as a perfect prototype for Polo's customers and licensees, management expects that the store's expenses will continue to exceed its revenues." From a confidential financial document on Polo Ralph Lauren Corp. prepared by the company.

91 "Everyone loves M&M's . . .": Ralph Lauren, A.I.

91 "Ralph is demanding . . .": Confidential source.

91 "Ralph was always . . .": Confidential source.

91 "The salespeople were . . .": Confidential source.

92 "Think of this . . .": Confidential source.

92 "I always see . . .": Mimi Avins, "The Good Life for 30 Years. Ralph Lauren Has Set the Standard for American Style," *Los Angeles Times*, 9/12/96.

92 "Now I think . . .": Ibid.

93 "stuff inside there . . .": "Ralph's Teepee," *W*, 12/1/95.

94 "Ralph is busy . . .": Confidential source.

94 "We work with . . .": Ralph Lauren, A.I.

94 "Every year the . . .": Confidential source.

95 "Ralph is the . . ." and following: Confidential source.

96 "Do I need . . .": Ralph Lauren, A.I.

97 "Ralph wanted the . . .": Teri Agins, "Gang of Five," *Avenue*, 9/89.

97 "When you see him . . .": Confidential source.

97 "There probably isn't . . .": Horyn, "Suiting Himself."

98 "gobbled up and . . .": Michael Gross, "Ralph's World," *New York*, 9/20/93.

98 "In 1990, Calvin . . ." and following: Teri Agins and Jeffrey A. Trachtenberg, "Designer Troubles: Calvin Klein Is Facing a Bind as Magic Touch Appears to Be Slipping," *The Wall Street Journal*, 11/22/91.

99 "Klein's reversal of . . .": Teri Agins, "Shaken by a Series of Business Setbacks, Calvin Klein Inc. Is Redesigning Itself," *The Wall Street Journal*, 3/21/94.

101 "preppy classics with . . .": Hilfiger Corp. press releases.

101 "Murjani's Polo-lite . . ." and following: Teri Agins, *The Wall Street Journal*.

101 "Every decade someone . . .": Trachtenberg, p. 220.

101 "He may have . . .": Agins, "Tommy Hilfiger," op. cit.

101 "To the consumer . . .": Vicki Vasilopoulous, "U.S. Designers Set Out to Redefine Themselves," *DNR*, 12/24/90.

102 "By setting his . . .": Amy M. Spindler, "Hilfiger's New Blueprint," *The New York Times*, 6/11/96.

102 "Tommy came down . . .": Michael Toth, A.I., 6/19/97.

103 "I haven't done . . .": Ralph Lauren, A.I.

103 "He chatted up . . .": Tommy Hilfiger, A.I., 8/5/97.

104 "They couldn't believe . . .": Jim Moore, A.I., 4/97.

105 "I saw products . . ." and following: Silas Chou, A.I., 8/5/98.

106 "Tapping into his . . .": Joel Horowitz, A.I., 8/18/97.

106 "From the beginning . . .": Ibid.

106 "Hilfiger's initial public . . .": Hilfiger Corp. stock prospectus, 6/12/92.

106 "We are just . . .": Silas Chou, A.I.

107 "Now I'm not . . .": Joel Horowitz, A.I.

108 "Four times a year . . .": The author attended Hilfiger's adoption meeting.

111 "We always bought . . .": Jonathan Van Meter, "Hip Hop Hilfiger," *Vogue*, 11/96.

111 "honest working people . . ." and following: Michel Marriott, "Inner-City Outer Gear, Urban Youth Take to Clothing of the Outdoors," *The New York Times*, 2/17/94.

112 "Andy knew that . . ." and following quote: Andy Hilfiger, A.I.

113 "The next week . . .": Ibid.

113 "He didn't use . . ." and following: Lloyd Boston, A.I., 8/5/97.

114 "Kidada speaks her . . .": Andy Hilfiger, A.I.

114 "Tommy Hill was my . . ." and following quote: Alex Foege, "Playboy Interview: Tommy Hilfiger," *Playboy*, 10/97.

114 "I feel proud . . .": Joel Horowitz, A.I.

115 "the number one . . .": According to spokesman from Oxford Industries, Hilfiger's shirt licensee, 8/97.

115 "Tommy is a . . ." and following quote: Ned Allie, A.I., 8/5/97.

116 "There are people . . .": Ralph Lauren, A.I.

116 "Tommy gives Ralph . . .": Confidential source.

116 "his salary would climb . . .": Hilfiger Corp. 1996 proxy statement.

116 "Ralph and I . . .": Alex Foege, op. cit.

117 "Tommy shrugged it . . ." Tommy Hilfiger, A.I.

117 "I sensed that . . ." and following quote: Ralph Lauren, A.I.

118 "Ralph knows the . . .": Susan Caminiti, A.I., 98.

118 "Is this going to be on the cover . . .": Ibid.

118 "And on one . . .": Spokespersons for Lauren and Hilfiger, A.I., 5/99.

119 "Lauren's first jeans . . .": Trachtenberg, pp. 200–201.

119 "As a matter . . ." Ibid. p. 202.

119 "The company rolled out . . .": Mary Ellen Gordon, "Double RL Hits Some Bumps Along the Way," *WWD*, 9/93.

120 "By the time . . .": Andy Hilfiger, A.I.

121 "Such were the . . .": The author attended Hilfiger's book signing in New York.

122 "I don't know . . .": Michael Toth, A.I.

123 "Friday night was . . .": The author attended the Hilfiger party.

124 "People around here . . .": Confidential source.

124 "It's a generational . . ." and following quote: Joel Horowitz, A.I.

125 "Maybe we can . . .": Silas Chou, A.I.

CHAPTER 4

127 "The press gives . . .": Giorgio Armani, A.I., 7/30/98.

128 "high-energy . . .": Armani press release, 9/19/96.

129 "an estimated $2 million . . .": Estimate provided by Armani officials. The Emporio Armani concert was largely underwritten by its licensees.

129 "He recruits my . . .": Sara Gay Forden, "Armani Ballistic as Forte Leaves Him for Calvin," *WWD*, 5/24/94.

130 "great complicity . . .": Giorgio Armani, A.I., 3/14/97.

130 "For the moment . . ." and following quote: Ibid.

131 "felt very young . . .": Ibid.

132 "an impressive $90 million . . .": Jay Cocks, "Suiting Up for Easy Street; Giorgio Armani Defines the New Shape of Style," *Time*, 4/5/82.

132 "changed his life . . .": Teri Agins, "Who Loves Armani? Actors, Car Washers, and Senior V.P.'s," *The Wall Street Journal*, 10/31/90.

132 "Armani is safe . . .": James Servin, "Look Who's Watching," *Harper's Bazaar*, 9/98.

132 "Change has to . . .": Suzanne Somers, *Italian Chic*, New York: Villard Books, 1992, p. 19.

133 "Armani changed the . . .": Patrick McCarthy, A.I.

133 "Armani put women . . .": Rosita Missoni, A.I., 3/6/97.

133 "The news from . . .": "Notes on Fashion," *The New York Times*, 7/18/83.

134 "Nicholas auditioned several . . ." and following: Colombe Nicholas, A.I.

134 "I know that . . ." and following: Patrick Robinson, A.I., 4/5/97.

135 "went through the . . .": Colombe Nicholas, A.I.

135 "We had our . . .": Patrick Robinson, A.I.

135 "I pay attention, . . ." Giorgio Armani, A.I.

136 "journalist Carl Bernstein . . .": Agins, "Who Loves Armani?" op. cit.

136 "Fashion is finished . . .": Rebecca Mead, "Giorgio Armani Designer," *New York*, 9/16/96.

138 "Celebrities work on . . .": Martha Nelson, A.I., 8/4/97.

138 "Versace loved the . . .": Hal Rubenstein, A.I., 8/97.

139 "wore Versace on . . .": Cathy Horyn, A.I.

140 "The Italian designers have . . .": Sara Gay Forden, A.I., 7/98.

140 "In Italy, we . . .": Armando Branchini, A.I., 3/9/97.

140 "There was no way . . .": Marie-France Pochna, *Christian Dior*, New York: Arcade Publishing, 1996, p. 161.

142 "Lancia charged us . . .": Nino Cerruti, A.I., 7/8/97.

142 "Cerruti's Paris boutique . . .": Ibid.

143 "What I could spot . . .": Ibid.

143 "fruitful years . . .": Cocks, "Suiting Up," op. cit.

144 "People were all . . .": Giorgio Armani, A.I.

144 "Armani had already . . .": Nino Cerruti, A.I.

145 "Kathleen was very . . .": Nino Cerruti, A.I.

145 "Hollywood is like . . .": Ibid.

146 "Gabriella is a true . . .": Pier Filipo Pieri, A.I., 1/21/97.

147 "Radziwill had mentioned . . .": Karen Stabiner, "Dressing Well Is the Best Revenge, or How a Former Reporter Went from Missouri to Milan—and a Job That Pays Her to Wear $2,000 Designer Suits," *Los Angeles Times,* 12/11/88.

147 "It'll be a . . .": *Los Angeles Times,* "Listen," 6/10/88.

148 "bought up a storm . . .": Marylouise Oates, "Marylouise Oates: Broadway at the Bowl: Bet on a Sequel," *Los Angeles Times,* 8/31/88.

148 "Costner turned . . .": Wanda McDaniel, A.I., 11/15/97.

148 "Catholic schools had . . .": Pat Reilly, A.I., 11/24/97.

148 "My players always . . ." and following: Ibid.

149 "Armani initially provided . . .": Ibid.

149 "made an adjustment . . ." and following: Ibid.

150 "also flew Reilly . . .": Confidential source.

151 "Lee Radziwill called to . . .": Bridget Foley, "CFDA: A Bumpy Trip to Its Lincoln Center Bash," *WWD,* 2/3/92.

151 "So maybe they . . .": Ibid.

151 "I'd almost feel . . .": Pat Reilly, A.I.

151 "looks like an . . .": Kevin Doyle, "Armani's True Confessions: The Magician of the Jacket, Giorgio Armani Is a Secret Dreamer Who's Putting His Fantasy on Display in His First Major Retrospective," *WWD,* 6/25/92.

151 "I had a business . . .": Ibid.

152 "The stars were . . .": Bob Mackie, A.I., 1/6/98.

153 "That dress was so . . .": Ibid.

154 "It's not so . . .": Wayne Scot Lukas, A.I., 10/97.

154 "hip, cool and . . ." and following: Ibid.

155 "On a night . . .": Glenn Close, A.I., 9/20/98.

155 "When I'm in . . .": Ibid.

156 "He was so . . .": Armani spokeswoman, A.I., 11/15/97.

156 "I like to keep . . ." and following quote: Giorgio Armani, A.I.

157 "According to its . . .": Armani spokeswoman, A.I.

157 "It started out . . .": Wanda McDaniel, A.I.

157 "she received, unsolicited . . .": Lisa Bannon, "And the Winner Is: Anybody Who Has an Oscar-Night Gig," *The Wall Street Journal*, 3/21/97.

158 "After the Escada . . .": Teri Agins, "Will Tom Hanks Wear Hush Puppies on Oscar Night?" *The Wall Street Journal*, 3/24/95.

158 "The maker of . . .": Ibid.

158 "I'm trying to . . .": Ibid.

158 "Gap sold thousands . . .": Gap spokeswoman, A.I., 1998.

158 "Mr. Armani is . . .": Agins, "Will Tom Hanks."

158 "We're cutting back . . .": Armani spokeswoman.

159 "The company's wholesale . . .": Armani spokeswoman.

160 "In 1998, several . . .": Heidi Parker, "Film Fashion Frenzy," *Movieline*, 9/98.

160 "can overhype . . .": Martha Nelson, A.I.

160 "Armani is synonymous . . .": Sara Gay Forden, A.I.

CHAPTER 5

162 "The consumer is . . .": Daniel J. Boorstin, *The Americans: The Democratic Experience*, New York: Random House, 1973.

163 "This was a moment . . .": Michael Francis, A.I., 1/97.

164 "the noisiest confrontation . . .": Peter Wilkinson, "Store Wars: Marshall Field's and the Bloomingdale's Invasion," *Vanity Fair*, 10/88.

164 "It'll be fun . . .": Ibid.

165 "Marshall Field's and a little . . .": Gary Witkin, A.I., 6/30/97.

165 "The ambiance is . . .": Gloria Bacon, A.I., 6/10/97.

165 "Customers [were] telling . . .": Dan Skoda, A.I., 7/22/97.

166 "When you go . . .": Gary Witkin, A.I.

166 "Establishing an identity . . .": Arnold Aronson, A.I., 8/12/97.

168 "about $70 million . . .": Janet Key, "Field's Keeps Legend Alive, Still Chicago's Number One," 9/9/85, *Chicago Tribune.*

168 "We had an . . .": Arnold Aronson, A.I.

169 "People would stop . . .": Phyllis Collins, A.I., 8/23/97.

169 "Miller's biggest challenge . . ." and following description: Key, *Chicago Tribune*, op. cit.

169 "You can't get . . .": Ibid.

170 "Disneyland of party . . ." and following: Jon Anderson, Barbara Mahany, Ron Grossman, "Social Studies: Chicago Pops the Cork on a Magnum Party Season," *Chicago Tribune*, 9/11/88.

170 "I'm not eating . . .": Ibid.

170 "I hope this . . .": Jon Anderson, Barbara Mahany, Genevieve Buck, John Teets, "Party Wars: 3,400 Cheer on the Blast on Boul Mich," *Chicago Tribune*, 2/25/88.

171 "This is the . . .": Ibid.

171 "If it's done . . .": Ibid.

171 Description of Robert Campeau's speech: Dorothy Fuller, A.I., 8/24/97.

171 "$7.5 billion . . .": Jeffrey A. Trachtenberg, "Campeau's Federated and Allied Stores Take Step Toward Leaving Chapter 11," *The Wall Street Journal*, 10/29/91.

172 "an 'ideal marriage' . . .": Genevieve Buck, "Can Crown Jewel Be Restored? Dayton Hudson Will Need Magic Wand to Revive Field's Mystique," *Chicago Tribune*, 12/25/95.

172 "Marshall Field's is . . .": Dorothy Fuller, A.I.

172 Descriptions of Field and Leiter and Marshall Field & Co.: Lloyd Wendt and Herman Kogan, *Give the Lady What She Wants: The Story of Marshall Field & Co.* New York: Rand McNally, 1950.

172 "marble palace . . .": Charles Collins, *Chicago Tribune*, 2/10/52.

173 "style expert . . ." and bustle dress: Homer Sharp, A.I., 2/23/97.

173 "I like this . . .": Wendt and Kogan, *Give the Lady What She Wants*, p. 237.

174 "Chicago gangster Al Capone . . .": Ibid., p. 355

175 "Kathleen was so . . .": Dorothy Fuller, A.I.

175 "we put them . . ." and following Carmel Snow quote: Ibid.

175 "Kathleen knew that . . .": Ibid.

176 "who swept through . . ." and following: Wendt and Kogan, *Give the Lady What She Wants,* pp. 204–207.

176 "came by the . . .": Ibid.

176 "Dayton Hudson was keen . . .": Gary Witkin, A.I.

177 "Never in their minds . . ." and following: Phyllis Collins, A.I.

177 "Gloria Bacon, a Field's . . .": Gloria Bacon, A.I.

178 "The Chicago customers . . .": Gary Witkin, A.I.

178 "Our buyers are your . . .": Homer Sharp, A.I., 8/23/97.

178 "Our buyers are lucky . . .": Dan Skoda, A.I.

178 "before television and . . .": Allen Questrom, A.I., 4/16/97.

179 "created the ultimate . . .": Philip Miller, A.I., 4/30/97.

179 "Most people don't . . .": Allen Questrom, A.I.

180 "or about a million . . ." Dayton Hudson Corp. 1997, 1998 annual reports.

180 "a show of . . .": Genevieve Buck, "Marshall Field's for Fall: Fashion and Theatre Share the Same Stage," *Chicago Tribune,* 5/8/91.

180 " 'Cause for Applause' was . . .": Genevieve Buck, "Fashion Show a Festive Affair with Patinkin," *Chicago Tribune,* 8/11/91.

181 "The way we . . .": Gerald Storch, A.I., 7/97.

181 "There were more . . .": Teri Agins, "Out of Fashion, Many Women Lose Interest in Clothes to Retailers' Dismay," *The Wall Street Journal,* 2/28/95.

181 "The way retailers . . .": Carl Steidtmann, A.I., 6/23/97.

182 "Never ones to . . .": Ann Hagedorn, "Will Many Go Mini? The Fashion World Awaits the Answer," *The Wall Street Journal,* 6/22/87.

182 "Claiborne spent hundreds of . . .": Irene Daria, *The Fashion Cycle,* New York, Simon & Schuster, 1990, p. 14.

183 "Nina Totenberg . . .": Ibid., p. 7.

183 "apparel prices fell . . .": Agins, "Out of Fashion," op. cit.

184 "Only about 20 percent . . .": Teri Agins, "Liz Claiborne to Close Stores but Problems Remain," *The Wall Street Journal*, 12/29/94.

184 "The average retail . . .": Agins, "Out of Fashion," op. cit.

184 "the more confident . . .": Susan Faludi, *Backlash*, p. 174.

184 "In women's apparel . . .": Agins, "Out of Fashion," op. cit.

185 Gap brand has been the second most popular brand after Levi's since 1991: Russell Mitchell, "The Gap," *Business Week*, 3/9/92.

185 Gap 1998 results from company reports.

185 "For years, we . . .": Patrick McCarthy, A.I.

186 "Fashion had ground . . .": David Wolfe, A.I.

187 "That is the big . . .": Patrick McCarthy, A.I.

187 "By 1996, discounters . . ." and following on Wal-Mart and department stores' market share: Ira P. Schneiderman, "Discounters Snag More Apparel Shoppers," *WWD*, 6/11/97.

188 "Outside of Bloomingdale's . . .": Terry Lundgren, A.I., 12/23/97

188 "is not growing . . .": Management Horizons report "North American Retail Outlook to 2001," 5/97.

188 "There are maybe . . .": Robert Buchanan, A.I., 3/97.

189 Description of Eileen Fisher's relationship with department stores: Eileen Fisher, A.I., 9/97.

190 "The worst thing . . .": Ellin Saltzman, A.I., 2/25/97.

190 "May has never . . .": Arnold Aronson, A.I.

191 "I can wait . . .": Dan Skoda, A.I.

191 "desperately need to . . .": Management Horizons.

192 "If we really . . .": Kal Ruttenstein, A.I.

192 "We give them . . .": Joan Kaner, A.I.

193 Banana Republic estimates are for 1998 from Richard Baum, Goldman, Sachs & Co., A.I., 3/99.

193 "We felt the . . .": Mickey Drexler speech at Goldman, Sachs & Co. Retailing Conference in New York, 9/11/98.

194 "Gap Gets It . . .": Nina Munk, *Fortune,* 8/3/98.

194 "We were promotionally . . ." and following quote: Dan Skoda, A.I., 8/22/97.

196 "In the old . . .": Hank Lorant, A.I., 9/11/98.

197 "They are now . . .": Dan Skoda, A.I., 9/11/98.

197 "We couldn't believe . . .": Confidential source.

197 "They're slowly . . .": Susan Chandler, "Field's Re-Wooing of Upscale Shoppers May Be Winning Strategy: Parent Has Seen Payoff in the Last Four Months," *Chicago Tribune,* 7/26/98.

198 "They recognized . . .": Ibid.

198 The author attended Field's 9/11/98 party in Chicago.

199 "Thank God, the . . .": Sugar Rautbord, A.I., 9/11/98.

CHAPTER 6

200 "No, I'm not . . .": *WWD,* 5/97.

200 "I don't watch . . .": Teri Agins and Wendy Bounds, "Donna Karan CEO Is Sobered by Wall Street Fling," *The Wall Street Journal,* 11/13/96.

202 "Women will decide . . .": Mimi Avins, "Karan Layers It on with Her New Line," *Los Angeles Times,* 10/30/96.

202 "talked her into . . .": Josie Esquivel, A.I., 97.

203 "It was all . . .": Confidential source.

205 "Unfortunately, we never . . .": Tomio Taki, A.I., 2/5/97.

206 The description of the road show and quotes from Karan are all from "Going Public," Donna Karan, *Vogue,* 9/96.

206 "She made it . . .": Tomio Taki, A.I.

206 At the $24-a-share June 1996 offering, Takihyo's 24.7 percent stake in Donna Karan was valued at about $127.5 million. By October, DK traded at around $15.50, making Takihyo's stake worth about $82 million.

206 "I have been a . . .": "Donna Karan's Agenda: Find a Co-chief Executive, Firm Up Licensing Deals," *WWD*, 6/6/97.

208 "The market has . . ." and following quote: Linda Killian, A.I., 4/14/97.

209 "Donna Karan's best . . .": Linda Sandler and Teri Agins, "Donna Karan IPO Got a Warm Reception but Designer's Earnings Outlook Is Uncertain," *The Wall Street Journal*, 7/1/96.

210 "Investors were starstruck . . .": Josie Esquivel, A.I. 5/97.

210 "Fashion companies can . . .": Arnold Cohen, A.I., 7/97.

210 "Puritan couldn't survive . . ." and following quote: Ibid.

211 "Kimmel personally pocketed . . ." and following: Thomas J. Ryan and Lisa Lockwood, "The Age of the IPO: Fashion Execs Wear Crowns of Royalty," *WWD*, 4/17/97.

213 "Columbia skirted the . . .": Thomas J. Ryan, "Columbia's IPO Wows Wall Street," *WWD*, 3/30/98.

213 "High fashion and . . .": Alan Millstein, A.I., 2/97.

213 "Donna is an . . .": Ibid.

214 "poured more than $10 million . . .": Tomio Taki, A.I.

215 "a terrible student . . .": Jennet Conant, "The New Queen of New York," *Manhattan Inc.*, 10/89.

215 "I was always a . . .": Ibid.

215 "But Donna was unfocused . . .": Ibid.

216 "Young Taki had . . .": Teri Agins, "Tomio Taki Is Hoping to Stay in Fashion," *The Wall Street Journal*, 8/30/88.

216 "he sent dozens . . ." Ibid.

216 "get the order . . .": Dexter Levy, A.I., 7/27/98.

216 "Oppenheim had no . . .": Ibid.

216 "Anne was legendary . . ." and following: Ibid.

218 "There are no . . .": Agins, "Tomio Taki Is Hoping," op. cit.

218 "sit wherever you . . .": Ibid.

219 "I wanted her . . .": Tomio Taki, A.I.

219 "it was always . . .": Ibid.

219 "I needed a . . ." and following quote: Teri Agins, "Woman on the Verge," *Working Woman*, 5/93.

220 "Go talk to . . .": Tomio Taki, Ibid.

220 "Unfortunately, the combination . . ." and following quote: Ibid.

221 "I design from . . .": Agins, "Woman on the Verge."

222 "In my opinion . . .": Stephen Ruzow, A.I., 2/98.

222 "Fortunately, her bread-and-butter . . .": Ibid.

223 "Karan was a . . .": Agins, "Woman on the Verge."

224 "intimately acquainted . . .": Conant, "The New Queen."

224 "What's business to . . .": Agins, "Woman on the Verge."

224 "insures that a . . .": Ibid.

224 "She would do . . .": Ibid.

225 "We creative types . . .": Agins and Bounds, "Donna Karan CEO."

225 "Donna is the . . .": Confidential source.

226 "In creating financial . . .": Tomio Taki, A.I.

226 "Whenever the costs . . .": Stephen Ruzow, A.I.

227 "She and Weiss . . .": Agins, "Woman on the Verge."

227 "We had so . . .": Tomio Taki, A.I.

227 "The scent was . . ." and following quote: Georgina Howell, "Donna's Prime Time," *Vogue*, 8/92.

227 "losses of $5.9 million . . .": Teri Agins, "With IPO in the Wing Is Donna Karan in Fashion?" *The Wall Street Journal*, 8/16/93.

228 "The fragrance debacle . . .": Tomio Taki, A.I.

229 Details of Leslie Fay accounting scandal: Teri Agins, "Loose Threads: Dress Maker

Leslie Fay Is an Old Style Firm That's in a Modern Fix," *The Wall Street Journal*, 2/23/93.

230 "So Karan, Weiss, and . . .": Teri Agins and Sara Calian, "Donna Karan Suspends Plan for Public Offer," *The Wall Street Journal*, 11/18/93.

230 "He wasn't credible . . .": Rebecca Mead, "Donna Sells Her Soul," *New York*, 5/6/96.

230 "burns my butt . . .": Ibid.

231 Gucci results from 1995 and 1996 offerings from Gucci Group press releases.

231 "The company's balance . . .": Donna Karan International stock prospectus, 6/10/96.

232 "For the use . . .": Ibid.

232 "advised against . . .": Josie Esquivel, A.I., and Tomio Taki, A.I.

232 "claiming that it . . .": Tomio Taki, A.I.

232 "if anybody deserved . . .": Ibid.

233 "Designer Holdings made . . .": Wendy Bounds, "Donna Karan Shares Sink After Pact with Designer Holdings Is Terminated," *The Wall Street Journal*, 3/6/97.

233 "The contract stated . . .": Arnold Simon, A.I., 6/11/97.

234 "We were on track . . .": Stephen Ruzow, A.I.

235 "Mori appealed to . . .": Jennifer Steinhauer, "Donna Karan in the Cutting Room," *The New York Times*, 6/28/97.

235 "didn't sit well . . .": "Karan Reflects on Her Week's Development," *WWD*, 8/4/97.

235 "But there was . . .": Stephen Ruzow, A.I.

235 "estimated $100 million . . .": Ibid.

236 "Employees saw many . . ." and following: John Idol, A.I., 3/10/99.

236 "But Karan had gotten . . .": Ibid.

237 "Consistency in menswear . . .": Stephen Ruzow, A.I.

237 "one-time fashion . . .": John Idol, A.I.

237 "ridiculous that DKNY's . . .": John Idol speech at Goldman Sachs & Co. Retailing Conference, 9/9/98.

237 "This is The . . .": Ibid.

238 "I'll pay for . . .": Confidential source.

238 "We may have . . .": Wendy Bounds, Donna Karan interview on Dow Jones News Service, 4/27/97.

238 "We've turned the . . .": Teri Agins, "Donna Karan Reports Much Narrowed Loss and Cost Cutting," *The Wall Street Journal*, 3/25/99.

239 "The post IPO . . .": Valerie Seckler, "Wall Street Runway, Why Some Stocks Fly and Others Don't," *WWD*, 5/11/98.

239 "to pull in $44 million . . .": Russ Stanton, "The Rise and Fall of Mossimo Giannulli," *Los Angeles Times*, 3/8/98.

240 "latter-day version of rat-packer . . .": Frederick Rose and Teri Agins, "Fashion Designer Becomes Fashion Victim on Wall Street," *The Wall Street Journal*, 10/23/96.

240 "shareholders headed into . . .": Frederick Rose, "Designer Mossimo to Wear New Title of Firm's 'Visionary,' " *The Wall Street Journal*, 3/6/98.

242 "I never believed . . ." and following: Robert Gray, A.I., 11/10/97.

242 "the Grays sold . . ." and following: Ibid.

243 "We're not going . . .": Ibid.

243 "You know we . . .": Gray speech to analysts at Robertson Stephens Retailing Conference in New York on 10/11/98.

245 Claiborne study: Al Shapiro, A.I., 1/98.

CHAPTER 7

247 "You don't have to . . .": Zoran, A.I., 2/98.

250 "amounted to an estimated . . .": Estimates from retail executives.

252 "Zoran recalled spending . . .": Teri Agins, "Uniquely Chic: If Zoran Doesn't Ring a Bell That's Fine with Quirky Designer," *The Wall Street Journal*, 5/8/95.

252 "was an equal . . .": *Marion Greenberg v. Zoran Ladicorbic*, State Supreme Court of New York, 7/1/83.

252 "who was initially . . ." and following: Ben Brantley, A.I., 97.

253 "didn't consider Zoran . . .": Ibid.

253 "Zoran is a man . . .": Ibid.

254 "You need to . . .": Agins, "Uniquely Chic."

254 "He wanted to . . .": Ibid.

255 "I want you . . ." and following: Cathy Horyn, A.I., and Zoran, A.I.

255 "I told him . . ." and following: Lauren Hutton, A.I., 11/12/97.

257 "With their implicit . . .": Ben Brantley, "Zoran Zeitgeist," *Vanity Fair,* 3/92.

257 "There was this . . .": Ben Brantley, A.I.

257 "I am your . . .": Agins, "Uniquely Chic."

258 "You like to look . . .": Zoran, A.I., 3/95.

258 "give jewelry . . .": Agins, "Uniquely Chic."

258 "Woman should be . . ." and following: Zoran, A.I.

258 "Zoran has an incredible . . .": Ann Free, A.I., 95 and 5/97.

259 "If they want . . .": Zoran, A.I.

259 "Arena logged . . .": Roberta Arena, A.I., 95.

259 "I feel that . . ." and following: Nancy Friday, A.I., 97.

260 "One Bendel's client . . .": Ted Marlow, A.I., 4/29/97.

260 "They are separating, . . ." and following: Agins, "Uniquely Chic."

261 "Zoran believed that . . .": Zoran, A.I.

261 "Garratt maintained all . . .": Sandra Garratt, A.I., 3/98.

261 "Garratt's first year . . ." and following: Diane Reischel, "Units Creator Wrapped up in Legal Woes," *Los Angeles Times,* 5/4/90.

262 "I knew I could . . .": Zoran, A.I., 3/97.

262 "Labels scratch . . .": Agins, "Uniquely Chic."

262 "$14,000 in 1998 . . .": "Designer Agrees to Label Fine," *WWD,* 7/28/98.

263 "it was more typical . . .": June Horne, A.I., 3/97, and Gary Galleberg, A.I., 3/97.

264 "great success with . . ." and following: Agins, "Uniquely Chic."

264 "Zoran grew into a . . .": Joan Weinstein, A.I., 7/97.

264 "understands his . . ." and following: Ibid.

265 "His seamstresses kept . . .": Agins, "Uniquely Chic."

265 "I close up . . .": Ibid.

265 "More than 25,000 combinations . . .": Zoran, A.I., 2/98.

265 "the best mills . . .": Gary Galleberg, A.I.

266 "But they don't . . .": Ann Free, A.I., 4/95.

266 "I had heard . . ." and following quotes: June Horne, A.I.

267 "The most time . . .": Zoran, A.I.

268 "I was intrigued . . ." and following: Gary Galleberg, A.I., 6/17/97.

270 "The tab for . . ." and following: Agins, "Uniquely Chic."

271 "Is kitchen available?" and following: Author attended the 3/7/95 dinner in Milan.

272 "hadn't been profitable . . .": Bill Blass, A.I., 7/1/97.

EPILOGUE

275 "Companies that stumble . . .": George Anders and Scott Thurm, "The Innovators—The Rocket Under the Tech Boom: Heavy Spending by Basic Industries," *The Wall Street Journal*, 3/30/99.

276 "The alarms were . . .": From Peter Jacobi speech to the American Textile Manufacturers Institute, 3/13/99.

277 " 'war of the handbags' . . .": Thomas Kamm, "War of the Handbags Escalates as LVMH Revives Gucci Quest," *The Wall Street Journal*, Dow Jones News Service, 6/10/99.

277 "The brewing battle . . .": Thomas Kamm, "Gucci Watch: Behind the Competition for Luxury-Goods Firm Is a New European Ethic," *The Wall Street Journal*, 3/22/99.

278 "Cardin insisted that . . .": "Pierre Cardin Says Prefers to Sell to Italian Group," Dow Jones News Service, 3/15/99.

278 "This company has . . .": Teri Agins, "Polo Ralph Lauren Agrees to Acquire Canadian Chain," *The Wall Street Journal*, 3/2/99.

279 "The Hilfiger organization . . .": Hilfiger spokeswoman, A.I., 5/99.

279 "which generated $17 million . . .": Susan Chandler, "Outsourcing Risks, Rewards: The Decision to Farm Out Production of Frango Mints Has Left a Not-So-Sweet Aftertaste in Chicago, but Field's Is Hardly Alone in Retailing or Other Sectors in Taking That Route," *Chicago Tribune*, 3/14/99.

279 "This is the candy capital . . ." and following on zoning proposal: Gary Washburn and Susan Chandler, "A Taste of Politics of Field's Daley Message Hits Target on Frango Jobs," *Chicago Tribune*, 3/12/99.

Ballard, Bettina. *In My Fashion*. New York: David McKay, 1960.

Bender, Marilyn. *The Beautiful People*. New York: Coward McCann, 1966.

Birmingham, Nan Tillson. *Store*. New York: J. P. Putnam Sons, 1978.

Brady, James. *Superchic*. Boston: Little, Brown, 1974.

Coleridge, Nicholas. *The Fashion Conspiracy*. London: William Heinemann, 1988.

Daria, Irene. *The Fashion Cycle*. New York: Simon & Schuster, 1990.

Fairchild, John. *Chic Savages*. New York: Pocket Books, 1989.

Ferragamo, Salvatore *Salvatore Ferragamo, Shoemaker of Dreams*. Florence: Centro di Della Edifini srl, 1985 (originally published 1957).

Forestier, Nadege, and Ravai Nazanine. *The Taste of Luxury*. London: Bloomsbury Publishing, 1992.

Grumbach, Didier. *Histories de la mode*. Paris: Éditions du Seuil, 1993.

Gruppo GFT. *Emanuel Ungaro*. Milan: Electa, Milan Elemond Editori Associati, 1992.

Jarnow, Jeannette A., Miriam Guerriero, and Beatrice Judelle. *Inside the Fashion Business*. 4th ed. New York: Macmillan, 1987.

Milbank, Caroline Rennolds. *Couture: The Great Designers*. New York: Stewart, Tabori & Chang, 1985.

Mirabella, Grace. *In and Out of Vogue*. New York: Doubleday, 1994.

Morais, Richard. *Pierre Cardin*. London: Bantam Press, 1991.

Pochna, Marie-France. *Christian Dior*. New York: Arcade Publishing, 1996.

Rawsthorn, Alice. *Yves Saint Laurent*. New York: Doubleday, Nan A. Talese, 1996.

Ricci, Stefania. *Salavatore Ferragamo: The Art of the Shoe*. New York: Rizzoli International Publications, 1992.

Roscho, Bernard. *The Rag Race: How New York and Paris Run the Breakneck Business of Dressing American Women*. New York: Funk and Wagnalls Co., 1963.

Rubinstein, Ruth P. *Dress Codes: Meanings and Messages in American Culture.* Boulder, Col.: Westview Press, 1995.

Sices, Murray. *Seventh Avenue.* New York: Fairchild Publications, 1953.

Somers, Suzanne. *Italian Chic.* New York: Villard Books, 1992.

Trachtenberg, Jeffrey A. *Ralph Lauren: The Man Behind the Mystique.* Boston: Little, Brown, 1988.

———. *The Rain on Macy's Parade.* New York: Times Business, 1996.

Traub, Marvin, and Tom Teicholz. *Like No Other Store . . . the Bloomingdale's Legend and the Revolution in American Marketing.* New York: Times Books, 1993.

Vienne, Veronique. *French Style.* Columbus, Oh.: Express, 1993.

Vreeland, Diana. *D.V.* New York: Alfred A. Knopf, 1984.

Wendt, Lloyd, and Herman Kogan. *Give the Lady What She Wants: The Story of Marshall Field & Co.* New York: Rand McNally, 1950.

index